Dancing in the Dark

Dancing in the Dark

Words by Howard Dietz

Quadrangle/The New York Times Book Co.

For Lucinda

Acknowledgments

Carol Southern helped me get this book together and I could not exaggerate to what extent she helped me. Virginia McTernan has been of great assistance for many years in times of typographical errors. There are others whose good hands I fell into, such as Melvin Parks who arranged an exhibition of my songs and paintings at the Museum of the City of New York. Walter Wager of ASCAP who gave sage advice. Martin and Selene Levin whose editorial knowledge served me in many decisive occasions. Frank Campbell of the Metropolitan Music Library and Ann Murphy who made an appreciated contribution which could have been better if it weren't for a horse called Secretariat.

I am grateful to many other people but especially Arnold Weissberger, Marian Spitzer, Jerry Griffin/Bill Richards and Jackie Adams of the Museum of the City of New York, Paul Myers and Maxwell Silverman of the Theatre Collection New York Public Library, Chester Kopaz, Norman Kaphan of MGM and John Springer of the Springer-Bettman Archive.

Contents

Foreword

by ALAN JAY LERNER

More than the crocodile—the kangaroo and the bald eagle are becoming extinct in our time. We in the painted jungles of the theatre are also faced with our own disappearing species. One is "the star." The other is "charm." And not only is there no game preserve for either, but lately charm has been critically outlawed on the grounds of criminal literacy.

It is also true that the growing extinction of these precious species of life is not unique to the theatre alone. God knows that politics is suffering from its own lack of Lunts, Alice Bradys, Laurette Taylors and Bert Lahrs. Compared to Churchill and DeGaulle, Wilson and Heath are "rep" and Pompidou is an understudy who can barely keep the curtain up. Next to Roosevelt or even Kennedy, Nixon is the Chicago company (of the Capone era at that); and in Russia they have to have two fellows alternating in the same part.

In industry, the titans have been reduced to captains and as a rule only achieve name billing when they get to court. (Trials have always been sure-fire.) I expect General Motors to be demoted any day now.

As for that other quality of life known as charm, I can only shrug sadly and chalk it up as another victim of that creeping nastiness called modern civilization.

In the theatre I cannot help but link "star" and "charm" together because each somehow had the ability to carpet-ride us far away from the noisy beat of the doldrums of life; one, by the pulse-quickening excitement of a larger-than-life presence; the other, by delicious, enchanting seduction. And each in its own way brought joy to our lives.

All these thoughts come to mind, at least to my mind, when

I think about the man whose reminiscences are contained within the covers of this book. Not that he is a star; although as a companion he is. To paraphrase his famous line: "A day away from Tallulah is like a month in the country," seeing Howard Dietz is very much like a month in the country. The reason they come to mind is because of that special gift of charm that is so characteristic of his lyrics.

In the 1930s, when I was at school I was induced into trance by the pipes playing "Dancing In The Dark," "Where Or When," "Just One Of Those Things," and "Embraceable You." To me, an exotic aphrodisiac was a pair of great legs on a girl in the front line. And the gurus who led me on to the next plane of happiness had nice Occidental names like Gershwin, Rodgers, Porter, Hart, Berlin, Dietz and Schwartz. I knew every song and every lyric they wrote, including the verse and second chorus, as well as I did the Lord's Prayer. And I knew them within a week after each show opened. I remember even then as I listened to Howard's lyrics and sang them to myself as I walked down the street (which, incidentally, is what good popular music is supposed to make you do), that aside from their obvious wit, rhyming legerdemain, style and at times philosophic tenderness, they were the most charming lyrics in the world. They had that special grace, that warm elegant glow that hung a smile around you.

> *"You're never lonely when you love only one.*
> *You're only lonely having two or none. . . ."*
>
> or
>
> *"If there is someone lovelier than you,*
> *Then I am blind,*
> *A man without a mind. . . ."*
>
> or
>
> *"I'll face the unknown.*
> *I'll build a world of my own.*
> *No one knows better than I myself*
> *I'm by myself, alone."*

Howard is the Fred Astaire, the Chevalier, the Molnar, the Lubitsch of lyric writers. When he and Arthur Schwartz joined hands with Fred and Adele Astaire for *The Band-wagon,* it is no wonder it became about the most enchanting revue ever produced. Years later, when I finally met him and we became friends, I quickly found out where all that charm came from. He is a walking reservoir of it. A warmer, wittier, more life-loving and life-giving human being never came down the pike.

To those who will be meeting him for the first time in the pages of this book, I can only say, "Dear reader, you are about to meet one hell of a fellow." To those of us who have long loved him and admired him, this book is not only filled with his memories, but the best of ours.

ALAN JAY LERNER, *Centre Island, N.Y., January, 1974*

HOWARD DIETZ

January 8, 1974

Dear Alan,

When I received your introduction to my book I was in the hospital. When I finished reading the introduction I went home.

As ever,
Howard

A Word Before

This book is named after the title of a song I wrote with Arthur Schwartz. It seemed to fit the chaotic organization of the text. It is not chronological, although it makes an effort at it. It is not grouped by subject matter, although it is somewhat so. I just thought that a person who lived so many working lives ought to set down some of those adventures. If one writes for any length of time, covering a number of pages, a bit of the truth can't help creeping in.

I seemed to have observed, then copied. I saw newspapermen at work, so I became a correspondent. I saw advertising men at work, so I became an advertising man; publicity people at work, I went in for publicity. I saw painters at work, so I bought some canvases and covered them with oil. I saw musical shows I liked and I became a lyric writer. I read books by my friends and I decided to write my own, so here it is.

Right at the Start of It

othing memorable happened until I was seven, when I stole the month's wages of Lizzie Kutchardy, our Hungarian housemaid. Her pocketbook lay open on the bed in her tiny bedroom, and I couldn't resist the temptation, knowing that our baseball team was pathetically short of equipment. It was a shame to do that to Lizzie, who had always been on my side against the family; but the situation was urgent, and so, aided by Herbie Wolf, an unhysterical accomplice and a good shortstop, we spent the loot at Davega's, the sporting goods shop on 125th Street and Sixth Avenue, right around the corner.

It was foolish of me to think that such a prominent inside job could possibly remain a secret. I returned home carrying some of the hot merchandise—fielding gloves, bats, big league balls and other exhibits of armed robbery. Lizzie led me by the ear to Davega's and demanded that they take back their goods or she would brand them a receiver of stolen property or a fence, or a corrupter of youth. I was grateful that she didn't tell my father as she threatened to. I was so scared by her tongue-lashing that I never pilfered anything again in my life, excepting some sandwiches in the Exchange Buffet on Park Row where they were in slots and you used the honor system in declaring what you had eaten. I also have been guilty of buying 10 subway tickets and cutting them into 11 parts.

My father was the punitive type, an eye for an eye, or a mouth washed out with soap. I always had the feeling that my father wasn't really my father and he always had the feeling that I wasn't his son. I was terrified at the thought of him in possession of clear evidence calling for punishment. I didn't mind Lizzie telling Mother, who was bravely striving to hold the family together, an impossible task when all she had to work with was spit. The loyalty to her of her four children was a source of irritation to Father. These four included my brother Charles, who was 10 years older than I, and still is. He had left high school and was looking for a job. My sister Roberta was 12, red-headed, flirtatious and attracted to boys. She learned to play "doctor" at a premature age. Sadie was 10 and agreeable, her life bound up in a scrapbook, mostly clippings from theatrical publications. She wrote to prominent actors and actresses for their autographs. When I was sent from the table by Father she helped Lizzie smuggle food to me.

The trouble was no laughter. Mother constantly cautioned against frivolity unless Papa was in a cheerful mood, which was seldom. We were, however, an underground that trafficked in family jokes and the jokes were all on Papa. We were on different wavelengths. He was European, born in Russia, and though he had traveled a lot before coming to America, there was a difference. We mimicked his somewhat musical accent. Coming to New York, he found a niche for himself in the jewelry business and managed to court and marry Mother, who was too good for him. In fact she was perfect, except for her needless attempts at keeping up with the Joneses—the Jewish Joneses—buy now, pay never.

We lived in cycles of Manhattan, inheriting neighborhoods as they became passé, from Yorkville to Harlem, to Washington Heights, to West End Avenue, to Riverside Drive. The apartments had fancy names, such as "The Cambridge," "The Oxford," "The DePeyster," "The Riviera." When we got integrated, we would move. As a result, I got to know kids from all over town—marble shooters, button pitchers, stoop handballers, and other dazzling athletes who used the city for an outdoor gym. Occasionally, while playing in the gutter, not thoroughly swept by the white wings, we would get brushed by a brewery Percheron, a Stanley Steamer, or even a glass-enclosed Baker Electric. We would pick ourselves up, unbothered by the accident, and get on with the game.

The streets aren't macadam playing fields anymore. They

are double parking lots, and teenagers don't play one o'cat, prisoner's base, or ring-o-levio. The girls don't play potsy. Mothers don't lean on cushioned window sills anymore, and exchange views and gossip while keeping an eye on the street scene below.

The family sort of fell apart. My brother got a job as a drummer for a variety of merchandise which kept him on the road, and he sent me boxes of local taffy from New Orleans, Detroit, Cleveland and Cincinnati. My sisters got married to commonplace wage-earners and moved to New Haven, and other havens outside Manhattan.

My father's presence became unpredictable. Occasionally he would turn up and take my mother to the Metropolitan Opera, although he had only a pretentious feeling for music. He wanted to be able to say he had heard Caruso, and would even hum "La donna é mobile" in an alien key.

My mother played bridge-whist with her ladies during the afternoon, and when Papa died in his late 70s, she managed her life alone, though a guest in a hotel with cooking odors. When she was wasting in stamina, she called my sister Sadie on the hospital phone at seven in the morning.

"I'm feeling so bad," she said. "I feel I'm going to die."

"I'll be right over," said Sadie.

"Are you coming *right* over?" Mother asked.

Sadie again said she would be right over.

"Then," said Mother, "on your way here stop at Barney Greengrass's and get me some smoked salmon!"

While not a wit-conscious wit, she said some memorable things. Her last words, her children at her bedside, were fervent: "The 10 years since your father died have been the happiest years of my life."

My school and street life was a carbon of any New York neighborhood kid. I had fist fights with the block bully, Georgie Bartlet. In 1904, I was for Teddy Roosevelt, Georgie was for Alton B. Parker, and when the election returns endorsed my crusade it became dangerous to walk to school. It wasn't so safe when you were there.

SCHOOL DAYS

At public school
I made no sense
But learned the art
Of self-defense
From kindergarten
to 6B
I went to P.S.
103
And what with all
The cons and pros
I left there
With a broken nose
Continuing
The local war
I went to P.S.
24
My tongue
As usual
Was glib
I left there
with a broken rib
I went to P.S.
165
The only ones
Who there survive
Are those whom Darwin
Termed the "fittest"
The students who
The hardest hittest
I left there
With a souvenir
A slightly
Cauliflowered ear

I held my end up
If you please
With several
Pyrrhic victories
It's give-and-take
The golden rule
At any New York
Public school.

Scoreboard watching at Lenox Avenue and 125th Street and weekend excursions to Van Cortlandt and Central Parks for baseball, tennis and soccer were habitual. Our 124th Street baseball team, the Orioles, had one distinction, a girl pitcher. She was speedy Margaret McGinnity, the niece, or daughter, of the famous Giant, iron man Joe Mc-Ginnity, who they said pitched several doubleheaders, all shutouts. I was Margaret's catcher, and have a broken nose to show for it. Only sissies wore masks in those days. Later we emulated Roger Bresnahan, the New York Giant back-stop, who did, and I even saved up for a chest-protector and shinguards. A couple of us wrote a song which was a parody of the raging hit, "Oh, You Beautiful Doll." Our song was "Oh, You Oriole Team."

I was a dyed-in-the-wool baseball fan, and my stars were Christopher Mathewson of the New York Giants (everybody worshipped "Matty") as well as Rube Marquard, who once won 19 straight. Hal Chase was the first baseman of the New York Yankees. He was left-handed and lightning fast, and one time when there were many injuries, Chase played second base, unusual for a left-hander as the throw after fielding a ground ball loses a step to the runner. Chase was involved in the Black Sox scandal and was never heard of again.

6   Great stars were indicted for throwing games. The most

regretted by us was "Shoeless" Joe Jackson, who had a strong following among the teenagers. Jackson was walking to his trial in the Chicago court house and one kid on the line was heard to cry out:

"Say it ain't so, Joe."

The theatre, the movies, and printers' ink were mysterious worlds that brushed my consciousness early on.

The movies and I were to live together throughout my adult life. They were born before I was, but we were both childishly young when we began our big affair. The first one I remember was at the old Eden Musée on West 23rd Street. The kinematograph, as they called it, was a special novelty. The memory comes back vividly in images of trains, trotting horses, cowboys and Indians flickering across the screen.

Not long afterward, I saw *The Great Train Robbery*, first epic of the celluloid, presenting one whole reel of derrying-do with pistols, masks, and enough suspenseful action to rivet attention more readily than current dawdling dramas shown on wider screens, but with narrower plots.

Every Sunday I went to the Nickelodeon and the Nicolet. If I had my timing right, I could catch the bill at the Nickelodeon, which was a one-reeler, and then sprint to the Nicolet where I could see another one-reeler, and spend the rest of the day glued to the stereopticon where I saw women in lewd poses as well as prizefight pictures. I got to know many popular songs and I still remember the ones I heard then more accurately than later when song-writing and show-writing became my designated profession.

One of my favorite actors was John Bunny, a character star with great personality. When he died his pictures were at once withdrawn from the screen. It was thought that the public would resent seeing its dead favorite moving about as though alive and kicking. I waited impatiently for them to be released again. The industry soon learned that the public resents nothing except boredom.

The Musée held other fascinations, too, and presented a great attraction to the 10-year-old mind. Mostly the Musée consisted of wax works like Madame Tussaud's in London. There was a policeman at the entrance who looked so real, you were certain he was alive; but it was dangerous to poke his bulk, because there was the story of someone who had done that one day, and he turned out to be real after all.

There was a Chamber of Horrors—all that the name promised, but better than the Chamber of Horrors was one celebrated attraction that particularly interested me. It was the automatic chess player. This was a highly polished carving of a pubic-bearded turbaned oriental in porcelain, who sat with crossed legs behind a metal box which contained the board and the metal pieces. His arm moved swiftly but precisely over the chessmen. You made your move, and he immediately made his. Whenever a game was being played, it was accompanied by a steady buzzing sound like an electric razor. He always won or had a stalemate. If you made an illegal move or any technical mistake, his jerky arm would sweep all the pieces aside. This was all done, supposedly, by an elaborate mechanism hidden within. The area seemed too small to allow for a human hiding place, but one doubted the pertinence of those wires and cogs which you saw moving when the figure was in action.

Edgar Allan Poe, years earlier, wrote a novella called *The Mechanical Chess Player*. He was convinced, as I was, that a live player was inside; but to fit in, he had to be no bigger than a midget. It seemed too much to ask, but no one could help asking it. My mysterious mechanical expert was handled in a showmanlike fashion by one Mealzl. It had appeared in Europe at the end of the century for all the "crowned heads." It had played celebrated matches with continental masters and had never been beaten, although it had allowed its opponents several stand-offs.

Years later in 1939 when I had acquired a reputation as publicity director for MGM, my services were solicited to promote "Agib," a mechanical figure similarly oriental, who played checkers instead of chess. Agib's manager offered me $500 weekly, plus a small percentage of the receipts. I countered with a more generous proposition. I would outline a detailed exploitation plan for no money at all, if he would reveal the secret of the porcelain Agib. This he refused. He explained that he alone held the secret, and divulging it would be trifling with his livelihood. He did agree to appear gratis at an Allied Relief Ball, a huge affair at the Astor Hotel, run by my then wife, Tanis. Agib's corner of the ballroom was a great mystifying success. He was continually winning against baffled opponents, who paid varying amounts a game for the privilege of playing. I spied all of that night, and when the figure was installed and removed, but I came up empty. The contents of Agib remained a mystery.

I can remember my introduction to the live theatre. My sisters and I were taken by Lizzie to see Richard Mansfield in *Monsieur Beaucaire*. He had been posing as a barber—I can't recall his plebeian appearance but I can still remember him as the Duc de Chateaurien darting about in silken 18th-century clothes, with a powdered wig. The theatre that Richard Mansfield played in was named after him and stayed "The Mansfield" until he died.

My theatregoing picked up circa 1910 when pocket money saved began to afford occasional visits to the balconies of a variegated assortment of shows. It was love from afar with many of the stage luminaries. I saw specimens of blood-and-thunder melodrama. Paul McAllister and Beatrice Snow were the stars of one. I was a vaudeville fan, and a regular patron of the Alhambra Theatre at 125th Street and Sixth Avenue. The bill followed the Colonial which was in the Sixties, and the Palace which was way downtown. The price was 25¢, the exact amount of my weekly allowance.

I was lucky enough to get into Townsend Harris Hall, the preparatory high school for City College, located on a beautiful Gothic campus at 136th Street and Amsterdam Avenue. It was a three-year school, but equal to four years of Clinton or Commerce. Its high scholastic standard created a prideful solidarity among undergraduates and alumni.

Exposure to the writers of the *Academic Herald,* the Townsend Harris Hall scholastic monthly, led to literary experiments. Together with the boys on the block, Bennett Cerf, Merryle Stanley Rukeyser, and others who have since made names for themselves, I managed to get out a neighborhood magazine, the *Twentieth Century Quarterly,* financed by extortion from the neighborhood storekeepers our families patronized. They all had to take ads. My short story in that edition showed no talent, but was remarkable for a coincidence: The name of the heroine was Elizabeth Hall, a pure invention, but the same as the name of the girl I was destined to meet and to marry, the first of three.

When I was 15, I got myself hired as a copyboy on the *New York American* by answering a want ad. I worked after school and during summer vacations. This was an excuse for me to play hooky from home and I sort of ran away, although those at home didn't realize I had gone, much less run away. I disguised myself with a new personality and lied a lot. It didn't get me anywhere except to Greenwich Village. I stayed at Mrs. Loughlan's at 80 Washington Place, owned by John Philip Sousa, and I learned to eat a lot of Italian dough. I didn't invite my brothers and sisters down. I was ashamed of the commonplaceness of my family, and I thought they might expose the lies I had told about myself.

My nouveau wealth from the job was a passport to the successful shows. I remember Julia Sanderson in *The Sunshine Girl*, one of the musicals that Charles Frohman imported from London's Gaiety Theatre and which was a huge hit. I was told that Donald Brian, the leading man, received $500 a week, a fortune in those days.

I doted on Ethel Barrymore, first seen in an old Pinero play about English theatrical life, *Trelawny of the Wells*. Then I saw her in a vaudeville act made from Barrie's tight one-actor *The Twelve-Pound Look*, about a wife who decided to become a secretary and walked out on her lord and master as soon as she accumulated twelve pounds, which was the price of a typewriter.

I've never forgotten Eleanor Robson in *Nurse Marjorie*. She married August Belmont, and her work for the Metropolitan Opera Club brought her into my life when I was writing the English versions of *Die Fledermaus* and *La Bohème*.

My favorite heroine was Irene Fenwick, especially in Sudermann's *Song of Songs*. Some years later, after she had married Lionel Barrymore and retired from acting, I met Miss Fenwick at a cocktail party. Fortified with martinis, I told her that she was the love of my life, and I had seen her show at least ten times, and I still dreamed of her. She said merrily, "Then why don't we go upstairs?" Assignations in those days were not consummated on the street level.

But most of my time out of school was spent at the old New York American-Evening Journal building on William Street in the shade of the Brooklyn Bridge. I had a sycophantic respect for reporters, and a hero worship for those with bylines—newspapermen like Frank Ward O'Malley who covered neighborhood affairs like the Mulligan Guards Ball, which was attended by Mr. and Mrs. Kid Broad and all the men about Flatbush, and Joseph Jefferson O'Neill who wrote parade stories that were more glamorous than the parade.

There was Lindsay Dennison who pulled together the loose ends of a crime, Charlie Sweeney who dared enter the domain of the Ku Klux Klan and take off their white sheets, and Herbert Bayard Swope who became executive editor of *The New York World,* and sent despatches from the front in World War I.

The sports staff alone had become a classic. Lean lantern-jawed Tad Dorgan, wearing a green eyeshade, was something of a genius as cartoonist and humorous interpreter of the fight game. Hype Igoe, squat, squeaky and likably dissipated, who was almost another Tad, was an artist who also practiced word swinging. There was Bill Farnsworth, the sports editor, and Sam Crane, the ex-baseball player who turned baseball reporter and kept going into his 80s. Think what you may of the general influence of the Hearst papers on American life, they employed talent in a big way, and certainly their sports pages gave a lot of pleasure to followers of the elusive pill, the 6-ounce glove, the pigskin and similar symbols of a way of life.

I ran errands for the great Arthur Brisbane, editor then of the *Evening Journal* and daily author of the most pontifical editorials ever penned by man. These articles never discussed or argued. They told you. Now and then there was flattery of the reader, so insincere that even in my early teens I could read the contempt between the lines.

But I was in awe of Mr. Brisbane as a successful man who had won his way by writing—or so I oversimplified it. And I had already decided that I wanted to be a writer of some sort. Why not follow in the footsteps of the balding, sharp-featured, cold-eyed titan of journalism whom I had actually seen in conference with William Randolph Hearst himself. (They were talking about John Purroy Mitchel, afterward mayor of New York, whom they helped supplant with "Red Mike" Hylan.) Mitchel's superiority had no more to do with the case than had W. S. Gilbert's flowers of spring.

One day I wrote an editorial myself and dared take it to

Mr. Brisbane in his private office. He read it over twice, nodded and told me that he liked it. It was a shameless imitation of his peculiar style, and it even dealt with a subject close to one of his favorite topics—the still-remembered thesis that the gorilla's superiority to man makes all human athletic prowess ridiculous. My subject was: "Can Man Do What a Monkey Does? Will the Simian Evolve?"

He said he liked this piece of apery, but if I had dreams of becoming his protégé and favored disciple, and I did, they gradually faded away. Of course, he didn't print my editorial and he never mentioned it to me again. The iron entered my soul as I realized that to him I was just another office boy.

But I wasn't just another office boy all the time. Justin McGrath, the steel-gray managing editor, noticed my alacrity in slipping pseudo-quietly about the city room serving reporters and re-write men. One day when his secretary, Harry Nicholas, was home with a cold, I was tapped to substitute for him. Although I couldn't take shorthand, I could type using the hunt system, and somehow managed to convince the unsmiling Mr. McGrath that I was not frightened when he stared at me through his pince-nez, as I did my secretarial tasks.

I Always Go to Bed at Ten

fter finishing my junior year at Townsend Harris, I decided to chuck it and work on a year-round basis on the *New York American*. I sought the advice of Mr. McGrath, who decided I would be making a mistake to abandon thoughts of going to college; as my prospects for a financial future estate were undeniable, I would need an education. He hinted that I might try the college entrance examinations to Columbia; after which event I might become, with his help, the university correspondent, and at the same time attend the newly launched Pulitzer School of Journalism.

The entire summer of 1913 was a cram session filling the gap of a year or more of preparatory study for entrance to the Columbia School of Journalism. It wasn't merely a matter of brushing up on what I'd been taught in high school. It was getting acquainted with unfamiliar Latin texts, solid geometry propositions and hallowed literature, the classically remote as well as the intimately recent. After much anxious doubt, all was well. I got the necessary fourteen points and was enrolled in the Class of 1917 and was appointed Columbia correspondent for the *New York American*. The pay, space rates at $7.50 a column, averaged about $20 a week. I was in a good borrowing position to pay my tuition fees. I touched a couple of uncles in preference to my father, who refused to be proud of me even though I wasn't costing him a penny.

Life at Columbia began with a feeling of discovered freedom. The campus belonged to me. I had been there before, but never with a sense of belonging. Its standing as an Ivy League University with hallowed traditions, its long line of fathers and sons, its graduate schools gave me a feeling of importance in being there.

As an embryo reporter, I poked into the corners of the college world; and chose first to see the squads of athletes trying out for the varsity teams. In a moment of delusion, I myself tried out for freshman tennis and crew. My showing was pitiful. Anton von Bermuth, also trying out, beat me 6–love, 6–love, and I wasn't off my game. In the crew department, despite my 105 pounds, I didn't show the executive ability required for a coxswain. I was told there were at least five competitors just as light and more water-minded.

I hovered around the barges and shells, however, until I got an interview with James C. Rice, the able but abusive head coach, who vented his scorn on anyone who thought the four-mile race too strenuous for college boys. I quoted him in many items that appeared in the paper and the coach was called to task by the stewards of the Poughkeepsie Regatta, who accused Rice of insensitive guardianship. "Damn it," said the coach, "when I was a boy, our boat club had a six-mile sculling race for octogenarians, and because the field was getting overcrowded they'd shoot the last two to finish."

Holding two jobs, what is now called moonlighting, was to become my way of life, but studying to be a journalist and being a journalist at the same time told on my classwork. New friends came to the rescue. Red-headed Francis Joseph Scully, as Irish as the sound of his name, was Columbia correspondent for the *Sun*, and together we formed a syndicate to serve each other and outwit Malcolm Roy of *The Times* and Ernie Ettinger of the *World*.

Roy had a corner on Columbia news. He knew all the trustees and officers of the university and had actually arranged to pay various fraternity members who would feed items to his typewriter. His tentacles reached out. When an important story came up, he'd often send copies to papers other than his own, including ours, on the chance that our coverage was insufficient. Occasionally, he'd succeed in breaking the *American* or the *Sun*, and Scully and I were put on the carpet. But though Scully was minus a leg from a basketball fall in high school, his guerrilla tactics had not suffered.

"Roy's Boys," as we called them, had their pressroom on the second floor of Earl Hall. Scully and I operated from his room in the dormitory. One night when Columbia played Cornell in a big basketball game for the championship of the Ivy League, I wrote Scully's story as well as my own, which required little more than differing leads, and delivered them to Park Row. Frank, meanwhile, went to Roy's press room, locked it on the inside and climbed down the drainpipe. *The Times* didn't have the story in the first edition, and Roy was called on *his* carpet. Keets Speed, the managing editor of the *Sun*, was delighted.

Columbia was between football teams at that time. The sport had been abandoned in 1905 when a fatal injury in a game at South Field frightened the trustees. Students were not supposed to die for dear old Columbia, except in song, but while injuries in the field of athletics are to be abhorred and guarded against, every Joe College wants his Alma Mater to give her all on the gridiron.

Scully and I agreed something was missing without a football team. The roots of a university are easy to plant. As in the O. Henry story, if you want to start a college, you buy 50 footballs, package some hashish, and open a saloon. Football had to be revived. We interviewed President Nicholas Murray Butler and many trustees, and after several tight-lipped receptions got a story: "They are thinking it over." Frank formed the Bring-Back-Football Committee which proposed that for the first five years, the Columbia varsity eleven should have an easy schedule, playing colleges that were not so violent, such as Williams and Wesleyan. Undergraduate mass meetings were held every few days. The light blue got the green light, and the Morningside hysteria was like an election bonfire. Columbia correspondents at $7.50 a column struck gold!

The journalism course made me a candidate for B-lit, Bachelor of Literature. It was a degree blended with the college A.B. curriculum, served up with experimental newspaper writing. The class made up a hypothetical newspaper called "The Front Page" from assignments meted out by students taking turns being editor. The slogan of "The Front Page" was a parody of *The New York Times:* "All the news that fits we print."

Despite my job on the *American,* I found time for other campus activities. I was on the board of the *Jester,* the comic monthly magazine. Also, for a brief time, I ran the *Spectator* column, "The Off Hour," in the daily newspaper. My own pieces often appeared there after being rejected by Franklin P. Adams, better known as F. P. A.

F.P.A.'s column or "colyum" called "The Conning Tower" appeared regularly on the page opposite the editorials in *The New York World,* having previously appeared in *The Evening Mail* and *The Herald Tribune.* It specialized in light verse and quippery. It was considered too highbrow by the editors, but many first-rate writers contributed to it. F.P.A.'s standards were high and the contribs, as they were called, competed in French forms and snappy couplets for a place in the Tower, at the top, if possible. F.P.A. spent most of his time playing pool at the Players Club. He had only one columnar rival and that was Don Marquis who later created Archie the Cockroach and Mehitabel the Cat in the *New York Evening Sun.*

Many of us at Morningside Heights were what the bullfighters would later call literary aficionados, passionate about trifling letters. We turned to F.P.A. first thing in the morning to see if we had made it, or if not who had. Among the most frequent nom de plume contributors from Columbia was Morrie Ryskind, a brilliant fashioner of quip and song, who signed himself "Morrie." He ran "The Off Hour" and was also editor of *The Jester.* He was an opponent of the fraternity system and hated the reactionaries who were particularly prevalent in the Ivy League. Even though his politics were left of center, he kept the campus amused. He was active in all election debates. He made rude speeches in front of Hamilton Hall. He was accused of being the author of the line about Nicholas Murray Butler, Columbia president, "Who is that dapper fellow in the sleek cutaway who may be seen crossing the campus every morning just before 9 o'clock? That is not our president, that is our butler."

It is said that President Butler and other members of the faculty and the Board of Trustees joined in a movement to expel Ryskind before the final examination. The morning and evening newspapers played up the Ryskind episode. His failure to pass the swimming examination was mentioned in the stories. At Columbia you couldn't get a degree unless you could swim.

Released from the confines of the University, he started leaning to the right and he later became a champion of Joe McCarthy. He published in a fortnightly magazine *The Freeman,* a parody of Kipling's "Fuzzy-Wuzzy," part of which read:

> *So here's to you, Joe McCarthy, you're a swell A-meri-can;*
> *You're a terror to the traitors an' a first-class fightin' man;*
> *Oh, bless him for the enemies he's made!*

His classmates would never have predicted that Ryskind would become a champion of Joe McCarthy and many reckoned that championing McCarthy was the same as championing Hitler.

He landed on Broadway where he collaborated on hit shows. I kept up a reasonably accurate correspondence with him for a while and we did a show, *The Merry-Go-Round.* Morrie later won the Pulitzer prize for the musical *Of Thee I Sing,* co-authored with George S. Kaufman.

The reign of F.P.A. was an era of golden laughter. While the contribution of F.P.A.'s light verse and paraphrasing was not profound, it was literature that stimulated a forum of readers who were proud of their standards. The contributors lived by a code of scansion and were united in a war against assonance. I struggled to belong to this group, and the acceptance of my contributions signed "Freckles" became increasingly unsurprising.

It was conventional, when contributing a poem or a paragraph, to use a pseudonym. Robert Simon signed his romantic verses "Leoceles." Louis Untermeyer signed his submissions "Daffydowndilly," Deems Taylor was "Sneed," Newman Levy was "Flaccus," Nate Salisbury was "Baron Ireland," Dorothy Parker was "Dotty."

Another contributor to F.P.A.'s column was Irwin Edman who wrote stately rhythms while he was studying to be a philosophy professor. He held cram sessions for us ordinary students and later on he joined the Columbia faculty. There were other campus poets, including Herman J. Mankiewicz of the well-known Mankiewiczes. Mank later wrote the Academy-award winning scenario *Citizen Kane* about the private life of the king of yellow journalism.

F.P.A. donated a watch to the contrib who wrote what he considered the best piece of the year and every year a banquet was held at a prominent tavern such as Allaires, or the Algonquin Hotel, or Cavanaughs. Frank Case, the owner of The Algonquin, was especially hospitable to those with literary talent and was enthusiastic over the annual event. A speaker from among the contributors would make the presentation of the watch. I first became aware of the great Robert C. Benchley when I heard him speak at the 1916 dinner. He started his speech with a sober delivery.

"It is only fitting in making the award of this watch, that I give you a history of the watch industry. It was started by John W. Watch in 1626 and the industry grew until the latest annual report revealed that in the fiscal year 1915 some 2 million-odd watches were produced, of which 20 percent were white and 22 were gun metal."

It was a convulsing delivery and Benchley's fame was immediate. A few years later he appeared in the Ziegfeld *Follies* with "The Treasurer's Report" taken from his F.P.A. dinner speech. Benchley had a great influence on his generation with his penchant for turning the pompousness of politicians into nonsense.

It was fashionable at school to get drunk and tell stories about your alcoholic excesses and we made a competitive pastime of drinking. The drinkers gathered at City Hall and drank a drink at every saloon on the way uptown. Every man selected his own drink. Saloons were plentiful, one on almost every corner. There were usually about a dozen contestants but their numbers grew less the further uptown they got. The time I won I drank beer which was on draught and got as far as 33rd Street. I left a trail of vomit and passed out victoriously in Herald Square.

"Seventeen J" was an argumentative class. Almost daily, our group would gather in a Furnald Hall dormitory and argue about capital and labor. The tuning fork for debate was Professor Charles Austin Beard, who had written *An Economic Interpretation of the Constitution,* giving a scandalous picture of the money-making patriotism of some of America's crocodilic founding fathers. John Hancock, we were told, had an interest in a tea company, accounting for the sabotage represented by the Boston Tea Party. We pictured ourselves as student radicals in the genre of the French and Germans of the 1840s.

Nobody cut Beard's classes. With more than 50 seated, the professor, leaning against the venetian blinds on the side-aisle window of the classroom, his eyes half-closed, began in a sepulchral voice:

"Today, we are going to discuss the position of the budget in state government. Now I am sure that the budget must seem a dullish subject, but if you will tell me how much a nation spends on its army, its navy and its public works, I will tell you as much about the people of that nation as I could if you gave me the collective writings of its philosophers and poets." Suddenly, the dullish subject became alive and for the first time I sensed the infinite potential of a college education.

The discussions that took place were sparked by the many new periodicals springing up. There was *The New Republic*, which gave us the liberalism of Walter Lippmann; *The Masses*, the socialism of Max Eastman, and several other periodicals such as *The Nation* of Oswald Garrison Villard, and the short-lived *Metropolitan* with John Reed.

Among my classmates, the most provocative was Charles Francis Phillips, who was well-versed in Marx and Engels and knew the plays of Henrik Ibsen, Gerhart Hauptmann and George Bernard Shaw seemingly by heart. At least he had a quotation to embellish his every point. My "by-heart" knowledge was French verse, W. S. Gilbert and Lewis Carroll. I began to read more provocative literature, and was an enthusiastic audience for *An Enemy of the People, Ghosts, Hedda Gabler*, and talked them out with Phillips.

I read everything Shaw wrote—his plays, his prefaces, his novels. I knew every episode in his biography by Archibald Henderson. I toyed with vegetarianism. I became a snob. I felt superior to those who wrote unradical literature, but what I wrote myself was so light you would have to hold it down with a paperweight or it would blow away.

"To a Bookworm" was typical of my ballads.

TO A BOOKWORM

You visit me often and every time
*   You raid and plunder my library*
Volumes of genius in prose and rhyme—
*   How many books have you pilfered? Gee,*
What a collection yours must be!
*   Books are the debts that never come due.*
Where are the volumes I used to see?
Why don't you "borrow" my bookcase, too?

23

A burglar coming to call must climb
  The fire escape or the balcony.
He risks a punishment for the crime;
You enter a house with more ease that he
(At times I even lend you my key)
And "borrow" a Sheridan, Shaw, or Sue
*An F.P.A. or a B.L.T.**
Why don't you "borrow" my bookcase, too?

Poems by Lindsay and Oppenheim,
  Untermeyer and Edgar Lee
Masters, and others now in their prime—
  Verse that's shackled and verse that's free
Traveled in classical company
Straight to the flat which belongs to you
  Out of the home which belongs to me.
  Why don't you "borrow" my bookcase, too?

At times you robbed me of two and three
  Priceless volumes, some old—some new,
The Britannica went—from A to Z
  Why don't you "borrow" my bookcase, too?

Phillips found me easily shockable. He said he intended one day to organize a union in his father's garment factory and lead a strike against the bosses. I asked him what was wrong with the working conditions. He said nothing was wrong, but every manufacturer should be struck against.

We had many arguments. I finally admitted I didn't know much about capital and labor but said I intended to find out by working as a laborer.

"How are you going to do that?" asked Charlie. I said with determination that the next summer vacation would find me doing manual work. To my surprise, Charlie said, "I'll join

---

* Bert Leston Taylor, columnist of the *Chicago Tribune*.

you," and we solemnly shook hands, forming a two-man union.

When the semester was over, I persuaded Frank Scully to protect my job on the paper by feeding the summer stories to the city desk of the *American*. I agreed with Phillips that we would hit the road. We took a dollar each, sandwiches and a change of socks and underwear which we carried in a paper bag. We lined up at the employment store of the Erie Railroad underneath the "el" tracks on 3rd Street. As protective disguise, we wore overalls, dirtied up our hands, faces, and clothes by rolling in the gutter, and were hired by the Italian foreman.

A group of us were conducted via the ferry to Hoboken and instructed to wait in a boxcar which was on a siding. Finally our mysterious journey began as our car, coupled to the locomotive, began to move. About 15 other gang workers were crowded in the car. They were all types. One old man looked like Velvet Joe, the then ubiquitous tobacco advertisement, who kept dipping his fingers into the granulated sugar in his pants pocket. Another had a harmonica which he played well. It was cold and frostbiting and Charlie and I clung together as we listened to the lonesome sounds of our train screaming through the night.

One of the men produced a bottle of gin and we were offered a sip. I had a paperbound book of Richard Aldington's poems in my pocket, but I didn't dare read it, fearing discovery and ridicule in this unliterary atmosphere. This is how Gresham's law works on people.

We rode all night and most of us fell asleep. The train slowed down at what seemed to be a whistle-stop. About eight of the gang swung off with professional jumps. We didn't see them again. It was made clear subsequently that holding a third of the labor shipped out was a high percentage. We stopped and got out in the early morning with a taste in the mouth like stale alligator pear.

We had arrived at Deposit, a town of 2,000, on the state

line separating New York from Pennsylvania, some 250 miles out of New York City. It was 5 A.M. and we were led to another boxcar divided by board slabs into oblong sleeping quarters for the workers. We were told that work started at 6, and our pay would be 20¢ an hour, or $2 a day, payable at the end of the week. As all the sleeping slots were occupied, we must try to rent a room in the town, but we were to be sure to return by 6. The foreman took Charlie and me aside and confidentially directed us to Mrs. Demoney on Front Street. This turned out to be favored treatment. Our college curriculum was showing.

Mrs. Demoney took in boarders at $1.25 a week, which was living beyond our means. She understood that we couldn't pay until we got paid and said we could have coffee with her husband John, who worked at the post office. The Demoneys were of Polish origin, and their one child, Doris, a blue-eyed blonde, not yet school age, took a liking to me, showing her good judgment. I decided to recite poems to her before she went to bed.

We reported to the work gang at 6 as instructed. Our job was to ease the roadbed and we were divided into teams of four. Two would lift the ties by applying leverage with iron pikes and the other two would fill up the space with shovelfuls of gravel. It seemed simple enough, and we felt important, as though we were wearing the "dear old paper cap that labor wears" in editorial page cartoons.

The foreman inspected the quality of the work and he switched Charlie and me from rakes to pikes. It was broiling in the June sun and we were grateful for the trains passing, which gave us a short rest. We'd mop our brows and watch the passengers go by. It seemed close to lunchtime when I asked Charlie the time on his Ingersoll watch he had hidden in his pocket. The answer was disheartening. It was only 9, and we had been working an eternity.

I managed to huddle with Charlie, who whispered that we'd better quit.

"But how?" I asked. We agreed on a plan. When the next train came along, we would be on the wrong side of the tracks and run for it while the train blocked us from the foreman. It was a cowardly idea, but comforting, and it succeeded. We ran as fast as we could toward the center of town.

We spent the rest of the day in the post office writing heroic accounts of our three hours as laborers, waiting for 6 o'clock when we could go back to the Demoneys as though all were well. They gave us beef stew and coffee and asked us questions about the job. Mr. Demoney was familiar with it as he had spent part of his early life working on the Erie. He looked at us suspiciously, and I was sure we weren't fooling him, but we got into his good graces when I recited "The Congo" to Doris, who enjoyed Vachel Lindsay's eerie sound.

During the night, the post office had been robbed of a loaded mailbag, and when we arrived there that morning we were put under lock and key by Si Wheaton, the tobacco-chewing sheriff of Deposit, who wore a black patch over one eye. We were held on a charge of vagrancy. Mr. Demoney, who was an assistant to the postmaster, came to our rescue, much to our embarrassment, and got us released. The sheriff gave us three hours to get out of town. We were grateful, but still determined to find out about labor.

We offered to pay Mr. Demoney for our board out of our original dollar, but he sensed our dire straits and was willing to do us favors because we had enchanted Doris. He suggested that we go to Whitney Point, 30 miles farther on. We could make it by hooking a ride on the afternoon train and we could get jobs in Borden's Creamery where there was a shortage of workmen.

We went to the local bakery and spent 10¢ on coffee cake before we boarded the whistle-stop train, and hid in the baggage car. It pulled into Whitney Point where, at the appropriate slowdown, we jumped off without falling, feeling professional and akin to our companions of two nights before.

Whitney Point was the size of Deposit, with transient laborers who left the job periodically and returned to it when they were desperate. We didn't give the appearance of being sturdy enough for the jobs we were to undertake, but we passed ourselves off as creamery men.

Six A.M. found us assigned to work in the icehouse where we had to buy rubber gowns, rubber hip boots and rubber gloves. These items totaled $8, which would be deducted from our pay, but we could sell them back on leaving. We were solemnly warned not to get the boots or gloves wet inside as they took days to dry and we would not be issued others. We soon realized that the rubber equipment was necessary, not just to comfort but to life itself. We stood knee-deep in icy water and bent over to heave the huge blocks of ice. Our job was sliding them into a machine which made cracked ice as a bedding for the bottles. We lasted until a bell clanged for lunch. As we staggered out aching into the fresh June day, we were handed our free bottle of milk. I was too tired to drink and lay down until the work bell sounded. When work was over Charlie told me gloomily that he had gotten his boots wet. It would be impossible for him to go back.

He walked me to work the next morning. It irritated me to think of him sitting in the grass or wandering at whim in this countryside while I had to work for the two of us. It was difficult, this first physical work, and I doubted that I could last long at it, but I had to try. After work, I trudged back to the boarding house, and was greeted by Charlie who had spent the day lying in the fragrant meadow with sandwiches and my Richard Aldington poems. He waved a paper and shouted that he'd written a magnificent poem.

"Do you want to hear it?" When I said nothing, he proceeded to recite:

Corn-colored grass on a wind-blown hill
That bends away as the breeze goes by
And up where the champagne heavens spill,
A field of forget-me-nots and I.

"What do you think of it?" he asked.

Without raising my head from the country-fried potatoes, I replied, "Pure shit."

I marveled that the men could do such cruel work for a mere 20¢ an hour. I became more and more indignant at the plight of the workingman including myself. I asked some of the other bottle boys why they didn't form a union: The company was unusually dependent on their workers. One man suggested that I talk to some of the other boys at lunchtime. Trying to recall Phillips's rhetoric on the dignities of labor, I presented a modest but manly plan for unionization —30¢ an hour and better working conditions.

I thought I had made an impression and was pleased to have understood the just grievances of labor. On the way home a few nights later, I was attacked at a turn in the road by some goons. Among them I recognized my first convert, just as he delivered a solid blow to the eye. It was a popular punishment and clearly a warning for the future.

I decided to work just long enough to accumulate the fare home and get Charlie to Binghamton. It took three weeks of back-breaking stick-to-it-iveness to amass the capital and I had no time to observe the reactionary workmen at work.

Back home I found both my sympathies for labor and my attitude toward honest work had changed. Though vague socialist feelings persisted, my yearning was now towards finding out about capital.

Charlie, from his outside vantage point, returned for the fall term, more passionately Left than ever and became a Communist. In 1917 he wrote a pamphlet advocating disobedience to the draft law but he escaped punishment by the expert defense of his counsel. He was sent to Fort Dix where he refused to put the uniform on. He ran away from the camp and, with a young girl from Barnard College, Eleanor Parker, swam across the Rio Grande, and escaped into Mexico. From time to time, I received letters from him signed with varying aliases. The last I heard, he, like his hero, John Reed, had gotten into Russia in time for the revolution.

There were a few others in the class of '17 who stood out. There was the aforementioned Herman J. Mankiewicz, who hailed from a school-teaching family in the slate mines of Pennsylvania. When he was 17, he scraped up enough to move to New York, where he had no difficulty passing the entrance examinations at Columbia. There was hardly an accomplishment Mank didn't boast of and most of his boasts were not idle. He had been a coal miner in Wilkes-Barre. Mank claimed he had read *War and Peace* in a single sitting, which is probably faster than Tolstoy took to correct his proofs. He was a sponge of useless knowledge. He could list, in chronological order, the last 25 governors of Pennsylvania and this feat was useful as it made him money in local wagers.

He particularly overtaxed my credulity by admitting to having spent the summer with the Pendelton roundup and hanging on to the toughest broncos. I didn't have the courage to cross-examine him as his stories always turned out to be true.

Mank was not a joiner; his ambition was to be a free-swinging heckler. Logic would have suggested that his politics be on the port side but he couldn't afford to conform to any rule of Darwinian origin. Having views was a form of intellectual therapy. It was clear, he said, that he was against the Right, the Left, and the Center, and the best party was one that was pro-Mank.

Mank paid his tuition and something more by turning his dormitory room into a lending library exclusively erotic. He charged $1 an hour for *Fanny Hill*, 50¢ for *The Memoirs of Josephine Mutzenbacker*, and so on down. On his door was tacked a sign which read, "Come In and Enjoy Yourself." Luckily Dean Fackenthal never passed that way.

Mank's attitudes were a waste of human timber. He was a natural student and he spent his time ridiculing his struggling contemporaries. He had no scruples; if he had had any, he would somehow have turned them to his advantage. He sabotaged his potential rivals and proved his literary ability by succeeding the brilliant Morrie of F.P.A. fame, running "The Off Hour" column in the *Spectator*. He always had something to say and I marveled at his glib verse that appeared regularly in his column. Each morning I shook my head like a losing heavyweight contender in his corner between rounds.

One of those mornings, I happened on a book of verse by Samuel Hoffenstein, *Poems in Praise of Practically Nothing*, and turning the pages I recognized what I had just read in Mank's column. I confronted him. He took the charge airily, saying that he believed in plagiarism and that Hoffenstein came from his home town in Wilkes-Barre; besides, he had given Hoffenstein several of his ideas in exchange. Determined to find whatever truth there was in such controversy, I called up Mr. Hoffenstein, who said that he had told Mank he could take what he wanted. This shook my leaning tower of literary values.

Mank was a menace. He majored in gambling, most of it off the track. It got so that one was hesitant to be seen with him, even merely crossing the quadrangle. Suddenly, he might hurry from your side into a dark vestibule where he would have an appointment with a bookmaker waiting to collect his due—or else! Sarah, the object of his affections, whom he subsequently married, received a threatening phone call from a gangster-like voice and became alarmed at the plight of her would-be husband. Making sense out of Mank was no job for a woman, but she could try.

Time passed, and school days passed, and a Broadway play had opened which was game for Mank's style of criticism. It was called *Merrily We Roll Along*, and was written by George S. Kaufman and Moss Hart. It told its story backwards, the last scene first and the first last.

"How can it be a hit," said Mank, "when it's about a writer who started as a great talent, writing about matters of social significance, coal mines and unions, and when he has a best seller succumbs to the fleshpots, even as you and I. The fleshpots include a showplace on Long Island, a wickerwork Cadillac in the driveway, a marble kidney-shaped swimming pool, around which are gathered the most beautiful girls in the world. The dazzling guests sip champagne and utter quotable phrases. The message of the play is this: How did the poor son of a bitch get himself into such a fix?"

Years later in 1934, the Columbia football team had won the right to play Leland Stanford in the Arroyo Basin. The absurdity of the contest was suggested by the odds, which had stretched to 33 to 1. For the occasion, Mank had become "Joe College" and covered every cent he could get his hands on. Columbia was considered so soft a touch that one partial to the underdog, or better still, the under-lion, was given as much as a 50-point handicap.

Mank was confident that Columbia had the team that could win. Sarah heard him boasting about the odds he had received, all the way from even up. Sarah sought out experts in the field of gambling, the bookmakers. They rarely gave advice, but she reminded them of the many wagers that Mank had lost on football, and when they heard the amounts that Mank was risking, they were won over by her beauty and charm and made an exception. They hedged for her.

The day of the game dawned grim and ugly. It rained all through the game, recorded in pigskin history as the biggest upset in collegiate football. Barabas, George Montgomery, all were heroes. Lou Little, the coach, invented what became known as the Statue-of-Liberty play, and the final score was Columbia 7, Stanford 0.

Mank was halfway drunk by this time. I ran into him as the fans were crowding out. "I've just seen Sarah, Mank." "Sarah *who*?" said the glaze-eyed Mank. "Sarah, your bride, remember?" I said. "What would she be doing here? You must be mistaken," Mank said. But she was there, terrified to confess that she hedged the bet.

The three of us went to my hotel suite. We didn't go to Mank's house because the telephone was cut off; besides, the hotel was more convenient for Mank's program for internal ablution. "You know who won today?" he said to every car they passed. Sarah tried to get in her "but." Mank wasn't listening. He continued, "At least 6,000 bucks, enough to wipe the chalky slate clean." Then Sarah, weeping, came out with her news. Mank said nothing. There was a long silence. I wanted to shorten the sermon of doom. "I just heard that MGM has bought three songs I wrote with Walter Donaldson," I said. I reached in my inside pocket and threw the check on the floor. "It was a smart victory for Columbia."

The silence decided that so generous a gesture deserved a reward. Mank spoke, "Sarah," he said, "dance for the gentleman."

nother character who colored my views was "B.," who was to become a main character in *The Enormous Room*, the World War I novel by the lower-case poet e. e. cummings. e. e. and B. shared the same cell in a French prison. cummings got off without a sentence, but B. was caught with what is called the goods. He had a copy of *Mother Earth* on him. *Mother Earth* was a muckraking magazine in English of, about and for Emma Goldman and her cause, aimed at support of the International Peasantry. From time to time her magazine would run out of paper and cease publication. Emma would explain that she had no machinery for making pulp as the capitalists had conscripted all that was available and bought up all the trees as well. The gendarmes thought the capture of B. a find. They searched the crevices of his apparel and came up with treasure—a photograph of Trotsky and Kerenski drinking a toast to each other.

I first met B. in the Furnald Hall dormitory. On the way to class, I heard the sound of deep snoring coming from a door slightly ajar. I looked into the room and cased it with a quick glance. It was bare except for a bed, on which, at a precarious angle and equally bare, was B. In one corner of the room piled up with care were at least 100 cakes of soap in their original wrappers. B., who had wakened, was now in a sitting position. He said without hesitation:

"Come in, sit down." He held a soap package to my nose. "Smell that." Then he went through wild college cheers for "Daggett and Ramsdell," "Yardley's," "Palmolive."

"Stick around while I get dressed, and we'll go hunting for the perfect smell."

B. wasn't a nut, he merely had his off-center moments which were manifest when he had a drop too much. He became fond of me and I of him. He was the first aesthete I had ever met. He introduced me to Baudelaire's poems, Lachaise, Arthur Lee, and other unconventional art.

Years passed before I saw him again, and even then he was drunk as in his undergraduate days. I thought of taking him to dinner but he was too drunk for that. Formerly a handsome fellow, his appearance was now marred by ugly teeth waving in the breeze. He explained that he meant to have some stainless-steel teeth made but he didn't have the money. With a burst of generosity I gave him $300 to get a set of choppers which he promised would send him on the wagon as well as teach him to bite.

More years passed and I saw him again in Greenwich Village when he knocked on my door, high as a kite, his teeth ugly as ever. I tried to close the door on him. He sat down on the stairway steps outside my door.

"You don't understand people like me." he moaned from outside. "You musn't let an alcoholic handle money. You should make a deal with a dentist in a case like this."

This idea sounded good to me, and I decided to take another chance on B. I called up his dentist and he thought I had the right idea. "By the way," I said, caught by an inspiration, "these teeth are made of stainless steel. Can I have engraved on them *property of Howard Dietz?*"

I didn't see B. again but I heard that he stopped drinking and became a great success. I like to think it was partly because he couldn't hock his teeth.

Love
is a Dancing
Thing

Love had come in the form of a brilliant Barnard girl, Elizabeth Bigelow Hall, who hailed from Virginia. Her mother was a working woman in charge of the office workers for United States Steel. She had solved the problem of the handicapped and underprivileged. She grouped them in various departments, all the blind, the paraplegics, and those who were retarded by language. Betty inherited her social conscience. She had worked on magazines for a few years before entering Barnard. She was four years older than I, and I was afraid she would kiss the campus goodbye after she got her B.A. Her periodic coolness suggested that I might be kissed goodbye along with the campus.

I met her and put her in the news. She was the honored representative of Barnard College students on the Henry Ford peace ship, the *Oscar II,* which planned to cross the Atlantic at the height of the Kaiser's *schrecklichkeit* and get the boys "out of the trenches by Christmas." It was a brave, if somewhat foolish, adventure on the part of the motor magnate, who wanted to make a contribution toward world peace. Though impractical, it showed a nobly sensitive attitude, even if a limited knowledge of history.

Miss Hall allowed me to interview her in her flat. On the parlor mantle was a photograph of her, which I asked for, but was refused. When she went out of the room for a few minutes, I jammed the photo into my pocket and left before she noticed that it was gone. The picture got a front-page, three-column display in the *American.* Furious, she got me on the phone that morning, calling me an "unmannerly, unethical earthworm, an unprincipled mosquito," and other invectives, quite unlike her customary gentle conversation that rarely resorted to epithet.

I stood on the pier as she sailed away and waved constant goodbyes but she didn't notice me. I was the last of the visitors to leave the pier. I didn't feel guilty somehow, only sad. I had had a compulsion to steal that photograph. Should I be denied a front-page by-line? It was my first by-line. My compulsion was humored.

It would have been nice to have pleased Miss Hall, and I went to the pier when the *Oscar II* returned to New York. She gave me a complete brush-off. I wrote a glowing account of her part in the expedition, but that did no good and she ignored me whenever we met, which was usually in the lunchroom at University Hall. I always said "hello" and gave her a big smile, until it got to be a game. I dented her composure, but wooing did not get on a compatible basis until we found ourselves face to face at the meeting of the editorial board of *Challenge,* a newly formed liberal undergraduate publication. She gave me a liberal smile for a change, and I saw her every day for about 19 years after that.

A windfall of $500 came my way in my junior year. I was the winner of a competition for the college man who wrote the best advertisement for Fatima cigarettes.

The ad I wrote pictured two men in dinner jackets standing beside a potted palm denoting a party. One has a happy expression on his face, the other has a not-so-happy expression. Not-so says: "Isn't this a stupid affair?" to which Happy, offering a cigarette, replies: "Do you think so? Then have a Fatima."

Several friends decided it was up to me to give them a banquet, and I chose Lorber's Restaurant where you could eat all you could eat for a dollar. Among those present were Bennett Cerf, Irwin Edman, the albino philosopher, Max Lincoln Schuster, who started the crossword-puzzle craze with the firm of Simon and Schuster. There were Merryle Stanley Rukeyser, later the financial editor of the Hearst chain of newspapers, M. R. Werner, author of *Barnum Brigham Young* and many other distinguished tomes, the political columnist George E. Sokolsky ("Sok"), who subsequently wrote a Chinese geography. Sok on campus declared himself an anarchist, but off campus made speeches in Yiddish for the Republican Party. Oscar Hammerstein of Rodgers and Hammerstein was there, as was Larry Hart of Rodgers and Hart.

Lorber's didn't profit from these eaters.

The Fatima advertisement was used extensively and I received letters of congratulations with offers of jobs from several advertising agencies. This was an opportune time to quit Columbia. I wasn't conscientious in my studies. I had neglected Professor Edwin E. Slosson's courses in physics and chemistry. It wasn't that I couldn't grasp the essentials. It was that the class was at 9 o'clock and I got to bed at dawn and imagined that I could melodiously snore my way to a degree. I would never find a more propitious moment to launch a career. Of the advertising offers the most attractive was that of the Philip Goodman Company:

Dear Mr. Dietz:

> *I have a small agency and pay meager salaries. There is little chance of advancement. If you are interested, come and see me.*

> *(signed) Philip Goodman*

While I knew nothing about advertising agencies, I was instinctively mindful of what Sinclair Lewis was saying in his novels. I applied at Goodman's, whose office was at 33rd Street and Broadway. It was the garment district and Goodman did a lot of advertising in *Womens Wear,* a trade paper that occasionally printed respectable stuff. It had a drama critic I got to know, named Kelcy Allen, who was noted for a remark he made at the opening performance of a *Macbeth.* When the Shakespearian character said, "Lay on McDuff," Allen was heard to say, "Lay off McBride!" McBride was a well-known ticket speculator.

40   When I met Goodman, he asked me if I was a reader. Did

I know authors? Had I read *Rasselas* by Dr. Johnson? I thought I was in the wrong place.

"What has this got to do with the job?" I asked nervily.

"A great deal," he said. "Anybody can get a job in advertising if you want to follow the usual boring lines; I want men who have had some truck with culture."

"You don't seem to have many men," I said, looking around the room and seeing no one.

We discussed Shaw's plays, the then-raging war on *Mrs. Warren's Profession*, Brieux's *Damaged Goods*, *The Soul of Man* by Oscar Wilde, and G. K. Chesterton's *Tremendous Trifles*. He thought most criticism of erotica was tommyrot. I left with an appointment for the same time next day. We never discussed the job or the salary or the hours. I went back to Furnald Hall somewhat bewildered, wondering if a job with Goodman was too chancy.

The Goodman office was a cubbyhole and Goodman's proportions took up a lot of it. The staff consisted of Miss Landsman and me. Miss Landsman, the secretary, was a dynamo. She did all the telephoning and filing and whatever there was to be done outside of the writing of advertisements and the selling of accounts. Goodman did that. Most of his accounts were cloak-and-suit manufacturers and though Goodman himself was an entirely different personality, he understood what would appeal to the transplanted foreigner who sold his merchandise at cost plus five percent. He had about 10 customers for whom he made neat layouts for folders and house organs. They were obvious philosophics in the manner of Elbert Hubbard and the copy in all the house organs was the same except for the masthead. It was pretty corny stuff, mostly in Old English type. Goodman made a profit of $300 a month on each house organ.

Goodman did not notice me much, but when he had a conversational urge, he would summon me to his cramped quarter and discuss the fat men of literature. It was an unusual situation and I did homework to be ready for Goodman. I read fat Balzac, and fat Thackeray. I equipped myself with literary anecdotes.

Goodman wanted to be a book publisher or a theatrical producer. He liked Don Marquis's "The Old Soak" from his column in the *Evening Sun*. Goodman wanted to make a play out of this character and I assumed the role of a go-between. I went to see Don Marquis in Lipton's Saloon. He was enthusiastic but didn't know how it would work out.

"I have never written a play," he said.

"Neither has Mr. Goodman," I replied. "You start without the handicap of knowledge."

Goodman's personality seemed to improve with the dawning of this new ambition. He had to raise the money, about $10,000, and he approached one of his garment customers, I. Guinzberg. Goodman used his slick approach. "Guinz," he said, "I'm going to make you create a coat and suit based on the style of George Sand; you'll incidentally put up the money for a play, it will only cost $10,000, and it will be a bombshell in the garment center."

"Why do I have to fool around with plays?" said Guinzberg.

"It will give you something to live for. Your money will be in safe hands."

"Whose hands will it be in?"

"Mine."

This dialogue ended with the loan of the money, and there were frequent meetings at Lipton's which gave Goodman the feeling that he was in an old English tavern. His greeting became heartier and he adopted the role of the portly bootlegger in Don Marquis's manuscript.

Through the atmosphere of the saloon and the cavalier company of reporters, Goodman and I got to talk to H. L. Mencken, George Jean Nathan, Joseph Jefferson O'Neill, Donald Henderson Clarke, Lindsay Johnson, Homer Davenport, and several other writers who had views on everything.

Goodman met Samuel Goldwyn and he became Goodman's

client. Goldwyn needed a trademark for his film company and asked us to design one. He did his producing in Fort Lee, New Jersey, and his home office was on Fifth Avenue and 40th Street opposite the library lions. One would think that the Goldwyn trademark stemmed from such an obvious influence, but Leo the lion, with the Latin *Ars Gratia Artis* (Art for Art's Sake) decorating his proud dome, was my idea, not Andrew Carnegie's. I got the idea from the laughing lion decoration in the college comic *The Jester*. The lion used in the magazine was a symbol of Columbia University, which in turn was taken from the lion on the crest of Kings College. That's powerful lineage enough for a film company.

Goodman had a large bright room for an art department. Commercial artists could use this area for free as a studio and Goodman would get their services for less.

I got to know John Held, Jr., the Mormon who invented the flapper, Hal Burroughs who made designs for the house organs, Stu Palmer who would imitate well-known draftsmen, Ted Ireland who was handsome and talented and a lover who made many conquests.

The most complicated was Ralph Barton, a fine line illustrator whose work appeared in *The New Yorker*, and many other publications. He was a favorite of editors Harold Ross and Henry Blackman Sell in particular. Barton came from Kansas City and was jealous of Thomas Hart Benton, who was also born in Kansas City. Barton pretended to despise Benton's work and he was a most unhappy man.

He had many women and married two of them. Ann Minnerle, who was only at home in a bed, and Carlotta Monterey, who left Barton and married Eugene O'Neill. Barton never got over Carlotta, but he managed to fall in love with Ruth Kindley, a department-store heiress who jilted him, sailing away on the very day that Carlotta arrived home from her honeymoon in France with O'Neill.

Barton used to sit in Goodman's art room and do his illustrations, telling intimate details of his excitement of the night before, but after this happened he stopped talking.

One night in his one-room apartment on East 44th Street, Barton wrote farewell letters to Carlotta Monterey and Ruth Kindley. He drew a diagram of his heart and tacked it to his drawing board. He drew profiles of Ruth and Carlotta and tacked those on the board too. Then he put on a gray silk dressing gown, got into his bed, laid the drawing board on his chest and shot himself with a .38.

The war was on in earnest and we were bound to get into it. I avoided the draft by enlisting in the Navy. It was important I marry Betty now to delay the call to the services. I lured her to City Hall and Mr. James Cruze, the city clerk, performed the ceremony. Fred Besel, a handsome sailor, was my best man. We had met him at a Greenwich Village dance hall "The Golden Ball of Isis," which was no place to go if you felt respectable and didn't want to have your clothes pulled off.

In Spuyten Duyvil, I had rented a barn for Betty which had been converted into a dwelling by Egmont Aarons and Josephine Bell, a couple who owned the Washington Square Book Shop. The Aarons had done an admirable job with the barn, which was carpentered to the hilt and every bit of furniture in the place was made out of boxes and barrels. It was clever and cost nothing. Mrs. Andrews, a friendly neighbor, had encouraged us in our domestic enterprise.

There was a fuel shortage in the winter of 1917, and our two-story barn with its bright colors and handmade furniture couldn't get any coal. We had no strong connections in the neighborhood; we had no pull. We slept in our overcoats and kept the gas oven going.

When the gas gave out, the porcelain in the bathroom cracked and pipes burst. We still needed a coalman and now we needed a plumber. Our drawing room became icy as a skating rink. Betty had a pair of skates which she put on and played hockey with a broom while I opposed her with the mop. In order to keep warm and make life bearable, we made everything into a game.

When we were confronted with the necessity of doing our personal chores, we could either go outdoors, where it was cold as kelcy or take to newspapers. We chose to be paper-trained, and made little packages, out-rivaling each other in neatness, making our parcels look almost gift-wrapped. We placed our handiwork outside the door and went downtown —Betty to her secretarial tasks at *Judge* and I to Goodman's.

Returning home at the end of the working day, we were greeted by our neighbor Mrs. Andrews. She was wringing her hands.

"Only a little while ago, a strange man came by and I was terrified. He took the packages and ran off. I hope they weren't valuable!"

Lawton Mackall, editor of *Judge*, which had become a market for my occasional contributions (those that weren't good enough for F.P.A.), without twisting my arm got me to write the lyrics for an operetta entitled *Behind the Front*. Carl Engle of the Boston Music Company wrote the music and Mackall furnished the book. I would sing the songs at the slightest provocation. They were Gilbertian, but all meter and rhyme and lacked blood. It was later performed many times in high schools and preparatory schools.

I had kept my job as college correspondent for Columbia while working for Goodman, but I no longer went to any classes and the time had come for me to honorably resign. I gave a complete report to Managing Editor McGrath. I told him it was difficult passing up $7.50 a column but I valiantly sacrificed this fabulous income for the love of country. I told him that I had been hired by the Goodman Agency, got

myself married to Betty Hall, had written songs for a published libretto, had quit Columbia and enlisted in the United
States Naval Reserve and was waiting to be called up. I
thanked him effusively for his guiding hand, and would have
told him all this sooner if I hadn't been so afraid of him. He
laughed and had a bottle of Chablis delivered to the doorstep
of the barn on Kappock Street, Spuyten Duyvil.

Before the call came I had what became a disastrous episode with Victor Arden of Ohman and Arden, who were arranging a vaudeville act for the Viennese singer and dancer
Lina Abarbanel. They needed the lyric for the title song
"Philopena." Louie Wyle, a small-time theatrical manager,
would pay $250. Breathless, I said I would try to write it,
and my lyric was the one accepted.

The sketch went into rehearsal on the day my name was
called by the Navy. I telephoned goodbye to Wyle, kissed
Betty goodbye and boarded a train to Norfolk, Virginia,
home of the Hampton Roads Naval Base. Betty worked on
Judge for the duration.

fter receiving the indoctrination by bath, hair-
shave and uniforms, two whites and two blues
and a blanket which we lodged in a seabag, we
were assigned to our barracks. We laced up our
hammocks with dangerously feeble knots. Subsequent days were spent marching to the music of my former
landlord, John Philip Sousa, which made marching in the
Virginia sun easier to take.

A cigarette lighter of the briquet type was in the back
pocket of my whites while I was marching to the "National
Emblem March." An officer in the glass house, which over-
looks the parade ground, noticed my mound of smoke. Step-
ping across the grinder, he ordered the drill stopped and
plucked a burning orange rope from my back pocket. It was

a laughing matter to all in my row. The incident was referred to as "Dietz's arson."

Correspondence from Betty informed me that *Philopena* was playing at the Palace, the world's premiere vaudeville house. It was my first theatrical show, even if the show was only one act, and I was dying to see it and collect my pay, but it was difficult to get a furlough or even a day off for at least a month after shots had been taken. I finally managed one 48-hour leave, and went to New York to see Wyle in his noisy building and collect my $250. I took a seat in the reception room, which was empty. The door to the office was opened by Wyle, who greeted me with enthusiasm.

"Take a seat," he said, "and I'll get to you as soon as I can."

I told him I had very little time. I had to get back to Hampton Roads by the morning if not sooner, as there was nothing more important to the Navy than punctuality. Wyle retired to his desk behind the wooden partition, and I waited an eternity before deciding to go in without an invitation. I opened the door, and was greeted by a room empty except for a desk and a chair. There was a door leading to the hall-way. Wyle had gone, flown the coop. I couldn't believe it. "There's no business like show business."

Betty put me on the train to Norfolk and said she would see a lawyer but I had no confidence. The atmosphere around Wyle was too fetid to approach.

Our company spent a week at Virginia Beach practicing on the rifle range. It rained every minute we were there. Living out of a seabag isn't fun, even when the sun is shining, but in the rain, with every piece of clothing soaking, with every dish of slumgullion making a tide on the platter, antagonism to the whole human race, especially that part of it which includes the Navy, was boundless. The wet rifle was loaded with wet bullets. A grim humor possessed us.

We returned to Hampton Roads after a week. Most of us

had bronchial disturbances from plopping our carcasses in the quickish mud. The officers, who had not gone to Virginia Beach, were stoical about it.

There came a night, about a month later, when our barracks was called out and we gathered in front of the glass house, seabags and all. Roll was called, and all the second-class seamen were lined up on their way to the shipyard— that is, all except me. An officer informed me that I was to be transferred to the History Building where *Navy Life*, the naval base magazine was published. Evidently there was something literary in my dossier. I was happy to be left behind; the rest of our company had been shipped to Honolulu where they coaled ship for the duration, while I wrote satirical-verse editorials of a feigned jingo sort. I was in a solid stone building and had a cot to sleep in instead of a waving hammock—the height of luxury.

There were some few gobs at *Navy Life* who invited friendship. Tommy Haines from Montgomery, Alabama; Eddie Ford from the Kansas City *Star;* Russell Iredel, a clever illustrator; Ted Rotzheim from Minnesota. Rotzheim had a friendly feeling for liquor, and managed mysteriously to get frequent passes and hang around the St. Andrews Club in Roanoke. He filled the History Building with the smell of gin.

Chaplain Knox would drop into our office occasionally and we'd all keep very quiet. I got up my courage and told him Lieutenant Huscke had appointed himself editorial supervisor of *Navy Life*, and that we couldn't get out a satisfactory magazine unless we had the feeling that it was our own and not the officers'. Huscke was removed from his editorship and we operated without a boss.

Then Tom Goodwin was promoted to an ensign, and he felt that as he was the only officer on the staff he was in absolute command. We were all working at our typewriters one day, when Goodwin in his ensign's uniform appeared in the doorway. He swept in and said, "Carry on, men."

None of us carried on. *Navy Life* members were not to be treated like gobs, and whenever Goodwin was in the room we would pretend not to hear what he was saying.

Lieutenant Harms was the next one to be appointed to look after the conduct of the staff of *Navy Life*, but he also misinterpreted his assignment. He thought of himself not only as an editor, but, worse still, as a censor. I was commissioned to go over the contents of the magazine with Harms before printing. This meant waiting until the lieutenant was good and ready to pass it on to the printer. When I told him this was to be a gob's magazine, not an officer's, he punished me by getting a petty officer to command me to lift a load of pig iron and put it three feet from where it had been and then put it back several times. Doan's Little Liver Pills had no effect on my back.

This physical assignment may have had something to do with my subsequent collapse. One morning about a month later, I woke up coughing and spitting, too feverish to keep my balance. The line at sick bay was getting formidably long and standing there became an ordeal. I made a suggestion to the corpsman who was sick himself. "Why not stick a thermometer in the mouths of everyone in line? Then you could decide who should have priorities."

These must have been my famous last words, for I woke up in unfamiliar surroundings a week later. There were 32 sailors in the sick bay barracks and many of them died.

When I was recovering, they gave me a tonic every afternoon. It was milk and brandy. I didn't care for the milk, but you had to get that in order to get the brandy. The tonic was one of the features of the place. A corpsman guarded it as if it were nectar. When temperatures became normal, names were taken off the list. My name had reached the "taking off" stage, but I worked out an ingenious plan of my own. On top of the list it said "Diet." I put a "Z" right after the word and so succeeded in getting my brandy long after discontinuance was due.

Armistice Day, November 11, 1918, was celebrated in the ward. There was chaos. Patients jumped from bed to bed, no matter how ill they were. I recovered and was subsequently discharged from the Navy.

The Columbia campus paper had printed a story to the effect that I was dead, and when I was riding to New York on the train, I met Freddie Pitts and his wife Alice, classmates of mine at the School of Journalism. They turned pale at seeing me. It seems that when I was in a coma, my condition had been misinterpreted.

Got a Brand New Suit

y honorable discharge from the service inspired an all-night drinking orgy in which Betty and I spent the $85 of Navy pay I'd saved. We woke up in Prospect Park, Brooklyn, which was an odd place to find ourselves. We were under a sheltering tree and had barely enough change to get back to Manhattan.

I had to get a job and couldn't look for one until I had a suit of civilian clothes and an overcoat. I didn't know anyone prosperous enough to touch for the amount I needed, but I cooked up a scheme with Mank who had been part of our celebration. He had a charge account at Brooks Brothers and I asked him if I could use it. Payday would surely come soon and they would settle for slow pay like the English.

I decided that Goldwyn Pictures was the practical company to attack. Earlier, Goldwyn had formed a partnership with Selwyn. When Goldwyn changed his name, he took the first syllable of his own "Goldfish" and the second syllable of "Selwyn" to make Goldwyn. Had he taken the first syllable of "Selwyn" and the second of "Goldfish," he would have had Selfish.

Gabriel Hess was the lawyer for the firm. He knew me from my prewar days with Goodman, and said he would try to help me get a job. Helen Hess, his wife, was a cozy companion, friendly to me, mainly because I laughed at her anecdotes. She had taken her seven-year-old daughter to a school that was almost exclusively gentile, but because her cast was somewhat Aryan, the headmistress decided to grant an interview. "I hope you won't mind, Mrs. Hess, if at Christmas we tell your little Elizabeth some stories about Christ." Helen said, "I don't know any stories about Christ that my little Elizabeth ought not to know."

She influenced Samuel Goldwyn into considering me for a job in the publicity department. I was given a chair and told to wait, that Mr. Goldwyn would see me shortly. The day went by and Mr. Goldwyn did not see me. Out of sheer boredom, I put a piece of paper in a nearby typewriter and wrote a letter to the editorial page of *The Evening Mail*. I selected *The Mail* because it ran the F.P.A. column. The letter was about Samuel Goldwyn, who had left Poland and gone to Gloversville, New York, where he had a friend, Abraham Lehr, in the glove business. I told about his success selling kid gloves, suede gloves, silk and woolen gloves. His success had shown America to be a land of opportunity. I said he would revolutionize the film industry with the newly formed Goldwyn Pictures Company. I reported for work the next day even though I hadn't been hired.

The letter appeared in *The Mail* two days later. I answered it using a pseudonym. I sent another letter with another pseudonym. Each letter was a plug for Goldwyn. Though I stayed at my post for four days, I did nothing that was not self-assigned. I wrote a letter from Sam Goldwyn addressed to George Eastman of the Kodak Company. In my Eastman letter, I pointed out that the Kodak Company could be a great benefactor to the film industry by inventing noninflammable film. I sent the letter into Goldwyn's office with a brief note saying, "This is the sort of letter you ought to write for its publicity value." Goldwyn liked that letter and he showed it to everybody who visited him. It took days before he mailed it.

He finally got around to sending for me saying he wanted to see the man who wrote the letters. I entered his office via the exit side and was standing on the carpet while he was dictating to his secretary. When he was through dictating, he looked up and asked what I was doing there. I told him that I had been writing letters about him for the past week and that these letters had appeared in several papers, and that he, Goldwyn, did not appreciate such good publicity. Goldwyn offered me a job which I stretched from the regulation $50 a week to $200 a week.

I promised Betty I would only stay on a salary until I

could write a book or a play or a song. But $200 a week would be difficult to pass up.

The publicity director at Goldwyn Pictures, when I got my job there, was Ralph Block, who didn't get as much as I got. But then he didn't apply under the same circumstance as my spectacular letter campaign. Ralph had been dramatic critic of *The Herald Tribune*. He was well read and aesthetic. Some would say he was too aesthetic to be a publicity man. He relied on me a great deal and, in fact, gave me no assignments, allowing me to shift for myself.

I would make a detailed synopsis of every current movie. I also wrote biographies of the actors and directors under contract. I serviced these to critics and editors. They appreciated the attention. Being useful is a good way to make friends.

Ralph didn't like his job and he petitioned the executives to transfer him to the studio in Culver City, California. I thought I would be his successor. But no. The sales manager, Felix Feist, preferred a man in a gray suit named George O'Neill. I found him intelligent and attractive. O'Neill kept a diary of what he had done each day, and he also made entries of what our rival companies had been up to in the way of stunts. But he lacked imagination. At the end of a working day, we would sit in his office and have a drink. I asked him how he got the job which was rightfully mine, although I didn't say that. He was frank. "I read an article in *Printers' Ink* on how the movies should be promoted. I studied it and memorized every point. I got a friend on the board of directors to propose me for the job. This was Francis Gudger, representing the Du Pont interests."

"Who wrote the article?" I asked. He didn't remember. I never told him I wrote it.

You had to be thick-skinned to work for Samuel Goldwyn. He had a temper and he would lose it often, especially when he was wrong. I got to know him on intimate terms. I saw him every day and admired him for his shrewdness. He also had good taste in pictures, which was surprising. A large percentage of the many jokes attributed to him was true. His secretary came to him and asked if she could destroy the files from 10 years back. He said, "Yes, but keep copies."

I first learned about exploitation, an important aspect of the movie business, from Hunt Stromberg, exploitation director. I sat in his office and my bewildered ears heard him dictating a letter of advice to theatre owners on how to promote a picture.

"Hire an elephant from a nearby circus," he said, "and have him parade through the town."

I couldn't help interrupting. "Suppose there is no circus? What does he do then?"

Stromberg gave me a scornful look. "That is exploitation. You tell the theatre a lot of things they can't do and let them select."

Louis Sherwin, who was the drama critic on the *New York Globe,* was hired as an editor by Goldwyn. I had written a criticism of a film for him and said it lacked punch. Sherwin asked me to define "punch." "Punch is an indefinable something without which nothing is successful. Jesus Christ had it, and so did Jack Dempsey, and Goldwyn pictures better have it," I told him.

I n my early days with Goldwyn, he created a subsidiary called Eminent Authors. Popular American novelists combined to write stories for motion pictures that were to be filmed in Culver City. Among those incorporated were Rex Beach, Rupert Hughes, Gouverneur Morris, Gertrude Atherton, Mary Roberts Rinehart, Basil King and Leroy Scott.

When Maurice Maeterlinck visited America, Goldwyn

wanted to annex the famed Belgian playwright, whose works included *Monna Vanna, Mary Magdalene, The Burgomaster of Stilemonde* and *Pelléas and Mélisande.* He had written, as well, *The Life of the Bee,* an unexpected departure, and was enjoying unprecedented contemporary fame for his *Blue Bird,* being performed at the Metropolitan Opera.

J. B. Pond, the agent, secured speaking engagements for the author for a coast-to-coast tour, but with the first talk at Carnegie Hall he was in trouble. Maeterlinck couldn't speak English, and indeed, could hardly speak French, his Belgian accent was so thick. He was reading from a script that had been written in phonetic English—"ainded" for ended, "ichou" for issue, and so on. While Maeterlinck knew what he was talking about, he didn't know what he was saying, and the effect was dizzying. The Master couldn't communicate, and in the middle of his much-heralded lecture, he broke down and made a conspicuous retreat from the lecture hall.

Professor Henry Russell, a Boston concert impresario, felt that opportunity had knocked, and he dashed to the Waldorf Astoria and got an audience with the author. Russell then urged Goldwyn to sign Maeterlinck to a motion picture contract. Goldwyn listened to the frock-coated Bostonian and made a most extravagant deal for the playwright's services. I was present at the negotiations; my accent was as good as anyone's there. Goldwyn listed the stipend of his eminent authors in order to give Maeterlinck the feeling that he would share the rarefied atmosphere of American literary lights and American substantial terms. To Goldwyn's surprise, Maeterlinck said he hadn't heard of any of those authors and mentioned George Bernard Shaw and James Barrie as English authors he *had* heard of. Goldwyn turned to me with puzzlement at the playwright's ignorance. "What is he, a dumbbell?" he asked.

However, an agreement was reached: Maeterlinck was to go to the studio and stay there until the outline of a scenario was completed. He was to receive $100,000, and the use of a house the company used for visiting celebrities in Brentwood. Goldwyn, who pronounced "Maeterlinck" as though it were a delicatessen item, cautioned the maestro against contributing anything like *The Life of the Bee.* He said the film public wasn't ready for that sort of thing.

J. B. Pond sued Maeterlinck for $100,000, and sought to stop him from lecturing. Maeterlinck considered his obligation to Pond at an end and blamed the agent for subjecting him to the embarrassment of his phonetic ordeal. He would henceforth be represented by Henry Russell and was determined to study the technique of picture making in his stay at Culver City preparatory to writing one original story a year for Goldwyn. He toyed with dramatizing the life of the ant, but abandoned the notion as it was too much like *The Life of the Bee,* which Goldwyn didn't want.

The first thing I did was to arrange a spectacular junket to take him from New York to California. I got President Wilson's private railroad car, "The Mayflower," placed at the disposal of the Belgian genius. This luxurious palace on rails was to stop at all the key cities on the Santa Fe Trail. In the party were Mr. Maeterlinck and his flaming red-haired wife, Mr. and Mrs. Henry Russell, and his business manager, W. R. MacDonald. I asked Edwin Justus Mayer, the press agent (who was, as well, a poet and playwright), to cover the trip. His aesthetic side would appeal to the Gallic giant. At one time, I had tried to get Edwin Mayer for $50 a week, but he was scornful in his refusal and asked for a hundred. "I can borrow $50 a week," he said. We reached a more generous agreement when I assigned him to cover this most unusual hegira.

The train left Grand Central Station, February 11, 1920. There were secretaries and stenographers on board, and the Maeterlinck special was a busy place. Mayer telephoned me from the train once a day and I kept abreast of the squabbles en route, getting a blow-by-blow description in fractured French. In Los Angeles the party was to be met by Samuel Goldwyn and welcomed to the studio. Henry Russell was not enthusiastic about banquets and speeches, as he planned to revive the personal appearance tour after Maeterlinck had finished his chore at the studio and had improved his speech, which couldn't fail to be improved.

I set out to get as much publicity as possible, as we'd paid dearly for it. Announcing his affiliation with Goldwyn, the poet in a braver dialectic declared: "America doesn't give the motion picture the artistic importance it merits." In Memphis, he predicted the return of beer and wine. In Kansas, Maeterlinck declared that the West was more civilized than New York. In St. Louis, Archbishop Glennon declared Maeterlinck's philosophy one of pessimism and falsehood, but the poet was catching on to the noisy political U.S.A.

In Dallas, the Goldwyn pictures division manager, Lou Remy, a Texas character who spoke "y'all," had arranged a big banquet to honor the artistic guest. He invited the governor of the state, the mayor of Dallas and other celebrities who wore 10-gallon hats and carried blue birds mounted on sticks. But Henry Russell was determined to discourage the public appearances. He gave orders for the train not to stop at Dallas, but to go on to Houston. Left stranded on the platform were Lou Remy and others of the welcoming committee. Remy's astonishment was great as the train swept past the Dallas station. When his rage fermented, he sent a telegram to Tom Shaw, the MGM man in Houston saying: MAETERLINCK SPECIAL JUST BY-PASSED DALLAS MAN ON BOARD HENRY RUSSELL MEET TRAIN AND PUNCH RUSSELL IN JAW. Remy received a return telegram from Shaw stating simply: DID.

As a postscript to this journey, Maeterlinck was flamboyantly welcomed in Culver City. He spent about two months trying to concoct a story. Finally, he came up with a page and a half of typewriting entitled, *The Power of Light*.

It was intended as a vehicle for the great Goldwyn stars but was quite abstract.

Goldwyn also tried to lure George Bernard Shaw into films. Ralph Block asked the novelist Hugh de Sellincourt to arrange a meeting and Shaw actually invited Goldwyn to tea.

De Sellincourt wrote a letter to Block describing the mad tea party. Shaw said, "I'm afraid we will not get together, Mr. Goldwyn. You are interested in art, and I am interested in business." I sent this letter back to our representative in London, who had it put on the wire. It was a mild sensation.

Our abode in those days was a street-level apartment in a brownstone building at 18 West 8th Street. It would have been a tranquil spot if it weren't for the clanging of the crosstown cable trolley cars just outside our window, so close you could almost touch them. There were two cars on the line, and each car had a conductor and a motorman. The cars used one track with a place to pass each other where the tracks separated. This place was right outside our window—where else? At 4 A.M., like a truce or a cease fire, the two cars rested and a crap game was immediately started. One motorman kept the accounts, the other furnished the dice.

When you had nothing better to do at 4 A.M. than watch the game, you could listen to a couple of Spaniards making love on the third floor, or you could watch the musicians emerge from their dark cellar cabarets, carrying brasses and cellos, just in case they should feel the urge to drop in at the "stay awake places" or maybe pick up some buddies and start a jam session in one of the trolleys.

The family upstairs were our landlords, unusual landlords, who loved music and poetry. They were Lou and Emily

Paley, and there were several artists in their family tree, including the essayist Simeon Strunsky, and George and Ira Gershwin, then unknown and unheard of, plus others who at the time were on the fringes of noisy accomplishment.

Emily Paley was a Strunsky, and very beautiful. Despite our proximity, it took a long time to get acquainted, and then it didn't happen until I accidently short-changed them on the rent. They loathed rent collecting, and assuming their most impersonal landlord attitude, they wanted to know who were we to think we could afford to hold them up. However, by the second month, we managed our way into their good graces. As they explained it, friendship was worth more than money, and we could take our time about paying the rent.

Our prize possession, which we acquired at an auction, was a crystal chandelier. Every Saturday night, there was a jam session in the Paleys' apartment on the second floor, the chandelier had the shakes, due to the rhythmic pounding of the piano on the floor above, which was our ceiling. One Saturday night, Betty and I were on our way to the theatre. Just as we were leaving, I decided to go upstairs and protest the tremors they were evoking from our chandelier. "If that chandelier falls, one of us might get killed," I said to Betty. I knocked on the Paleys' door. Someone opened it carefully and put his finger to his lips, cautioning me not to disturb the music. I saw about 40 people sitting on the floor around the Steinway, while a dark-complexioned chap was playing and singing in a rich guttural. I took a seat on the floor. My wife below, impatient with waiting, came upstairs to find out what had happened to me. I tiptoed to the door, put my finger to my lips and motioned her to come in and sit beside me. We never made the theatre and we stopped bothering about our chandelier. Instead, we became regulars at Lou Paley's Saturday night sessions, listening to George Gershwin's songs.

Among the regular Saturday night audience was Oscar

Levant, who was a substitute at the piano, playing Gershwin's music when George was not available—which was seldom, Samuel Behrman, the playwright, Alex Aarons, Buddy DeSylva, Golly Hayes and other men and women about Broadway and Washington Square. It was the scene of many a verbal battle about song and scores, librettos and operas. Oscar Levant could crush with a phrase. Of Sigmund Romberg, the operetta balladeer, he said, "He writes the kind of music you whistle on the way into the theatre." Newman Levy, the light-verse lawyer-poet asked Oscar if he thought Gershwin's music would be played a hundred years hence. "If George is around, it will," he said. Oscar's wife, Barbara Smith, was a great beauty, though she was not the type you would pick for the epigrammatic epithet maker. They were married nevertheless, and divorced almost as soon. Barbara married Arthur Loew, the son of Marcus Loew, the theatre magnate. Oscar telephoned her long distance, California to New York, and instead of congratulations, he asked her what was playing at Loew's State and when the feature went on.

Oscar wasn't a composer, he was a magnificent musician. However, he did write one song that had some popularity. It was "Lady Play Your Mandolin." "It's an advantage to have a limited output," said Oscar. "When George Gershwin is asked to play his repertoire, he plays all evening. I just play "Lady Play Your Mandolin" and I'm through."

I was fond of Oscar, but there was something about our twin natures which made us exchange insults. I told him that I wanted to make a date with him every day so that I would know where he was and could avoid the place.

Joe Gould was a village habitué. He borrowed his livelihood from many eccentric friends, particularly from Morrie Werner the biographer, whose greatest eccentricity was lending money to Joe Gould.

Joe was writing a history of the world and he would write

things like "I am sitting on the subway steps at Sixth Avenue and 42nd Street and a man with eyeglasses framed in teeth is walking by. I record the history of the world. That's the history of the world today."

He would go to the basement of Morrie Werner's house and call up, "Hey Werner, you got any money for me today?" He would assess people. "You owe me $15.00 on Wednesday, but if you pay me now, I'll knock off 10 percent."

One night Gorham Munson, Morrie Werner, and a few literary boys and girls dropped in at our flat on 8th Street, bringing with them Charlie Sweeney, who had just finished an exposé of the Ku Klux Klan. They had been celebrating and flattered our abode by singling it out as a port of call on so eloquent a mission.

Our big room was in a state of transition. There were close to 26 stacks of books on the floor and we were in the midst of alphabetically arranging them to fit the bookshelves.

Sweeney was fascinated by the books and started to dance among them, doing what he called a "book dance." Betty whispered that we were out of drink and we were well out of it. I thought it best to enter into the spirit of celebration and I stepped out to Spanish Willie's a few blocks away on 3rd Street under the tracks to replenish our supply.

The place was empty except for one customer who sat at a table with his head buried in his arms.

"Who's that?" I asked Willie.

"He's a chap who comes here a lot," said Willie. "He likes my muscatel. His name is Eugene O'Neill."

I gave a big "what!" and said I'd take him home. "He shouldn't be seen in this condition. Get me a taxi," I said.

While Willie delivered a bottle to 8th Street, I went to work on O'Neill. It was hard getting him into the taxi. He came alive for a few minutes when I asked him where he lived but he wasn't coherent enough to give me a clue. He'd fall asleep and I'd start all over again. He'd mutter a few mumbles and would fall asleep. I had to do something to protect the great man.

I finally decided to take him to our house. On the way, he came to and gave me his address. I told the taxi driver to deposit him at the Royalton and got out.

"This man is a great man," I said. "He's Eugene O'Neill. He wrote *Anna Christie* and *Beyond the Horizon.*"

"He looks like just another drunk to me, but I'll take your word for it," said the driver.

Back home all was serene. Betty told me that Sweeney had passed out as soon as he finished his book dance, and the others had left. Betty had instructions from Sweeney's family to wake him up and get him off on the 10 o'clock train the next morning to Trenton.

It was almost as difficult an arrangement as the night before. I got Sweeney into a cab in front of the Brevoort and told the driver to go to Penn Station. I bought a ticket to Trenton and deposited Sweeney on the 10 o'clock train. Then I went home, telephoned his wife, and went to bed.

At 6 o'clock that night I was walking to the corner at 11th Street and Sixth Avenue to get a newspaper. I passed Sweeney, back from Trenton, giving another staggering performance. I nodded to him but he didn't recognize me and passed right on by saying, "Hi ya, buddy."

I got to know the stage designer Norman Bel Geddes and saw a lot of him due to his having invented a game called "War." It was a sort of aerial chess. There were two opponents with their armies, navies and airforces; their soldiers, sailors and flyers operating on a scale of 1 inch to 10 yards.

I was the mastermind of one side and Norman of the other. He spent all his time neglecting his work in favor of planning moves and maneuvers. We finished only one game, but this one game lasted six months.

Norman had an apartment in the Bronx at Loring Place, and Betty and I moved up there to be near our opponents.

We played the game on a sort of table 14 feet long and 3 feet wide built especially for the carnage. Each side had a terrain, an equal number of mountains, streams, valleys and wooded shelters. Approximately midway on the table there was a barrier that reached up about a yard. You could get a 10-minute study of the opponent's formation by sacrificing five airplanes and climbing up the ladder to look.

We had a gallery that kept the score. There were stenographers at the halfway mark. We had enemies placed at strategic points and some of their moves were inspirational. Members of the War Department came up from Washington to observe Norman's strategy.

Among those who helped in the maneuvers were Bruce Bliven and his wife Rosie, Maxwell Anderson, Charles Lapworth who worked for me at MGM, Norman's brother, Dudley Geddes, Robert Flaherty, Myron Sterns, the writer, and many others who were fascinated by the game.

Living in the Bronx had its drawbacks and Betty couldn't stand it. It was too clean and cleanliness had no romance. After a few months we moved back to the Village where dust gathers.

Though I now worked for Goldwyn, I saw Goodman nearly every day. He had dissolved his advertising business and had rented a one-room office on Fifth Avenue. He was pleased to see me and told me about his good luck with *The Old Soak*, his first theatrical venture. He gave me a German operetta, *Die Beiden Nachtegallen* to adapt. I called it *Sylvia*. It was never produced but Goodman later used one of the characters from it in a show called *Poppy*. The character, which had some laughs, was that of a country faker. I thought it would be a good part for W. C. Fields who, while known only as a pantomimist, might be good with words, if they were the right words.

He had his first speaking part in the *Follies* and his act was teeing off on a golf course. He would get set for his golf shot when Shorty, his assistant playing a caddy, would tear the lining out of his hat. Fields, teeing off, would say, "When I was in the Canary Islands . . ." then, he would be distracted by Shorty.

Shorty began to get on Fields's nerves. In the dressing room after the performance, Fields said to him, "You're fired!"

Shorty's reply was "Then I'll get a job at RKO."

"They're all Jews at RKO," Fields retorted.

"They're not Jews," countered Shorty, "they're Roman Catholics."

"The worst kind of Jew," was Fields's clincher.

The libretto for *Poppy* was submitted to Goodman by Dorothy Donnelly, the actress who played melodramatic parts such as Madam X and also wrote musical shows. Goodman decided to produce it. I wrote Fields's part, the country faker who sold patent medicine. Fields was good in the part and he became a star.

I also wrote a song for *Poppy* with Arthur Samuels called "Alibi Baby" which was introduced by Louella Geer.

ALIBI BABY

Alibi Baby
Why do they call me baby
You'll have to own up
I'm quite a grown-up baby
I don't mind stating
This aggravating baby
Beats any fibber
I tell a glibber lie
Put to the test
I'm there with the best
Excuses
Truth is a myth
You cover it with
Abuses
I'll tell the world that I'm not a cripple
I lead a life not double but triple
And when I'm caught I alibi.

Miss Donnelly said she would use the dialogue and the lyric but would not give any credit in the program. Goodman persuaded me to give in and *Poppy*, starring Madge Kennedy and W. C. Fields, became a passable hit in 1922. Goodman couldn't see his way clear to paying me a royalty. He did give me a pipe which he said was very rare and valuable.

Is It
All a Dream

hil Goodman was an admirer of my light verse. He suggested to Jerome Kern that he get me to write the lyrics for a musical comedy they had in mind, which was eventually called *Dear Sir*.

I received a phone call from Kern, and couldn't believe my ears. "Is this Howard Dietz, otherwise known as Freckles?" the voice asked. I confessed that it was.

"Well, this is Jerry Kern, and I'm a fan of yours. I keep up with your stuff in F.P.A.'s 'Conning Tower.'"

A stage wait. I tried to make some sounds.

Then again: "Is this Howard Dietz?"

I managed to answer. "Is this really Mr. Kern?"

"Take a chance on it. Is this really the author of 'I've a Bungalow in Babylon on Great South Bay?'"

"Yes, Mr. Kern. I know by heart every song you and Mr. Wodehouse ever wrote, and I think I'm going to faint."

"Well, don't faint yet, not until you hear this. Phil Goodman thinks you're a better light-verse writer than an advertising man. We want you to write the lyrics to a show that Goodman says he'll produce. Is it a deal?"

I was speechless.

"Come up to Bronxville tomorrow and we'll go over the whole thing. Take the 11:22 train and get a taxi at the station. Charge the taxi to me."

Feeling like the butt of a practical joke, I went to Bronxville the next day and waited in the Kern library which I had heard about. It was one of the great book collections in the country. There were rare items, first editions of some of the greatest authors in the English language. There were Dickens's notebooks in his own handwriting with notations on some of the characters the old master had created. There were precious editions of Jane Austen, the Brontës, Mark Twain, and a whole catalogue of classics. In awe I tiptoed around the room, studying the shelves. It was hard to imagine musical trivialities being born in this atmosphere.

Kern appeared. He was short, about 5′4″, his hair was gray at the sides and he wore a brocade smoking jacket. To me, he looked like a giant ornamented with gold braid.

"Goodman wants to produce a musical from a book by Edgar Selwyn with a score by you and me," said the giant. "I intend to use some numbers I wrote for a few English shows that didn't come off, or rather didn't get on. Do you think you can put words to tunes, or being a poet, you might prefer to have me set the words to melody. Either way will suit. Autoxinus said that music was in the ear."

I hadn't a word to say, and Autoxinus was in another league I hadn't heard of.

"Let's go to the piano and I'll play you some of the songs that might go with the libretto for *Dear Sir*. That's a good title, don't you think? The plot has something to do with a charity ball where a beautiful girl is auctioned off."

He played what sounded like a march, then handed the piano copy to me. "That might be the opening chorus," he said. He found some more songs in the pile. "This might be what is called the icebreaker, this the love scene, this a comedy duet, this a useful jingle which can be used as a finale, a fast 4/4, or, depending on the mood of the score, it can be a finaletto, whichever you think. Of course you can add some special material which I will set. You might write a number called 'My Trophy Is You.' Of course you'll think it over, but I must admit that I'm terribly impressed with your reactions. Let's see, this is Wednesday. When do you think you can come back? Do you think Friday?"

I nodded yes.

Kern didn't offer me lunch. He didn't believe in eating while working. He did ask me if I wanted tea but I was too nervous to say yes. He loaded my arms with sheets of music which I kept dropping and ushered me to the taxi which had been summoned to take me back via the 4:54. He waved me a cheerful goodbye.

When I told Betty about the interview, she said it must

have been wonderful seeing those rare books, and cooked me a hamburger before I got down to work. My problem was complicated by my inability to play the piano. The one-finger method was torture. But I kept at it almost continuously from that Wednesday until Friday morning when it was time to go back to Kern's.

It now seems idiotic, but I thought I was supposed to write lyrics to all the music Kern had handed me before I saw him again. My credulity stemmed from a contempt for most popular song routines. It seemed too easy. I didn't realize the absurdity of this idea until I was in the train riding back to Bronxville and that imposing library. Surely he must have meant that I was to write just one lyric, not all of them. I folded the sheets and put them in my pocket in such a way that I could produce the songs one at a time.

When I arrived at the sacred doorstep, Kern greeted me with some enthusiasm and asked me if I had done any work. I nodded yes and drew a song from my pocket like tissue from a Kleenex dispenser.

"You've finished one? I don't believe it," said Kern. He conducted me to his piano and played it, but shook his head negatively from side to side. He played song after song. Finally he hit on a comedy number, a trio. It had been less difficult to set because it had a lyric penciled in—"If you will be my morganatic wife"—and this gave me the rhythm and rhyme scheme. The lines had been written by a man I heard of subsequently, named Noel Coward. The idea of the lyric I wrote was derivative: "If We Could Lead a Merry Mormon Life." It delighted Kern, and he sang it out loud.

Marital entanglements have often been maligned
But I confess that they have infinite delight
Furthermore I'd like to add to what you said
By saying that monogamy just whets the appetite.

Oh wouldn't life be lots of fun
If we could marry more than one
If to the wind the law was flung
And we could live like Brigham Young.

Zip then we'd slip into bigamy
Another slip-let'er-rip to polygamy
Boy would love make a pig o' me.
For almost every day I'd take another wife
If we could only lead a merry Mormon life.

If you had your pick of all the pearls of femininity
Just name a few that you would make your choice
First of all I'd like to have those paragons of pulchritude
Ann Pennington and blondish Peggy Joyce
O Mary Pickford I'd select
That is if Doug would not object
With curiosity I'm cursed
I'd like a bearded lady first.

Tut, nothing but for monogamy
Another tut and a pooh for misogamy
Boy wouldn't love make a hog o' me
For every pretty girl I'd capture for a wife
If we could only lead a merry Mormon life.

The master got off the piano seat and made a deep bow before me. "That number alone will make the score great," he said.

I plucked another sheet from my vault. Kern grabbed it and played it without headshaking. It was a comedy duet for a boy and girl and a solo for the leading man.

On our houseboat on the Harlem
Where the pleasure-seekers flock
Though it's stuck there
In the muck there
It's the best boat on our block

71

The breezes sweep along the shore
And tell us what they cook next door
On our houseboat on the Harlem
Off the coal and lumber dock.

Oh, what's the use
There's no excuse
For bed at night
When you can clown
And paint the town
Bright red at night
I'd slumber if I weren't
Just like a live electric current
A rest can be attractive
When I am older and less active
I'll keep awake
Until I take
My curtain call
Oh, what's the use of going
To bed at all.

"You'd better sign up for the show before you get out of my hands," he said, ushering me to my taxi.

"I've conquered Kern!" I shouted down the hallway when I got home. "You'll have rubies and pearls, triolets and ballades. . . . I am a genius!"

Dear Sir opened on September 3, 1924. Although it was not a box-office success, its reception indicated that I might have a future in the theatre. *The Times* and *The Tribune* gave the lyrics good notices and I was emotional about a new song style that had been invented by Jerome Kern and that is alive still.

Shortly after the opening of *Dear Sir* I received a letter from a man named Arthur Schwartz.

ARTHUR SCHWARTZ
Counsellor at Law
299 Broadway
Worth 3420

February 24, 1924

My dear Dietz:

*Beans Cerf, a friend of yours and mine, promised to intro-
duce me to you, but he is such a busy publisher these days,
I fear that he has totally forgotten me.*

*This is what's on my chest: I'd love to work with you on
songs for the Neighborhood Playhouse annual show, The
Grand Street Follies. I am developing contacts which are, I
think, going to lead to something worthwhile. As I told Beans,
I think you are the only man in town to be compared with
Larry Hart, and from me, that's quite a tribute, because I
know almost every line Larry has written. I think that three or
four tunes of mine will be riots in the Grand Street Follies this
year IF they have lyrics such as only Larry and you can write.*

*Don't be too amused at the fact that I speak of tune-writing
under a lawyer's letterhead. I'm giving up the law in a few
months to spend all my time at music.*

Sincerely,
(signed) Arthur Schwartz

And I replied to it:

HOWARD DIETZ

March 8, 1924

My dear Schwartz:

*As I have written a first show in collaboration with a well-
established composer, I don't think that our collaboration is
such a good idea.*

*What I would suggest is that you collaborate with an estab-
lished lyric writer. In that way, we will both benefit by the reputation of our collaborators, then when we both get famous,
we can collaborate with each other.*

It's nice to hear from you.

Yours,
(signed) Howard Dietz

73

eorge Gershwin had collaborated with most of the word men in Tin Pan Alley, and he felt the time had come when he should form a song-wedding with his brother Ira. The brothers had started working on the score of *Oh, Kay!* when Ira was attacked by his appendix.

George needed a substitute and selected me. I hadn't done much to deserve this compliment, though I had received good notices for *Dear Sir*. But P. G. Wodehouse and Guy Bolton who wrote the book for *Oh, Kay!* were willing to write the lyrics, and the producers, Aarons and Freedley, were partial to Wodehouse's style. Gertrude Lawrence, the star of the show, felt that George was fortunate to have such talented pinchhitters as Wodehouse and Bolton, but George wanted Ira to retain as much of the credit as possible. He chose me because I would be least demanding of both credit and money and I showed promise.

While the doctors were sawing away at Ira's midriff, I was submitting a variety of ideas to George. One of the more successful was the title of the best song in the show, "Someone to Watch Over Me." I wrote and was credited with two songs: "Oh, Kay" and "Heaven on Earth." I wrote the verse for the spiritual number "Clap Yo' Han's" and a lyric called "That Certain Something You've Got" but Ira changed the lyrics and called it "Oh, Kay, You're O.K. with Me." It was the title song of the show and the least distinguished. Ira made me a present of the credit for it. It was the opposite of plagiarism; we'll call it donorism.

George, realizing that any sum he paid me would have to come out of Ira's royalties, paid me next to nothing. It was decided that I was to get 1¢ for every copy of sheet music that was sold. When Ira sent me my first paycheck it was for 96¢. Some time shortly thereafter, Ira wrote asking me if I minded canceling the arrangement which involved a lot of bookkeeping for such small sums. I said no, I didn't mind.

I was very proud to work with the great Gershwin, and I would have done it for nothing, which I did.

fter *Dear Sir,* I decided to go slow in pursuing both press agentry and show business. I had better concentrate on one or the other and it had better be my job. But I couldn't resist putting words to good melodies and song ideas kept inviting me.

I met Jay Gorney, who later wrote "Brother, Can You Spare a Dime?" to words by Yip Harburg. Gorney was doing a show about the circus called *Hoopla*. The producer was Bill Dollan who carried a roll of bills the size of a grapefruit. He conducted all his business in cash, peeling off the dollars as they were needed. I wrote some lyrics for them.

Hoopla starred Bernard Granville, a tenor somewhat like John Steele, who sang ballads in the *Ziegfeld Follies*. We rehearsed in Stamford, Connecticut where we were going to have our tryout. The cast often gravitated to a saloon we had discovered, only Granville had discovered it more than we had. One of his roles was the character "Prologue" who appeared before the curtain in his clown costume. His speech was supposed to last two minutes but under the influence of the corner saloon he stretched it out to what seemed like two hours. Jay Gorney, the mild-mannered composer who thought two minutes was too long with Granville sober, stamped his foot in a rage.

The show deserved a better fate, as it is impossible to conceive of a worse one, but it couldn't overcome the unsober Granville stretching his opening-night speech. Several people left the theatre rather than sit through the dreary introduction. Finally when the show was underway the scenery fouled, causing another delay of 40 minutes. When the curtain descended at the end of the first act, only seven people came back for the second. The stage manager suggested that we pay back the few customers and use the 10 minutes we had to rehearse instead of paying overtime for a regular performance. Bill Dollan was sadly discouraged. Jay Gorney was sympathetic. "Cheer up," he said, "you set a record."

"What record?" asked Dollan.

"You had the shortest run in the history of the theatre." The show ran one act.

Goldwyn's office was on 40th Street and I used to walk up to the Algonquin to eat. But I didn't eat at the Round Table; I watched the Round Table eat. Although I rubbed elbows with the famous wits and playwrights, they didn't rub elbows with me. I was regarded as a publicity man, not as a creative artist. It was a frustrating relationship.

The Round Table emerged in the early twenties. Alec Woollcott, critic of *The New York Times*, was as much a pioneer as any of the cast. Frank Case, the propietor of the hotel, struck the proper tuning fork for so sensitive a gathering. There were George Kaufman, Marc Connelly, F.P.A., Heywood Broun, Dorothy Parker, Harold Ross, Bob Sherwood, John V. A. Weaver, the regular attendants. But they would often have distinguished guests, such as John, Ethel and Lionel Barrymore, or some actor who had only recently captured the public eye.

The Round Table made life in the city a bit more exciting than its mundane self. The group presented light, but original plays for themselves and their friends which were usually burlesques of current hits. I remember one show called *No Siree*, which was patterned after an English revue *Chauve Souris*. The acting was amateurish, but then it was done by authors who substituted puns and wheezes for acting. I was a devout fan and I grew up with them as a background. They accepted me as one of their group after I had scored hits with *Dear Sir* and *The Little Show* and had collaborated with Kaufman and Connelly.

It was easy to get a crush on Dottie Parker as she sent you flattering telegrams on your birthday, your show opening and whenever she thought you were slipping from her grasp.

Her equipment was witty telegrams, vers de société and kisses on the lips when you aimed for her cheek.

Her husband was Alan Campbell who was straightlaced and unlike what you'd expect from a possession of Dottie's. I told her she should have married somebody like Arthur Kober or me. "What would we do with Alan?" she said. Then she had a second thought. "Oh yes, we could send him to military school!"

One time Dottie and I decided to go to the Royalton to see Mister Benchley who was the most individual character I ever met. Benchley was half undressed and went on undressing to go to bed. Dottie said she was sleepy too, took off her hat and dress, and got into an enormous waste basket that looked like a giant's cradle made of leather. Dottie curled up. I said I was sleepy too, and, shedding my clothes, was starting to climb in with Dottie when Mr. Benchley's wife Gertrude made an unexpected appearance.

"Hello, Gertrude," said Dottie, "Howard and I decided to drop in."

Benchley was my hero. Nothing ever happened to him that wasn't interesting even in his dreams. One time he had to meet a train at five o'clock in the morning. He set the alarm for four. He dreamed he was a judge presiding at a trial, woke up at three, looked at the clock, and muttered, "I just have an hour to hear this," and he went back to sleep.

Heywood Broun was a critic, a columnist, and above all a man of honor. Of all the members of the Algonquin Round Table, he was the one you could trust the most. He was a shaggy figure. He wore the same suit every day. Deems Taylor, composer, painter and writer, a triple threat, said, "Heywood Broun looks as though he got up in the morning from a wrinkled bed, took the coal out of the bathtub, planning on taking a bath, then changed his mind and put the coal back in the tub."

77

But his size-16 shoes were impeccable. He had second run on the shoes of his friend Joe Brooks, the 250-pound football coach at Columbia, shoes that were made by Lobb and Company of London. Joe Brooks could afford to have his shoes made to order and Heywood Broun couldn't—that is, he couldn't as long as there was someone around who could.

While I was not a bosom companion of Broun, I felt very close to him in general outlook. I voted much the same ticket and had similar taste in entertainment. I was puzzled when he turned Catholic. I should have realized he had fallen in love, and religion went with the bride. However, this is not a papal narrative; it's a story about an impromptu dinner party at a speakeasy called The Casanova.

Joe Brooks was buying the drinks and ordering dinner for a dozen gathered at the refectory. Brooks was introducing his new blond secretary to the intelligentsia present: T. R. Smith, the editor of *The Century* magazine, Alan Jackson, the film editor, and Dorothy Parker. Tom Smith, superior mind though he was, was telling a dirty story, using four-letter words to make the analogies more vivid. Joe Brooks frowned at the pornographic turn to the conversation. Brooks felt he had better protect his secretary, who was mentally fragile, so he told Smith to leave the table. "Tom hasn't said anything offensive," Dottie Parker said.

"Shut up, you goddamn tart," said Brooks.

I felt an obligation to interfere. I walked around the table, passing Broun and others on the way. "Take that back," I said. I punched Brooks in the belly six times and after a while he noticed that someone was pounding on his stomach. He casually lifted his left hand and knocked me down. My lower lip stretched itself out and I looked like a Ubangi.

I managed to get Dottie to a taxi, or she me, and we went to her apartment in the Fifties. She made a bonfire of Racquet Club hat bands and other reminders of Joe Brooks and for the next hour my lip came in for intensive nursing.

The doorbell rang. There was Heywood with a face that put mine to shame. It looked bumpy, like coffeecake with currants. "What happened?" said Dottie, horrified at the devastated landscape.

"I felt an obligation to wage war against Brooks for insulting his betters," said Broun. "When I got home and in bed, I reflected and decided it would look cowardly of me if I didn't avenge Dottie. I got up and wrote him a note: 'You can hit little guys like Dietz, but you can't hit a man your size!' I went to his apartment and slid the note under the door, but he opened the door and confronted me. He tore open the envelope and read the note.

" 'I'm going out,' Joe called back to his secretary, 'but I'll only be gone a minute.'

"He took off his jacket and I took off mine. The right fist was lifted this time, and when I was on the floor, he walked over my face. I lay on the carpet till the Marquess of Queensbury limit had been reached. Then I got up, put on a jacket and said, 'Goodnight, Joe.' It wasn't until I got out on the street that I realized I had Joe's jacket on. I decided not to go back. I came over here to your comforting care."

"That was very brave of you," I said.

"No, you were the brave one," said Broun.

I sat there nursing my drink. "When I stepped into action," I said, "what made you sit still?"

"I'll tell you," said Broun. "Joe Brooks wears the same size shoe that I do and they're very expensive. They're made in London by Lobb. When you were heading toward Brooks, I was thinking about what I'd do for shoes if I hit him."

Lucius Beebe was the first of the gourmets in my world. Until Lucius came along, most of us thought a steak was a steak and a chop was a chop. We didn't know what Bearnaise meant and aesthetes were opposed to philistines. He built up quite a following. He was on the editorial staff of *The Herald Tribune* and he came to work in gentleman's tailoring.

Lucius, arbiter of elegance, arranged a bachelor dinner at the Princeton Club for his friend Tony Williams the night before he was to marry Peggy LeBoutillier. Twenty carefully groomed men-about-town dressed in tuxedos with Lucius alone in full dress setting off his well-known diamond boutonniere; he headed the refectory table where a great amount of wine of various vintage was being consumed.

I was embarrassed at being the first to succumb to the spirits.

Lucius looked askance as I left the table and headed for the bathroom. On the way back to my seat, I whispered in his ear, "Don't worry Lucius, the white wine came up with the fish."

 got to know Dorothy Parker by way of F.P.A. I got to know F.P.A. by way of Robert Benchley. I got to know Benchley by way of Heywood Broun. I got to know the elite of the speakeasy clientele by way of the Volstead Act.

Dorothy Parker and I were standing on the sidewalk during the intermission of a Shubert opening night when the great Alexander Woollcott, his rotund figure draped in an inverness cape, came toward us. I say "us" but I mean "her." Woollcott rarely wasted his minutes on anyone less than a potential celebrity, and not being very potential, I had already been introduced to him for at least the tenth time.

"Why don't you two come over to my apartment after the curtain comes down, when this mountain of crap is en route to Kane's warehouse? You can have a drink with Junior while I'm writing the obit, and then perhaps a game of anagrams, that is, if this faylow" (meaning me), "I never remember his name, can spell." Dottie asked me if I wanted to do that. I was tongue-tied, but the arrangements were made.

A mongrel dog without a license came to the edge of the curb and did his stuff out of sheer nervousness. Mrs. Parker apologized for him. "It's the company," she explained, bowing toward Woollcott.

Woollcott finished his review in nothing flat, and sent

Junior, his worshipful mulatto, to the drama desk of *The Times*. "Now, how much will we play for?" he asked, rubbing his hands in anticipation. "You are outclassed, young man, but you can write off your losses as an admission fee to a select circle. I expect you are very rich." It was an attempt at brow-beating, but I didn't fold. They were big-time word makers and the experience might be worth the price.

Some remarkable takes were made. Dottie made Point with a K, into Inkpot. Woollcott took Pouches with a Y, and made Chop Suey. "I acknowledge my genius," said Woollcott.

I protested. "Chop suey—two words?"

"Are you trying to cross me?" he said, escalating his glance into a glare.

"I wouldn't dream of it," I said, "without an alpenstock."

The next day, I received a letter containing a small check, my winnings, and a note:

> *Dear Howard,*
>
> *We used to have a servant named Lena Dietz. I wonder if by any chance you are related.*
>
> Yours,
> A. Woollcott

It was the beginning of an attentive friendship, as I could judge by the number and caliber of clever insults launched in my direction. I became a regular at his Sunday breakfasts where I met the by-liners of the city and its theatrical stars. For Woollcott it was always a command performance. He worked at his friendships, and despaired when any one of his chosen group misinterpreted his abuse. Au fond sentimental as Shirley Temple underneath that biting exterior, he refused to be criticized himself.

Woollcott was the organizer of the Neshobe Island Club which owned a small island in Lake Bomoseen in Vermont. If you were tapped for it by the master, you paid your $1,000 entrance fee and became one of the ten owners of the unique vacation spot entirely surrounded by the most entertaining wits, including Charles Brackett who wrote a novel, *Entirely Surrounded*, based on the locale.

The Island, as it was intimately called, was not really beautiful. The water around it was not too invigorating and the foliage was a dusty green, as in a city park. Despite its lack of features, it was romanticized by the cast of characters who lived there in the summer.

The list of owners included Thornton Wilder, Alice Duer Miller, Charles MacArthur, Charlie Lederer, Irving Berlin, Harpo Marx, Harold Ross, Ray Ives and Joe Hennessy who ran the place. Many others came as guests if they had the official approval of Alexander Woollcott. It was only just for Woollcott to be in command. He had organized the club and built the one attractive house, paying half the cost out of his own pocket.

But his most valuable contribution was his energy, expended in old-fashioned games and pastimes to which he assigned a more liberal and cultural tone. The game "Murder," for example, had resourceful examiners prosecuting criminals, who defended themselves in entertaining ways. Many of the cross-questions were slightly irrelevant. When I was just married to my second wife, an elusive young lady, Charlie Lederer acting the opposition lawyer, asked, "In this temporary arrangement you call your marriage, did you make a settlement to forestall a precipitous divorce?"

Croquet was the leading daylight sport, and we brought this game up to a gambling pitch by the doubling method. You could get "destroyed" by having your ball sent sailing into the lake and it required a lot of skill to recover your position.

We played "Cops and Robbers." In one memorable game, Charlie Lederer and I were the robbers and sedate Alice Duer Miller was one of the cops. Charlie and I followed the

rules of the paper chase. We carried with us scraps of the

Sunday newspaper and dropped a scrap every 20 yards. When we ran out of our clues, we headed for the water, took our clothes off and swam around the island. Alice spying the two nudes was not the least embarrassed and chased us home. Those were the days when undressiness had shock value although it did not seem to shock Mrs. Miller, the propagandist author of *Are Women People?*

The most beautiful guest we had at the island was Rosamond Pinchot. For some inexplicable reason, Rosamond had centered her affection on me, and she sent me odd keepsakes, such as pinned-up butterflies. Her letters were interesting only because they were unexpected. Though an heiress, she had no conceit and was unaware of her great beauty.

I took her to the Island with Woollcott's permission. Alex was secretly delighted that a rich person should come under his thumb. His respect for me increased that such wealth should value me. He spent the entire time of Rosamond's visit insulting us and Rosamond would burst into tears at sudden moments. Woollcott was delighted, mainly because he didn't believe in tears; he could not conceive of anyone being deeply offended because he was never deeply offended himself. Rosamond ran away from the Island to escape Woollcott's clutches. She jumped into Lake Bomoseen and "struck out for Corsica" as Dottie put it. How she managed to get to her New York apartment in a wet bathing suit, I'll never fathom. I didn't cross-question her because she would have burst into tears.

Dorothy Parker arrived at the Island one day with a huge suitcase which, when opened, contained only a large picture hat. She spent a week at Lake Bomoseen practically naked. Her figure was as eloquent as her verses.

Telegrams arriving from the mainland were delivered by Will Bull, the one-man link between Woollcott and the mainland. Woollcott had many hates among the men and women about New York, and some of them crowded him closely. He would have found the thought of Elsa Maxwell coming to Neshobe a hovering storm. To annoy him, we sent a message via Will Bull reading.

PLAN TO SPEND WEEKEND NESHOBE NOT SURE DICKIE GORDON COMING BUT MY ARRIVAL CERTAIN LOVE ELSA

We all expressed pleasure at the impending visit of Miss Maxwell, but Alex packed up and started for New York. We tried to explain that we had played a joke, but Alex said, "I don't know when you're lying and when you're not; I'm going to New York."

Into the Twenties

SUPPER AT SUNDOWN

Communing with nature in 1902.

talented amateur minstrel show in 1912. RIGHT TO LEFT: Howard Dietz and Bennett Cerf.

izabeth Bigelow Hall, my first wife, who was game for anything. When the crash came
d we had lost all the money we had, Betty took off the bejeweled bracelet I had given her
an extravagant gesture. Saying, "This might as well go too," she dropped it in the john.
ummoned the plumber and resented his bill for $60.

LEFT TO RIGHT FRONT ROW: George Ephraim Sokolsky, Merryle Stanley Rukeyser, M. Lincoln Schuster, James Danahy.

SECOND ROW: James Marshall, Eliott Sanger, me, Francis Joseph Scully, Silas F. Seadler, Ralph Biddle, George Hough, Joseph Risley, Louis R. Mann, Harry Tove, David Robinson.

THIRD ROW: Tom Black, Alan Temple, James Robinson, Donald McGregor Stern, Fred Pitts, George Roberts.

FOURTH ROW: Morrie Ryskind, Palmer Smith, Fenton Johnson, Wayne Wellman, George Wickersham, Ben Heyman, Clarence (Ike) Lovejoy, Ralph Bevin Smith.

*Class of 1917 ~ School of Journalism
Pulitzer Foundation ~ Columbia University
May 27th 1917*

M. R. Werner, lifelong friend. Author of *Barnum*, *Brigham Young* and other works. Herman J. Mankiewicz, friend, wit, journalist and screen writer.

MGM

ilip Goodman, advertising agent and Broadway producer. My first boss and father of Ruth
etz.

Jerome Kern, the stylist leader of theatrical composers, also was a collector of rare books. When he sold his collection the John Quinn Galleries took in $1,600,000 for the Kern library. Kern moved to Hollywood where he gave up the study of rare book catalogues for the racing form.

Walter Donaldson, composer of "Yessir, That's My Baby," "Blue Heaven" and many popular songs. I wrote "Jungle Fever" with him. Donaldson wrote four of the first five million songs sold annually by the Feist Corporation. Donaldson was careless with his drinking habits and frequently got lost. The Feist Company had him shadowed to keep communication with him.

hat George is to music Ira is to words.

ere is no better way to spend an evening than listening to George Gershwin at the piano.
rtunately for his audience, he seldom was away from it. He played his own tunes to
's special lyrics and though his voice was sheer gravel it was special entertainment.

F. P. A., who injected the literary note into journalism.
Dorothy Parker, who wore picture hats.

ywood Broun, who had clean thoughts but unpressed clothes.

TOP: The old Morocco bar. Esther Jackson, now wife of Alan Grant, Lucinda Ballard, Tokio Payne; back of them, Daphne, then wife of Geoffrey Hellman, and Freddy Payne. To one side, Eleanor de Liagre Labrot, now Mrs. Brian Ahearne.

Charlie MacArthur and Helen Hayes with daughter Mary in the days of their exuberance in joy. He wrote plays with Edward Sheldon and Ben Hecht.

JEROME ZERBE

MG-29025

Bob Benchley. Man about town, who submitted his *Treasurer's Report* to Broadway.

Woollcott, the Island, entirely surrounded by water.

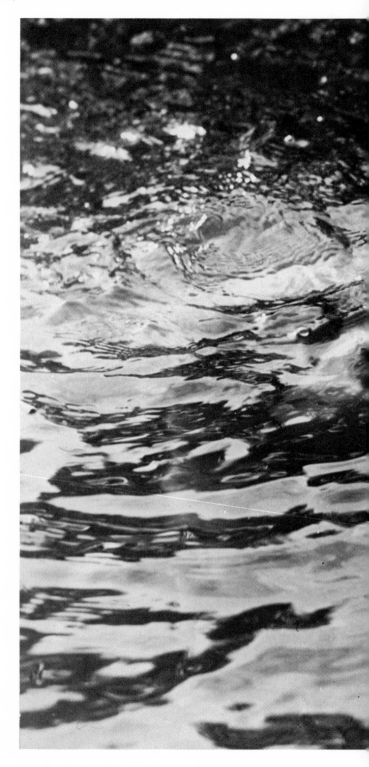

Croquet at the Island. Beatrice Kaufman, George's wife, Woollcott lining up his shot and Harpo Marx (without his wig). Harpo and I won the match and Woollcott was furious. He accused Harpo of trickery and went to New York for a rest. As he left for the mainland in Will Bull's speedboat, he shouted, "Goodbye to you two Jews. I hope I'll never see you again." But he was disappointed. He saw us almost every day.

In 1914 Mrs. Patrick Campbell created the role of the Cockney flower girl in *Pygmalion,* on which *My Fair Lady* was based.

FACING PAGE:

TOP ROW: George Oppenheimer, librettist and critic, at Charlie Lederers, a wit who wrote *The Thing* and other screenplays.

Marc Connelly, playwright and author of *Green Pastures.*

BOTTOM ROW: George Backer, friend, author, and political adviser once wed to Dolly Schiff, publisher of the *New York Post.*

Alice Duer Miller, author of poems and novels including *The White Cliffs of Dover.*

LEFT TO RIGHT: Irving Caesar, unknown girl, Jane Swope Brandt (seated), Maggie Swope, George Backer, Hannah Williams Kahn (who sang "Cheerful Little Earful" and later married Jack Dempsey), and Roger Wolff Kahn.

Lucinda Ballard.
Ellin and Irving Berlin, the romantic marriage of the 1920s.

New Sun
in the Sky

I still thought I had to decide whether I would become a lyric writer or a motion picture promoter. Walter Wanger, who was the head of Paramount Studios in the East, offered me a salary as publicity director, escalating in five years to $2,000 a week. The offer was attractive but I was working on shows and Wanger wouldn't allow any moonlighting. Goldwyn was indifferent to my working hours. He despised clock watching.

At the same time, I wanted to make war on Paramount, which was a sort of monopoly. I hired the most powerful stereopticon lens in the city from a man named Ludwig Kraus, who had a theory that on a cloudy night the lens could flash a sign in the sky. The Capitol Theatre was owned by Goldwyn Pictures. I had lantern slides of various sizes made with the words GO TO THE CAPITOL. We picked a perfect night for it, took the lantern up to the Capitol roof and aimed at the clouds. But the result was incoherent; the light appeared but no image was discernible. We had better luck with *The New York Times*. We swung our lamp around, and lit up the rear windows of *The Times*, blinding the people standing inside. Then we flashed the sign on the Paramount Theatre. It came out precisely and violently: GO TO THE CAPITOL. *The Times* sent a man up to the Capitol roof and what he saw inspired him to write a 3-column story starting on the front page.

The next day Wanger offered me $2,000 a week, which I refused. I went home and told Betty who wasn't impressed. Marcus Loew was, and raised my salary to $350 a week.

Paramount produced 104 feature motion pictures a year. They catered to theatres which changed their programs weekly and bi-weekly. The other producing companies didn't produce enough features to enable them to compete with Paramount. Metro produced 20, Goldwyn 20, and United Artists and Universal had the rest, still short of the quantity which would make for security. A merger was in the wind.

Samuel Goldwyn was encouraged by Marcus Loew to sell out the Goldwyn Pictures Corporation. When he left the company we had founded to become an independent producer, he wanted me to come with him as his assistant, but I was too sensitive for the assignment.

The stockholders virtually paid Sam $2 million to become an independent producer, and he became a mighty good one. Among the pictures he produced on his own were *The Children's Hour, The Best Years of Our Lives, Guy and Dolls* and several other hits. In the agreement Sam was not allowed to call his company the Goldwyn Pictures Corporation for 10 years.

The Goldwyn Pictures Corporation Sam left behind merged with Marcus Loew of the Metro Company and they lured Louis B. Mayer, who had Irving Thalberg under contract, to become the talent department. Nicholas Schenck, who was Marcus Loew's associate at Metro, became president of the merged corporation. Metro-Goldwyn-Mayer became a triple threat. I was a particular pet of Schenck and went along with the new company as director of advertising and publicity.

Nicholas Schenck and Joseph Schenck were brothers, and continuously solicitous about each other. They were born in Russia, the only Jewish family in the small town. They managed to pull strings and scrape enough money together for passage to New York. They had studied chemistry in Russia. Shortly after they landed in America, they opened a drugstore at 110th Street and Madison Avenue. They spoke English with a foreign accent; despite this handicap, they made friends and were shrewd in their transactions.

One Sunday they took an excursion to Fort George at 168th Street and Amsterdam Avenue, and stopped in for a drink at a corner saloon. Nick made conversation with the bartender and found out that the real estate surrounding them was all solid rock. This gave Nick an idea, and he asked the bartender who owned the land and how he could be reached.

The next day, Nick and Joe went back to Fort George to visit the owner. They told him the rock would provide an ideal foundation for a roller coaster and they wanted to build an amusement park. They convinced the owner that it was an opportunity to make some profit and sold shares to the bartender too, convincing him that an amusement park would be a boon to his business. They built the roller coaster and were the first to ride on it. It had an effect on the neighborhood as it attracted many people, especially on Sundays. The Schencks had tremendous imagination.

Joe became president of 20th-Century-Fox, and Nick became president of Metro-Goldwyn-Mayer. The Schenck brothers controlled the leading companies of the motion picture industry.

Joe was a philosopher who had a comic sense. He was not opinionated and he gave good advice, such as, "If four or five guys tell you that you're drunk, even though you know you haven't had a thing to drink, the least you can do is to lie down a little while."

Of the two brothers, Nick was the sounder. He was friendly and generous but more conservative than Joe, probably due to his being married to a level-headed beauty named Pansy Wilcox. Joe was less reliable than his brother but he gave good racing tips. Joe was married to Norma Talmadge, the most popular star in the twenties, but he didn't stay married, which may be why he got himself into so many jams. He was a big gambler and was pursued by tax collectors.

Years later when I had to spend more time on the West Coast, I was a frequent visitor to Agua Caliente on the Mexican border, which was owned and operated by Joe. One weekend I went there and lost $3,000 playing dice and roulette. I was very depressed and glad to get out of the place. Joe offered to take me back to Los Angeles. We left on Sunday night. I couldn't get the losing out of my mind; I wasn't rich enough to be casual about $3,000. I said to Joe, "On a crowded weekend like this one, the casino must clean up."

"No," said Joe, "there's no predicting how the house will come out. For instance, this weekend we had a profit of only $3,000."

he new company was an immediate success. The men largely responsible for this were Nick Schenck, Mayer, and Thalberg. I got along well with these mighty executives though they did not approve of my cavalier regard for office hours.

"You come in late," said Mr. Schenck.

"But I go home early," I answered.

Thalberg produced many hits and made many star attractions to go with a slogan I wrote: "More Stars Than There Are in Heaven." Success is a contagion and MGM attracted the outstanding talent. By the end of the silent era a majority of the directors, writers, producers, as well as players, belonged to MGM.

Such a galaxy of stars had never been gathered together by any one company and never has since. There were James Stewart, Margaret Sullavan, Irene Dunne, Lucille Ball, Hedy Lamarr, Katharine Hepburn, Greer Garson, Susan Peters, Lionel Barrymore, Harry James, Red Skelton, Mickey Rooney, William Powell, Wallace Beery, Spencer Tracy, Walter Pidgeon, Robert Taylor, Gene Kelly, George Murphy, Van Johnson, Marjorie Main, Robert Benchley, Reginald Owen, Esther Williams, Spring Byington, Gladys Cooper, Lana Turner, Judy Garland, Charles Laughton, Laraine Day, Robert Young, Ann Sothern, Margaret O'Brien, Herbert

Marshall, Robert Walker, Clark Gable, Robert Montgomery, Melvyn Douglas, Lew Ayres, Johnny Weissmuller, and others.

MGM had a large publicity staff. There was a great deal of logrolling and back-scratching. When I was put in charge, I borrowed a sign which had hung over the desk of Harold Ross, the editor of *The New Yorker*. It said: "Don't be famous around here."

With the merger, the industry became alive with competition for publicity. I was in need of an assistant and had my eye on Pete Smith who was a freelancer. He was working for Douglas Fairbanks at the time and was doing a spectacular campaign for *The Mark of Zorro*. Hearing the noise he made in Chicago, I decided to go to Chicago and cook up interest in *Remembrance,* but *Remembrance* couldn't be as cookable as *Zorro.* I really wanted to talk to Smith.

I had plastered the town with one-sheets. I had a sign on every lamp post, but Smith sensing that I was on his trail, plastered his billboards over mine. I met up with Pete in the Ambassador Hotel bar. He said he would work for me for $500 a week. As I was getting only $350 a week, the situation was embarrassing, but I told Smith that he was hired and could go to work on *Remembrance* as soon as he finished the work on *Zorro.*

I had to get a raise. Marcus Loew invited me to his Glen Cove estate, "Pembroke," and Sunday morning he took me for a walk through his grounds and greenhouses. I amazed him with my knowledge of the rarest flowers. He told me I was an exceptional young man to know botany as well as publicity.

Several days later the head gardener asked Mr. Loew, "Who was that dark-haired fellow in the conservatory Saturday night reading plant labels with a flashlight?"

I got the raise anyhow.

Pete didn't last long as a press agent. He made capital of his country voice and left publicity for the short-subject field. The indefatigable Howard Strickling took his place. I had met him in 1924 in Europe where he had done a snow job publicizing the director Rex Ingram, who had discovered Rudolph Valentino.

My job as chief of publicity was for the most part routine disseminating of items about pictures and stars. But now and again there was a chance of doing a spectacular publicity stunt.

We were planning to distribute an early Edgar Rice Burroughs *Tarzan,* the first one to star Johnny Weissmuller. Johnny leaped easily from limb to limb in the dangerous thicket but had to struggle to memorize his one line: "Me Tarzan, you Jane." He deserved first billing in that masterpiece.

I got Harry Reichenbach, the nonpareil of movie promoting who ranked with Barnum as a ballyhoo artist, to carry off the job. There was nothing he wouldn't do to crash the front page.

Reichenbach, knowing his way around the jungle of press agentry, arranged with the Hotel Belleclaire, a family hostelry in the Seventies, to rent a suite for Walter Beckwith, the great lion tamer. Beckwith was registered as T. R. Zan and had his "concert grand piano" hoisted to his suite. The piano case was a cage for the largest lion in captivity—9 feet long. When it was deposited in his sitting room, Beckwith called room service and ordered 15 pounds of raw beef, top sirloin and filet mignon. Five aproned waiters carried the meat on trays. When the lion smelled the beef, he let out a roar and headed for his meal. The waiters, dropping their loads, clattered down the stairs and frantically retreated to the kitchen, wringing their hands and falling over each other in terror.

The story broke big and the stunt was talked about for weeks. The press, which is vindictive when duped, didn't mind being used on this occasion because the lion was tame and appealed to the children living in the hotel. Beckwith gave them confidence, and they stroked the lion's mane.

When we publicized *Love* with Garbo and Gilbert, I got a professor at Columbia, William Marsden, to do a psychological experiment to determine which women were the hotter —blondes or brunettes. It became a subject of vital concern to the press across the nation. We filled the Embassy Theatre with emotional girls in their blooming twenties, mostly from the chorus, and had several interns in white jackets pass down the aisles with systolic blood-pressure gauges. They were listening to the beat of the feminine heart, blondes and brunettes, as the girls watched erotic scenes from the Garbo and Gilbert film. The stunt was a great success and all seven of New York's daily newspapers shouted out the news that blondes were hotter than brunettes. The redheads challenged the blondes, but the dew was off the rose, and we didn't run the idea further.

After Lindbergh made his historic flight to Paris, Pete Smith, who was heading the studio in Culver City, called and asked if I approved of renting a transatlantic plane similar to the "Spirit of St. Louis." His plan was to make a flight across the country with Leo the lion. He looked fierce but was the oldest lion in captivity and had only one tooth. The Humane Society in California prohibited the flight at first, but Pete argued with them and said they shouldn't make a snap judgment. He said they should put themselves in the lion's place and have a trial flight. Believe it or not, the committee from the Humane Society took a test flight in the airborne cage and granted permission for Leo to fly. Martin Genter, who won the Dole prize for his flight to Honolulu, flew the plane in a tribute to Lindbergh and the lion. Unfortunately, Leo never reached his destination as the plane crashed in the Tonto Basin in Roosevelt, Arizona. No one was hurt but the plane.

The lion was sent out to the Barnes Museum of Southern California. He has long since died a hero's death.

reporter whom I'd admired since my copyboy days, Donald Henderson Clarke, flirted with a job in my department. When he came to see me I had to stand at a distance, or he'd intoxicate me. Our promotion machine was dragging, and I decided an unsober talent like Clarke would be an asset.

So Don went to work as a publicity man. He was virtually his own boss. He had great contacts and came and went as he pleased as long as he got in touch with me by telephone every day and left word where he could be reached. He professed a great admiration for me, and I was duly flattered.

During this time Nicky Arnstein, the husband of Fanny Brice, was wanted for embezzlement, and Clarke had Nicky in hiding in a Bronx boarding house. The entire police force was looking for him. *The World* carried a box each day which screamed out, "Where Is Nicky?" It was an important political football for the police department. Clarke brought in sandwiches two or three times a day, and kept Nicky informed of the world outside. Nicky, who had led a secret life, was proud of the publicity. He was a dapper fellow, quite handsome and had rings and watches and chains and gold rivaling Fort Knox. He was far from happy in his dingy one-room compartment. He told Clarke that he was going to give himself up.

"What good is it?" said Nicky. "This room isn't any more comfortable than the cell they'll put me in and the food will be better because it couldn't be worse. I appreciate your good intentions towards me, Don, but I've reached the end of my rope."

"If you're going to give yourself up, do it my way," said Clarke. "Tomorrow is the police parade and I'll arrange for you to march in it. I want to see how many blocks you have to march before they notice you in their midst."

Nicky said, "What have I got to lose?"

So Nicky marched in the police parade, with Don Clarke and a male secretary taking notes. They marched from 110th Street and Fifth Avenue to the Washington Square arch without being discovered. Don had to take Nicky himself to the police commissioner's office before an arrest was made.

After Nicky had served his term and gotten out on parole, Don and I encountered him in the men's room of the Hotel Plaza. "Nicky," said Don, "I want you to meet the greatest guy in the world, Howard Dietz." "Howard, I want you to meet Nicky Arnstein, the greatest crook in the world."

"I wouldn't say a thing like that, Don," said Nicky.

"Don't be so goddamn modest," said Clarke.

Don's drinking became a problem; it was a pity to see him staggering around. I got in touch with Dr. Scott at Bloomingdale's Sanitarium. I had heard they had only room for three alcoholic patients. I acquainted the doctors with Clarke's worth, and the doctor agreed to take him. He was given a thorough psychiatric examination. Dr. Scott said he suffered from overfrankness. "When I told him that many patients indulge in excessive masturbation he said, 'Not as much as I do.'" Clarke learned to stop drinking, but he continued to live at the sanitarium and commuted to my office. He said he was beginning to like sobriety and was thinking of writing a novel.

"It should be easy," he said, "I could write one in three months."

I bet him $1,000 that he couldn't write a 50,000-word book in three months.

"Done and done," said Clarke.

Three months later they published *Louis Baretti*. It was trash, but it was a best seller. He wrote *The Housekeeper's Daughter* and *Millie* and he was enchanted by a new world of letters. He moved out to California and lived on the beach at Malibu. He would get up at 3 o'clock in the morning, go down to the beach, and write there until 8 o'clock at night.

A doctor told him he had cancer, and Clarke said it was no worse than a bad cold. Nevertheless, before he succumbed he gave the money that he didn't need to cancer research.

Executives have a special vanity due to the fact that they are not as talented as the staff they executive over. They have to enjoy pushing people around. Louis B. Mayer, while no Demosthenes, could organize the pebbles in his mouth and shout his way out of a tight corner.

He had a booming delivery. He was a master at changing the subject. It didn't matter whether two were present or 200, he always had the floor. On those rare occasions when he decided to let the other fellow speak, he only pretended to be listening. He used facial expressions to show he understood.

He would say, "I thought of that," whenever by accident he recognized the newness of a new idea. He fumbled with props on his desk or on his person—a watch chain, his tortoise-rimmed glasses, a fountain pen—and such fidgeting weakened his audience. Though he didn't admire me because he thought I was too soft and had "class," I liked his gluey stick-to-it-iveness which made his mind a valuable property. Mayer was extravagant. It is likely that he never thoroughly read a script. He was a great gambler for high stakes but a poor gambler for low stakes and as with most Hollywood executives, the larger the gamble the more attractive it became.

In 1927 I went with Mayer to an MGM sales convention where he was to make a speech. The sales managers gave him a big hand. Pressing his luck with his captive audience, Mayer called for questions and suggestions. "It's a free country," he said, "and it's yours as well as mine." Damned generous of him.

117

Bob Lynch, the fearless character who guided MGM's destiny in Philadelphia, raised his hand. "I have a suggestion," he said. "Why don't we stop making the Marion Davies pictures? They're a drug on the market. I know she's a blue-eyed blonde but she doesn't get us a quarter."

It was Mayer's ball. "That's a good question," said L. B., "and I'm glad you asked it." The sweat came out in beads. "Marion Davies is a dear friend of William Randolph Hearst, the powerful publisher, whose good will is an enormous asset to MGM, Mr. Dietz will verify my statement. W. R. is the son of the late George Hearst, the United States Senator from California. As a young man, the senator left Missouri and trekked Westward Ho and contributed to its winning. He had followed in the footsteps of the pioneers of the Northwest Passage. The Northwest Passage is a great subject for a film, Spencer Tracy will play it to the hilt. William Randolph Hearst, let me remind you, has rid the United States of the Yellow Peril. He championed Thomas Alva Edison, who made his first motion picture in the crude Black Maria which was an enclosed stage which turned as the earth turned and kept the light in focus."

Someone gestured from the doorway. I was handed a slip of paper on which was written: "Lindbergh has just landed in Paris." I eased myself to the platform and handed Mayer the note as he was delivering his peroration: "It's men like Hearst who have made America what it is"—he glanced at the note which had been placed in front of him—"and this very moment, Charles Augustus Lindbergh flying a one-engined airplane, 'The Spirit of St. Louis,' has landed at Le Bourget Field just outside Paris, the greatest and most daring achievement in all aviation!"

Pandemonium broke loose. When the applause had subsided, Bob Lynch was heard to say: "Well, it was only a suggestion."

Sweet Music to Worry the Wolf Away

In 1929 Tom Weatherly, a man-about-Broadway, had the idea for *The Little Show,* and got the backing of Dwight Deere Wiman, a solvent theatrical producer. He was so solvent that he had a wickerwork Rolls-Royce built for him. It was the most expensive-looking car ever to appear in traffic. He went traveling in it to various events. It was equipped with a bar, and this to Dwight was its most important equipment. Later he gave it to his daughter Trink, who used it regularly until termites set in. It was made of rare wood, fitting for termites living in a Rolls-Royce.

His new venture, *The Little Show,* was to be a revue, but not in any respect like the rhinestone creations with huge staircases of Flo Ziegfeld or Earl Carroll, the G-string titivator. If it was to be compared to any show, it got its inspiration from *The Garrick Gaieties.* It was to be topical and artistic, a witty travesty in the leitmotif, if possible.

Wiman and Weatherly were talking over their project in Tony Soma's speakeasy on West 49th Street and I happened to be holding up the bar in a position that wafted their conversation my way. I careened over to their table and told them that if it was a show they were discussing, they had better take my advice and not do it.

They weren't offended and seemed amused at my brazen interruption. I told them of the shows I had worked on, *Dear Sir, Poppy, Oh, Kay!,* and *The Merry-Go-Round,* that I hadn't made a nickel, and that I was lucky I had a job to turn to. I told them I was a publicity man for MGM pictures, that I wanted to make a better living, but evidently show business was not the way. I recited to them a few verses of a poem I had written about plays that close called "Lament for the Failures":

> *Sing a lament for the plays that fail—*
> *A dirge for the shows that fold.*
> *A tear on the bier of the flops of the year*

And the ticket that couldn't be sold.
Requiem sound for the overly ribald—
The "ball in the air" that was faultily dribbled—
And the play that had little to say.
Wringing of hands for the major fiascos,
The Saturday sundown of would-be Belascos
And the scenery carted away.
Sing a lament.
Sing for the actors who practiced in vain
Lines that were labeled inept or inane.
Sing for the orchestras down in the pits
Playing the numbers that sounded like hits.
Sing for the authors who wrote in the dawn
The "doctors" who came when the patient was gone
Sing for the backers who put up the dough—
One for the backer and two for the show.
Sing with your faces way down to the floor
The dancers, directors, the deans of decor.
Sing a lament.
Sing a lament for the plays that fail
For Sullivan and McBride.
But make it a wake for the critics' mistake—
The Beautiful One that died.

Weatherly wasted no time. He invited me to throw my lot in with them and to write the lyrics for *The Little Show*. I said, "Nothing doing," but if they would guarantee me a minimum of $100 a week against ½ percent of the gross, I'd consider it. Weatherly agreed. He said he had signed Fred Allen who was an original and inventive comic and would set the mood of *The Little Show*. He also had Clifton Webb, the soigné interpretive vaudevillian and Libby Holman, the swarthy, sloe-eyed houri.

He said he wanted me to meet a composer named Arthur Schwartz. I got Weatherly and Wiman in a taxi and took

---

* Prominent Broadway ticket speculators.

them to the Village where I showed them Arthur's letter and the copy of my reply. Weatherly felt it was fate brought us together.

Arthur and I got along well. He sympathized with my desire to write revues. They involved short spurts and no plot construction. It was easier for someone who was doing it as a sideline. Sometimes I would suggest a title and even a rhythm with a melody. But more often he would write a tune first. We weren't touchy about criticism. I would say, "The tune stinks." He would say, "The lyric is lousy." We aimed to please each other. We figured that if we succeeded, there were a lot of people like us. Schwartz was a great judge of lyrics. He had an editorial mind and an ear for the fitness of sound.

We took quarters in a hotel, that is to say hotels. To suggest where our scores were written would sound like a guide to the hostelries of Manhattan. "Hostileries" would be more like it because the complaints poured in from paying neighbors who were wrestling with slumber while we wrestled with our highly perishable wares. Working into the night, the sound of the piano, however muted, endlessly repeating the same strain, penetrated the walls to an unwilling audience. We worked on borrowed time waiting for the manager to knock at the door. We became wandering minstrels, moving from room to room, hotel to hotel. The Warwick, the St. Moritz, the Essex House.

"They don't like what I'm playing," said Arthur sadly.

"That must be it," I replied. "They never complain about the lyrics."

The first number we completed together was a satire burlesque of the movie theme songs that were cluttering the airwaves at the moment and making it difficult to breathe. A widely popular one of the moment was called, "Woman Disputed, I Love You." Our song was "Hammacher Schlemmer, I Love You," and got over well in the show. It was the kind of number that didn't belong in musical comedy but was suitable for a revue. The hardware company liked it too and that Christmas they sent us a box of tools tied with a Christmas ribbon and a merry card reading "Dietz and Schwartz, we love you."

HAMMACHER SCHLEMMER, I LOVE YOU

When skies are frowning,
And when skies are gray,
Then you feel blue, so it seems—
But there's a thought that
Can chase clouds away—
It is the song of my dreams:

Hammacher Schlemmer, I love you—
You're like a sweetheart to me—
Hammacher Schlemmer, above you
No other firm e'er could be.
Your business deserves devotion that is loyal—
I love you just like a fellow loves his goil—
So always remember,
Hammacher Schlemmer—I love you.

(patter)

When I was but a little lad,
Before I'd lived to ten—
I showed a streak of something bad
But that—oh, that—was then.
And now I've grown to be a man
I've grown to man's estate—
And something's come into my life
That's fine, it's more than great
Then came the war—and with the rest
That came from North, East, South and West
I went and tried to do my best
'Twas love that made me stand the test
Oh yes, I did my bit it's true,

123

But did no more than you would do
I was inspired by something big—by
Something that's real and fine and true.
You've often heard the phrase, I s'pose—
'Ten little fingers, ten little toes'—
They came to me, and I was proud—
I told my luck to all the crowd.
I told them that the boy who was bad
Had grown to be a father—yes, a dad,
Supporting a beautiful wonderful wife
With the salary from a firm that gave me life—

So always remember Hammacher Schlemmer,
I love you.

When Arthur and I thought we had finished the score of *The Little Show* we found that Webb wasn't satisfied. He wanted a number that was more perverse, a number he could deliver all alone in full-dress suit and a spotlight. He said it should be a lyric with suave romantic frustration. Webb craved parts that were virile and sensuous. He was not virile or sensuous offstage, but onstage he knew what moods would work for him.

The management was inclined to humor him, so Arthur and I went to work in our tiny room on the 20th floor of the New Yorker Hotel. I asked Arthur to play the tunes in his vast repertoire, but not to sing any lyrics. I wanted to interpret the mood of the number without a distracting influence. In about an hour a melody, just what I wanted, escaped from the upright.

It was a tune Arthur had written for none other than Lorenz Hart who became the outstanding word man of popular show songs. They had both been counselors at Brandt Lake Camp, a resort for boys in the Adirondacks. They wrote the camp show and one of the songs was that melody called by Larry, "I Love to Lie Awake in Bed." It was a well-turned lyric, peaceful and moonlit, and quite the opposite of what Clifton Webb wanted.

> *I love to lie awake in bed*
> *Right after taps I lift the flaps*
> *Above my head*
> *I let the stars shine on my pillow*
> *Oh what a light the moonbeams shed*
> *I feel so happy I could cry*
> *And tears are born*
> *Within the corner of my eye*
> *To be at home with Ma was never like this*
> *I could live forever like this*
> *I love to lie awake a while*
> *And go to sleep with a smile.*

I made it into a song about a different kind of bed, which sang of blue pajamas and forbidden fruit, comparatively poisonous.

I GUESS I'LL HAVE TO CHANGE MY PLAN

> *I beheld her and was conquered at the start*
> *And placed her on a pedestal apart*
> *I planned the little hideaway*
> *That we could share some day*
> *When I met her I unfolded all my dream*
> *And told her how she'd fit into my scheme*
> *Of what bliss is*
> *Then the blow came*
> *When she gave her name as "Mrs."*

> *I guess I'll have to change my plan*
> *I should have realized there'd be another man*
> *Why did I buy those blue pajamas*
> *Before the big affair began?*
> *My boiling point is much too low*
> *For me to try to be a fly Lothario*
> *I think I'll crawl right back and into my shell*

125

Dwelling in my personal hell
I'll have to change my plan around
I've lost the one girl I've found.

But on second thought this resignation's wrong
Most women want the one who comes along
With love that's secret and more true
Than they're accustomed to.
And besides it gives a most romantic edge
When one is sort of hanging on the ledge of abysses
So methinks I do not mind if she's a Mrs.

I guess I'll have to change my plan
Supposing after all there is another man
I'm glad I bought those blue pajamas
Before the enterprise began
For all is fair in love and war
And love's a war—that makes it fairer all the more
Forbidden fruit I've heard is better to taste
Why should I let this go to waste
My conscience to the wind is tossed
I've found the one girl I've lost.

It became for Webb the first of a series of solo flirtations which inspired Alexander Woollcott to refer to Webb as "the general futility man." I struck back for Webb by alluding to the *Times* critic as "Louisa M. Woollcott."

This was Schwartz's first hit, but he didn't know it at the time. We thought it was lost in that Sargasso Sea of songs that have popular quality but no popular success. It seemed to have made the Flop Parade, until three years after the show had closed news reached us that it was being sung in a London nightclub by a team called De Lys and Clarke. They called it "The Blue Pajama Song." When their act was scheduled to appear in New York, Arthur and I went to see it at the Place Pigalle. De Lys came to our table before he and his partner went on. "I've brought a song over from England that I'd like you boys to hear," he said. "We're killing audiences with it."

"Who wrote it?" Arthur inquired.

"I don't know," said the singer, "it dropped in from nowhere. Someone like Noel Coward."

After it was sung and the audience killed, De Lys came back and asked what we thought of it. Arthur, too annoyed to shed light, said, "I think it's the best song someone like Noel Coward ever wrote."

Even the music publisher was unaware he had a hit on his hands. People were asking for "The Blue Pajama Song." The publisher called up Arthur and asked if he had heard of such a number. "Dietz and I wrote it," said Schwartz. "You published it three years ago, and I want to congratulate you on the effortless way you go about making a song hit."

Another sensual show-stopper in *The Little Show* was "Moanin' Low," a dramatic musical playlet staged by Webb for Libby Holman and himself. The music, a dark blues-like throb, was composed by Ralph Rainger who played in the orchestra pit. I wrote a lyric which really wrote itself.

MOANIN' LOW

I feel too bad
I'm feeling mighty sick and sore
So bad—I feel,
I said: I'm feeling sick and sore—
And so 'fraid!
My man don't love me no more.
Day in, day out
I'm worryin about those blues
Day out, day in,
I'm worrying about bad news.
I'm so afraid!
My man I'm goin' to lose.

Moanin' low
My sweet man I love him so
Though he's mean as he can be
He's the kind of man
Needs the kind of woman like me.

127

Gonna die
My sweet man should pass me by
If I die where'll he be?
He's the kind of man
Needs the kind of woman like me.
Don't know any reason
Why he treats me so poorly
What have I gone and done?
Makes my trouble double with his worries,
When surely I ain't deservin' of none.
Moanin' low
My sweet man is gonna go.
When he goes, Oh Lordee!
He's the kind of man
Needs the kind of woman like me.

The Little Show opened in Asbury Park on April 30, 1929. Arthur and I took a train which stalled en route and we didn't arrive at the theatre until the final curtain.

Dwight Deere Wiman and Tom Weatherly greeted us in the lobby. Wiman was plastered and Weatherly had a glum face from which emerged disheartening words.

"It's just as well that you missed it," said Tom. "If I were you, I'd turn around and go back to New York. We'll close Saturday."

"As long as we've come all this way," I said, "we might as well take in tomorrow's performance, and I'll collect the $100 you guaranteed me." Dwight brought forth a $100 bill. "It's the show of a century," he said, handing me the prize.

The next night, with a heavy heart, we saw the show. It played to an almost empty house, but despite this great handicap, there was genuine enthusiasm for the three leading players, Webb, Holman, and Allen. From the moment that Allen as Prologue imitating the character in *Hoopla* appeared in an inverness cape, until the full stage finale, the performance was refreshing, anything but a failure.

The audience gave show-stopping hands to "Hammacher Schlemmer, I Love You," "Moanin' Low," and "Can't We Be Friends," the last composed by Kay Swift with the lyric by her then husband, the banker James Warburg.

"All I can say," said Weatherly, "is that what was a flop last night looks like a hit tonight." "That's all you're allowed to say," said Arthur.

I handed the $100 bill back to Wiman. "This payment was premature," I said. The show came to Broadway and played at the Music Box for nearly two years.

o one in the theatre was more discussable than Libby Holman, who came from Cincinnati and was game for anything. She was a child prodigy and had gone to law school at the age of 16 but decided that she preferred a career on the stage to the law courts.

She started in the original *Garrick Gaieties,* a revue with an original score by Rodgers and Hart. She caught the public eye and ear in *The Merry-Go-Round* singing "Hogan's Alley" with music by Jay Gorney which got all the notices.

Though she had studied law, she was a frivolous personality who appeared in the nude in her dressing room, and, therefore, had a lot of visitors. Libby was so nearsighted she couldn't see anything more than 2 inches away from her. She somehow found her way out onto the stage, but she could only get off by clutching the curtain as it came in and going off with it.

MGM was making *Trader Horn,* and the company was sailing for Africa on Friday. *Trader Horn* was part talkie and part silent. The actors had to be both. It was Wednesday and I had to find someone to cover the assignment from a press point of view.

I had a date with Libby who had just finished a tour with *The Little Show* and was getting ready for *Three's a Crowd.* She was as free as air and felt responsible to no one. She was

129

used to keeping her men waiting. I called for her and ultimately got her into a taxi. She wanted me to take her to the Algonquin Hotel where she would pick up a chap named John McClain who was a reporter on *The Sun*. McClain was leaning on a lamp post in front of the Algonquin and was in a temper. He had been waiting an hour. "That's the trouble with these Broadway queens," he said, "the fewer the better; I want to go where it's clean."

"How would you like to go to Africa on Friday?" I asked. "MGM is making *Trader Horn* and I'm looking for a press agent to go with the company." We had forgotten about Libby even though we were talking across her.

"Don't you think you might tell the driver where to go?" she said. "Never mind that," said the driver, "this is interesting."

McClain actually went to Africa. He had no experience with press agentry, but the log of *Trader Horn* was published every Sunday in *The New York Times*. McClain became well known.

Libby became well known too, not only for her stage manner, but for her individuality. She did outrageous things. For example, one Friday she said she was tired of being nice and proposed that on the weekend at the Henri Souvaines to which we were both invited we should act disagreeably instead of our usual selves. I said I didn't think I could carry it off. "Well, try," said Libby. Mabel showed us the garden and Libby said, "I hate flowers." Henri, who is a well-known composer, played one of his songs and Libby said, "I don't like what you're playing." Mabel caught on to her line and said to Libby, "I don't like you." It was the beginning of a great friendship.

Libby fell in love with Zachary Smith Reynolds who hailed from West Virginia and was part of the well-known cigarette family. Smith, 20 years old, was possessive and jealous of Libby, and Libby had no sense of loyalty. Those who knew her predicted dire results from this irrational knot. They didn't have too long to wait before tragedy stormed the ancestral home. Smith shot himself to death after a wild party. The authorities questioned the circumstances of his death. Libby went into hiding and it was months before she would see anyone. A legal dispute over young Reynolds's $25-million estate took place when the will was read. The Smith Reynolds family contrived that Libby receive just $750,000, a mere fraction of the fortune. Reynolds's first child Ann was awarded $9 million and Christopher, Reynolds's posthumous child 6. The balance was left to charity.

Arthur and I intensified our collaboration after *The Little Show* and our names began to go together. I have been asked several times how it was decided whether we should bill ourselves Dietz and Schwartz or Schwartz and Dietz. I explained that it depended on which of us was nearest the printer.

Arthur's father had insisted he study law and Arthur did as he was told. He zipped through public school and Boys' High. At 16 he received a scholarship from N.Y.U. and $100 a year from the State Board of Regents. He got his A.B. and M.A. He taught English at the High School of Commerce while he was taking his law course at N.Y.U.

All this time, tunes kept bothering him. During the preparations for the bar examination he once whistled aloud in the classroom. There is no evidence that Harold Medina, the celebrated jurist who taught the class, broke into a soft-shoe dance, but the melody was the right one for it. It later became known as "Shine on Your Shoes."

If it weren't for the persistent melodies that entered his ear without knocking, Arthur Schwartz might have climbed to some dizzy height, even to Attorney General. The man who was later to write "Dancing in the Dark," "You and the Night and the Music," "Something to Remember You By," "I See Your Face Before Me," "If There Is Someone Lovelier Than You," "I Guess I'll Have to Change My Plan," "I Love Louisa," "Alone Together," "That's Entertainment," and many others, was a junior partner in a law firm, but those melodies kept interrupting. Rude little rhythms would bother his head and on his desk would be notations on sheets of music paper that lived secretly in a drawer.

Arthur's first client was the father of Lorenz Hart of Rodgers and Hart fame. Pere Hart would start a new business every few months and had to have a new lawyer for each project because he never paid the old ones. But Arthur was more than repaid by his acquaintance with young Larry. It led to the first song for which he was ever paid. Larry wrote a lyric called "I Know My Girl by Her Perfume" and they sold the song outright for $75 to a vaudeville act called Besser and Amy.

For most of the Schwartz songs I furnished the lyrics. After about 500 lyrics, you get to know the composer. If you can stand it that long you must like him.

Despite the success of *The Little Show*, Dwight Wiman and Tom Weatherly did not want to repeat the three stars, Webb, Holman and Allen. Wiman and Weatherly wanted the title *The Little Show* to be the star. Schwartz and I were signed up for *The Second Little Show*, but we also made an arrangement whereby the three stars would appear in a show written and supervised by me. That meant by Schwartz also.

I made an arrangement with Walter Batchelor, the agent, to find a producer. Max Gordon turned up and he had the backing of the prominent producers, A. and L. Erlanger. We called the show *Three's a Crowd*.

While Arthur and I were working on the score, he played a tune he had written in England to the words of Desmond Carter, a prominent London lyric writer. He played the song very fast.

> *I have no words to say how much I love you*
> *That's my excuse, I have no words*
> *I've got a cottage and a room with a view*
> *And H. and C. but I've no words*

I would beg for you, break a leg for you
Lay an egg for you, like the birds up in a treetop
I wrote a song to say how much I love you
I've got the tune, but I've no words.

Arthur didn't seem to think much of the melody. He was convinced it couldn't be used. I suggested he play it in ballad tempo, but every time he repeated it he seemed to play it at a gallop.

"You can't make a ballad out of that," said Arthur, "it's a tinkly chorus number."

"No, it's just right," I said stubbornly, "play it again as slowly as you possibly can, you'll see."

He had to repeat it many times before I got him to slow down to the pace I had in mind. Finally, he got the tinkly tempo out of his system and I wrote the words to "Something to Remember You By." Libby sang it to a sailor played by Fred MacMurray, who had a band called "The California Collegians" which was also the chorus.

SOMETHING TO REMEMBER YOU BY

You are leaving me
And I will try to face
The world alone.

What will be will be
But time cannot erase
The love we've known.

Let me but have a token
Thru which your love is spoken.

You are leaving me
But it will say you're my own.

O give me something to remember you by
When you are far away from me, dear
Some little something meaning love cannot die
No matter where you chance to be

133

Though I'll pray for you
Night and day for you
It will see me thru like a charm
Till your returning.
So give me something to remember you by
When you are far away from me.

We used only one outside contribution, a number called "Body and Soul," which I thought was solid material for Libby. Johnny Green wrote the music and three lyric writers collaborated on the words. I wrote some of them at Libby's request.

When *Three's a Crowd* opened in Philadelphia, Libby was hopeless in it, and she rearranged the billing on the poster and pinned it to the wall of her dressing room: "Clifton Webb and Fred Allen in Two's Company."

Something had to be done to salvage the potential star material in Johnny Green's masterpiece, "Body and Soul." With the composer's consent, I lured Ralph Rainger down to Philadelphia. Rainger had written "Moanin' Low" with me and had a special feeling for this type of dark number. Libby, coached by Rainger, experimented with all types of delivery, but it was not until the last night in Philadelphia that they hit on a way to present the song. When the show opened at the Selwyn Theatre on Broadway in October, 1930, "Body and Soul" was a show stopper.

It Better Be
Good

From my first view of it in my Greenwich Village days, I had coveted the house on West 11th Street, number 18. It was a classic brownstone with five saplings to provide shade and many people considered it the finest small house in New York. Whenever I was in the neighborhood, which was not infrequent, I had the feeling, unmoneyed though I was, that one day that house would be mine. I asked a friend in real estate how much this dream house would cost. He told me that it wasn't for sale and what was a beggar like me doing dabbling in real estate. I told him that one day I would be rewarded for my dabbling.

The man who owned it was Charles Merrill of Merrill Lynch, Pierce, Fenner & Bean. I used to sing a song, "Merrill Lynch We Roll Along," whenever I passed the building. Merrill was willing to sell for a price—the price was $65,000 which was $65,000 more than I had. But then, like in an Alger story, I suddenly ran into scads of money. *The Little Show* and *Three's a Crowd* were both hits and I had gotten several raises at MGM. I paid $40,000 in cash to Mr. Merrill's agent and got a $25,000 mortgage. Mr. Merrill sent me a note saying he hoped I'd be happy in the little house on heaven street. He couldn't have all that money without being sticky.

Betty and I moved into the house on April 9, 1930, and I lived there until September 3, 1958.

The house was one of several built by the same architect, all on the same level. Since it was a small house, I rented the second floor at 20 West from Miss Anne Edgerly, a descendant of the first owner of the houses in the 1840s. We cut a doorway through the common wall. The result was a room 44 x 40, just the right size for a gala. Betty arranged for Dorothy Rodgers, the wife of the great composer Richard Rodgers, to decorate the interior. Dorothy was a great beauty and a handy girl to have around the house. The library, which was entirely paneled, was a work of art.

We had entertaining servants as well as guests. Martino, though he was a good cook, conducted his amours in the kitchen; that accounted for the slowness of the service. Then there was Jane who in her spare time was working on a novel entitled *Leona or The Wolf Girl.* For some inexplicable reason she never showed up on Mondays. The nearest I got to an explanation from her was this, "Since Sunday is my only day of pleasure, Monday is my only day of rest."

Several well-known people lived on the block when we moved in. There was Morris Ernst, the lawyer, at 32 West 11th; Howard Lindsay and his wife Dorothy Stickney, vastly talented in the theatre; Jane Bowles; Donald Ogden Stewart. Lawrence Langner and his wife Armina Marshall lived at number 14 and old Mr. Sullivan of the law firm, Sullivan and Cromwell, next to us at number 16. Oliver Smith was around the corner and down the street at Fifth Avenue lived the costume designer Lucinda Ballard, whom I later married.

The success of *Three's a Crowd* inclined Max Gordon to try again with a revue but I did not easily persuade myself to go along. Revues are difficult to do. Each scene starts from scratch and too much talent is required. The song score in a show with a plot has a thread to hold it together and the plot itself provides cues of a sentimental or comic nature; the simple declarative love song can be reprised with telling effect, whereas in a revue a reprise is just a repetition. I decided that another revue would be too much. But Max was persuasive. In a moment of weakness I said I would write another revue if George Kaufman would agree to collaborate on the sketches. He had written the best comic playlets—"The Still Alarm" which appeared in *The Little Show* was a classic. George agreed and we began working.

Though the work went well and Max was fortified with Kaufman's presence as co-author and director, he was not yet confident of Schwartz's ability to deliver a complete score. And the show involved an investment of $160,000, a huge sum then. But when Arthur played the melodies to "I Love Louisa," "New Sun in the Sky," and "Dancing in the Dark," a relaxed smile appeared on his face. "It's a pleasure to go broke with you boys," he said.

Max had signed up Fred Astaire for *The Bandwagon*. I called on him, and in the corner of his room was an accordion. Fred said he could play it, so I scratched out a lyric called "Sweet Music to Worry the Wolf Away" and Arthur set it. I said to Fred, "We're going to go into rehearsal with *The Bandwagon* in four months. I want you to play this tune on the accordion. Don't play any other tune. You're going to know this one so well when you dance and accompany yourself in the opening number you'll be dazzling. But you'll be even more dazzling when you dance without the accordion."

I took Fred up to Harlem and told him there was a hoofer up there in a club called "Step-In" who had some complicated steps he might want to look at. The hoofer did a special step and Fred picked it out to suit his feet. "He can dance," said the hoofer, "does he want a job in the club?"

I decided to use a revolving stage and consulted the director, Hassard Short. He wasn't sympathetic at first, but when I told him that I intended to use the revolving stage for theatrical effects rather than merely for scenic changes, he was won over.

The show's opening chorus in Philadelphia was most unusual. The curtain was already up as the audience came in. On stage the company took seats—a reflection, as if in a mirror, of the audience arriving. The ushers on stage wore costumes identical to the ushers in the aisles below. Gradually the theatre seats on stage as well as in the orchestra were filled up and as the lights were dimming, the company sang in strict unison, "It Better Be Good."

It better be good
It better be good and funny
It better be good,
It better be worth the money

It's getting so that every show to
Which I'm passionate to go to
Makes me sore
They advertise and ballyhoo 'em
When you finally get to 'em
They're a bore
So what's more!

It better be gay
It better not be too arty,
It better be gay
For this particular party

I haven't liked a show since Lord knows when
And even if it's good I might not like it then.

It better be good
I'm just beginning to yawn!
The show is on
It better be good.

The revolving stage revolved and we presented in capsule form a complete Broadway show, the kind of revue with sketches and songs that audiences had become used to. It was what *The Bandwagon* was not.

Fred Astaire and Adele then played a domestic scene, "Sweet Music to Worry the Wolf Away." Fred sang and accompanied himself on the accordion and the long weeks of rehearsal paid off. "Sweet Music" was Fred and Adele's first song and dance number and it was well received with its tricky couplets.

And when I remind you what
Mischa Elman made his fiddle do
You'll get an inkling of what
This kid'll do

The song ideas were presented with the revolving theme throughout. Children played in the park with hoops. Tilly Losch did a ballet, "The Beggar's Waltz." In the finale of the first act was "I Love Louisa" which had a German merry-go-round. Fred was the beggar and as he was carried around by the stage, he turned into a prince.

The two numbers I most liked were "Miserable with You," performed by Adele Astaire and Frank Morgan, and the ensemble number "Confession."

MISERABLE WITH YOU

She: *I just came back from a funeral.*
He: *How was it?*
She: *It was nice.*
He: *I'm glad you had a chance to enjoy yourself.*
She: *I hear you bought a gun and you're planning to destroy yourself.*
He: *Mm-hmm—*
    That's true
    And how about you?

She: *You talk about your trouble,*
    The trouble I've got is double.
      Oh, when will this depression be thru?
    Each day it's getting tougher,
    But since I have to suffer
      I might as well be miserable with you.

    This cough I've got is hacking,
    The pain in my head is racking,
      I hardly need to mention my flu—
    The Board of Health has seen me
    They want to quarantine me.
      I might as well be miserable with you.

Father, Father went and forged a check
   So they put him away.
Mother, Mother fell and broke her neck today:
   Hey, hey!
Between my aches and sneezes,
My groans and my grunts and wheezes
   I guess you see the reason I'm blue—
The doctor says that maybe
I'm going to have a baby
   I might as well be miserable with you.

He: I've been run over by a taxicab.
She: How was it?
He: It was nice
She: I'm hoping that at least they will operate.
He: I'd like to get the name
         Of the poison that your Popper ate!
She: Okay—what say
         We take it today?

He: You talk about your trouble,
         The trouble I've got is double—
            I'm wanted for murder or two.
         It seems that during Lenten
         I killed a guy in Trenton!
            I might as well be miserable with you.

         The outlook sure is gloomy,
         The landlord's about to sue me
            To get the rent that's long overdue—
         There's nothing quite as mean as
         Avoiding those subpoenas!
            I might as well be miserable with you.

         Sister, sister stole a string of pearls,
            She is funny that way!
         Brother's wanted 'cause he raped two girls, they
            say—
               Hey, hey!

My misery is utter,
I'm practically in the gutter.
   And yesterday I heard something new—
Mama, when she was plastered,
Admitted I'm a bastard.
   I might as well be miserable with you.

"Confession" was sung by a six-girl and six-boy choir singing in a cathedral set designed by Albert Johnson.

CONFESSION

Boys: *Let me be your father confessor,*
Girls: *Yes sir, yes sir!*
Boys: *Tell your innermost thoughts to me*
Girls: *That will be hard to do.*
Boys: *Would you mind if I gathered closer?*
Girls: *No sir, no sir!*
Boys: *Let your innermost thoughts come free,*
        It will comfort you.
Girls: *If you find you are shocked at the truth,*
        Excuse it on the grounds of youth.

Girls: *I never kissed a man before*
Boys: *Oh, isn't that a shame?*
Girls: *I never kissed a man before—*
        Before I knew his name.

Girls: *I never had a taste for wine,*
Boys: *Oh isn't that a sin?*
Girls: *I never had a taste for wine*
        For wine can't compare with gin.

Boys: *It's nice as nice can be*
        Our faith is at last restored
        To find that vice can be
        Its own reward—

Girls: *I always go to bed at ten*
Boys: *Oh isn't that a bore?*
Girls: *I always go to bed at ten, but I go home at four.*

"I Love Louisa" was written for the chambermaid in the St. Moritz Hotel where Arthur and I were working. She loved our music and would hang around whenever it was played. Our suite was the dirtiest suite in town. She never cleaned it. Her name was Louisa and she was our inspiration.

I LOVE LOUISA

He: *How I love a glass of beer!*
Boys: *More beer!*
He: *Beer goes very good with beer.*
Boys: MORE beer.
He: *When I'm drinking*
        Beer I'm thinking
        Ach—life is dear.
        But there's someone I love
        Even more than beer:

        I love Louisa,
        Louisa loves me;
        When we rode on the merry-go-round
        I kissed Louisa!
        And then Louisa,
        Louisa kissed me;
        We were so happy, so happy and free.
        Ach, Gott! but she's a
        Beautiful Louisa—
        Ach, when I choose 'em
        I love a great big boosom!
        Some day Louisa, Louisa will be
        More than just a fraulein to me.

He: *Frenchmen love a glass of wine*
Boys: MORE BEER!
He: *English think that whiskey's fine,*
Boys: MORE BEER!
He: *When I comb off*
        All the foam off
        I drink a toast
        To the Germans and the Madchen I love most:
          (Repeat refrain, I Love Louisa)

When we wrote "Dancing in the Dark" I thought it was a good song but I thought it was dull. I debated whether or not we should use it in the show. There seemed to be no way of staging it.

It was sung by John Barker in evening clothes. There were mirrors all around so that Tilly Losch could dance with her reflection. Time and applause have taken the dullness out of it.

DANCING IN THE DARK

Dancing in the dark
Till the tune ends
We're dancing in the dark
And it soon ends
We're waltzing in the wonder
Of why we're here
Time hurries by—we're here
And gone;
Looking for the light
Of a new love
To brighten up the night
I have you, love,
And we can face the music together,
Dancing in the dark.

What though love is old?
What though song is old?
Through them we can be young!

Hear this heart of mine
Make yours part of mine!
Dear one,
Tell me that we're one!

In general, Adele was more popular than Fred, but when she told me she would shortly get married to Lord Charles Cavendish in London, I thought she should be subordinated to Fred so as not to leave too big a hole in the show. I discussed it with Mrs. Astaire, their mother, who agreed. Adele began to come in late for rehearsals, and I told her if she came in late again, I would spank her in front of the entire company. I spanked her.

When *The Bandwagon* was in its closing week at the New Amsterdam Theatre and about to begin its road tour, there were a few other cast replacements to be made besides Adele. Tilly Losch, the star of the ballet, was the biggest problem. Tilly looked irreplaceable. She had been the partner of the great Harald Kreutzberg and had arranged ballet for Charles B. Cochran and Max Reinhardt in London. She was a great beauty, poetry in motion.

Not knowing a suitable substitute, I held auditions for each member of the ensemble and came up with Florence Chambecas, a lovely girl of eighteen who was excitingly graceful. Too good, thought Tilly Losch. There were three solo dance numbers to be covered: "The Flag Dance," an arrangement of "Dancing in the Dark," and a story called "The Beggar's Waltz." Tilly said we ought to have a separate dancer for each of the numbers, but I wanted to try Florence and believed she could do them. I pointed out that if we gave Florence the opportunity to perform before a paid audience, it would be a much better experience than practicing on a bare propless stage. Fred Astaire said he would practice "The Beggar's Waltz" with her.

Tilly didn't want Florence to wear her costumes, and to appease the explosive Viennese artist, I told Florence to get fitted for new ones and be ready to go on Monday night and play out the last week before the show went on the road. Miss Chambecas, knowing this might be the opportunity of a lifetime, gave a magnificent performance. Max Gordon was out front, I was out front, and of course Tilly was out front. We got into a huddle after the show. We all agreed, with the exception of Tilly, that Florence was a godsend and her performance saved the show. I said Florence was to play all week. Tilly said she was playing the last Saturday night performance.

The Post printed a paragraph about Tilly not going on the road. She thought that Howard Benedict, the press agent for the show, should have stopped the item from appearing in print and should at least have sent out a notice that Miss Losch had decided to go on the road after all.

Saturday night was the eve of doom. Florence appeared in her costume for the flag dance and waited in the wings. Tilly came down in her flag costume. I joined them, announcing bravely that Florence was to do the number. Frank Morgan and Helen Broderick were on and their sketch was a blackout. I took hold of Tilly and motioned to Florence to go on. Tilly struggled in my arms and scratched my face, but I held her firmly all through the number. When it was over, I released her and she ran up the flight of stairs to her dressing room.

I told Florence she had done magnificently well, a worthy road-company replacement for the great Tilly Losch and that her salary was quadrupled.

Then I took a position at the bottom of the stairs and waited for Tilly. She appeared at the top with her head in the air and started down with great dignity. When she got to the bottom, I linked my arm in hers and held it as in a vise. I asked her if she'd ever seen a burlesque show. It was an odd question. Caught off guard, she said she hadn't. There was one playing across the street on 41st Street. I led her directly to it and we never mentioned her ballets.

My professional experience with the Marx Brothers was brief, but intense. Chico, whose Italian character used words like "biggida" and "wotsa matta you," was a gambler offstage; we played bridge up to 50¢ a point. The silent Harpo was talkative in real life and was a good golfer and croquet player. He carried wickets, balls and mallets in the trunk of his car, and he would often set up a game in Central Park. He was careful with his money and had a portfolio of blue-chip stocks, partly the payoff on election bets. Zeppo was a businessman and became the agent for the family. Groucho, as we know, was quick-witted and made puns and spoonerisms until you longed for a cliché. One of his remarkable ad-libs was made when he was quiz master of his program, "You Bet Your Life." A big scientist was explaining that a single fly could multiply itself about a quarter-million times in a month. Groucho quickly suggested, "Imagine what a married fly could do."

After their musical *The Coconuts,* written by George Kaufman, they stopped doing shows and went into pictures. But they still retained their kinship with vaudeville and they toured in an act while their picture script was in the writing stage. The act was a hardy perennial, but though still a show stopper the time had come for a change. When Kaufman and Morrie Ryskind, who had written shows for them, were not available, they decided to try me out, as they liked the revues I had put together, *The Little Show* and *The Band Wagon.* I worked on a skit called *Said the Duchess,* which Groucho thought had possibilities. I agreed to write and direct it.

I didn't realize what I was in for. The act was a war act. It began with the four Marx Brothers harmonizing beneath a lamp post on a side street. Each time they'd hit a high note, the lamp post would move away. Their song is interrupted by a martial air on a bugle, and American flags pop out of every window. They say, "It's war," and solemnly shake hands as

147

they say their goodbyes and go off in different directions. They meet again behind the front and Harpo chases the girls in the canteen, Groucho plays cards with Chico for Madame Dumont, who is no prize, while Zeppo sings a ballad entitled "In the Heart of a Flower and You." The boys get captured as spies, but they manage to don bulletproof vests, and their invulnerability frightens off the enemy. With one thing misleading to another, they finish back at the lamp post, which tries to move away from their high note. But this time, it is held firmly by the quartet as the curtain closes.

It was agreed that we would rehearse at the Times Square Theatre at 12 o'clock every day. Twelve o'clock, the first day, came and went, but no Marx Brothers were in sight. At 1 o'clock Harpo showed, but as his act was a self-invented pantomime, he had to perfect his own routines. The next day Chico and Zeppo appeared, but no Groucho or Harpo, and you can't have the four Marx Brothers without them. On Wednesday, they all appeared, but they were a half hour late, and it was matinee day. Getting a quorum together, and on time, began to look hopeless.

Groucho suggested that we have lunch at the Hotel Astor where we could talk it all over. His suggestion was adopted, but so many people came over to our table for autographs that a feeling of frenzy invaded my brain, and I decided we'd best call the whole thing off. But Groucho wasn't discouraged and as we passed through the hotel lobby, he went to a door engraved "Manager's Office," which he opened and ushered us into. The office was empty, the manager probably had gone to lunch.

We draped ourselves around his desk on his oak chairs and began talking sense. We were there for about five minutes and had dismissed the trespassing when the door opened and the manager came in, startled at the sight he encountered. Groucho opened a desk drawer, took out a box of cigars and stuffed one in the manager's mouth. Chico gave him an insurance solicitation. "I represent the Liberty Bell Insurance Company established in 1776. Our $10,000 policy has the lowest accident and health rate you can find anywhere. If you lose an arm we pay you $75 a week and let you keep the other arm. Lose a leg, we teach you a time step like Peg Leg Pete and get you a week in vaudeville. Kick in the shins, 10¢." Chico gave the manager a kick and a dime.

Harpo called me up and said he had found the perfect place to practice. It was the penthouse apartment of a man-about-town called Jack Troutman. "Be there about 9 o'clock," he said, "and we'll whip this thing into shape." Promptly at 9 I arrived. A five-piece band was playing and there was dancing. Harpo was seated in a plush chair with a beautiful girl sitting on an arm of it. There was a backgammon set in front of Harpo. We made no comment on the vaudeville act. "Want to play backgammon?" said Harpo.

"What'll we play for?" I asked.

"We'll play for her," said Harpo, making the first move.

I won the game and the lady left Harpo's chair and seated herself on the arm of mine.

I made no further calls for rehearsals. *Said the Duchess* is one of those scripts that remains in the writer's trunk.

Something to Remember Me By

The acquisition of Greta Garbo by MGM was an accident. Louis B. Mayer had gone to Sweden to sign up the noted director, Maurice Stiller, and Garbo was thrown in with the deal. She was 19 in 1924, and you had to stare to latch onto her beauty; but once latched on, you lost your poise in her presence. She didn't speak except when necessary and you found yourself talking nonsense to make conversation. She used no makeup, and we weren't used to natural coloring in those days. Her hairdo was casual as a drunken driver's, but if you were facetious about her orbs and molars, you'd have to throw something over your left shoulder to assuage the fates.

She wore a comfortable stained suede suit, the same suit every day, unless she had more than one of that material and design. She was carted around by the MGM press contacts to meet the editors of the fan magazines. They weren't impressed, but Walter Wanger of Paramount tried to purloin her from MGM, offering to double the $300 a week she was getting. Garbo probably would have accepted this offer if it weren't for her mother, Mrs. Gustafson, back in Stockholm, who believed in living up to the contract she had signed for Greta who was a minor.

Garbo was not enchanted by the motion-picture people in Hollywood. She would wander aloof among the two-dimensional buildings on the back lot, and she spoke the approximate truth in her interviews and panned Hollywood. I wasn't paid to pan Hollywood and it was important to harness this free spirit. I insisted that a member of the publicity department be present at every interview. Garbo said if she weren't allowed to speak freely, she wouldn't have any interviews, and she didn't have any interviews for the next 48 years, and most likely never will.

This negative decision turned out to be the best publicity notion of the century. Loneliness is Garbo's most important product. Many stars have tried to emulate her technique. For a while, it was a common sight to see glamour girls walking on the back lot acting like they wanted to be alone, but their lack of sincerity defeated their intention. They were left alone and didn't like it.

John Gilbert was an outstanding star in the silent era and his partnership with the most beautiful actress in the movies, whose individuality dated from the film appropriately titled *Love,* had made Garbo-Gilbert a frequent column item. They were the biggest box-office attraction in *Flesh and The Devil* and *The Divine Woman* and would have continued so if the talkies had stayed away from the door leading to tragedy.

Few knew the details of the private life of the glamorous couple although I was one in whom Gilbert confided. He told me that Garbo was too much for one man and often left his side on evenings when lovers should be together. He tried to stimulate her interest in him by going out on his own. I ran into him at Luigi's Saloon in Hollywood, holding up a corner of the bar.

"What do you think of her?" he said.

"I think she's the most glamorous thing I ever saw," I replied, underestimating her.

"When I said 'I'm going out,' the only thing she said was 'I'll leave the door open, Jack!' What do you say to a girl like that?" Jack asked me.

"I don't know," I replied. "What *do* you say?" I was delighted at being a part of the plot.

"I didn't know either," said Jack; "I said 'I'm going out to sleep with Anna May Wong!'"

" 'I'll leave the door open, Jack' was all she said. What in hell do I do?"

"It's obvious," I said. "You sleep with Anna May Wong!"

Talkies were on the ascendant, there were nervous actors, and elocution teachers were in demand. Garbo was beginning to talk but Gilbert had squeaky pipes and I felt sorry for him. I believed his love affair with Garbo was doomed, which it was.

Some years later I was a guest at a small dinner party given by Diana Vreeland, then editor of *Harper's Bazaar* and Garbo was present. Out of nervousness at being seated next to the most glamorous of stars, I told of an adventure I'd had the night before when I played a hoax on a girl I took for a drink.

I told how an oriental gentleman in flowing robes and a turban was working his way toward us, obviously telling fortunes by interpreting handwriting. My companion was all for having her fortune told. I saw some folding money pass and being too stingy to part with $5 for what I thought was nothing but fakery, I said, "If you must have your fortune told, *I'll* tell it. I'm the greatest interpreter of handwriting in America. I tell devastating truths and I'm afraid of my own perceptiveness."

I had Sheila write a 50-word paragraph on the back of the menu. I told her it had to be an original composition, nothing previously memorized, possibly a letter to a friend. After a black look from turban, I set out to prophesy and predict. Oblivious to everything but the penmanship, I drew inferences from every "T" and dot. To my astonishment, my client was sobbing. By guesswork I had hit on hints of her disappointments in life and love. I felt like the very aged man a-sitting on a gate. "I do not dare to write as funny as I can."

When I finished my story, everyone at the dinner table was excited. Each wanted me to tell his fortune and had already written the 50 words. I managed to elude them, but Garbo was insistent. "Can I come to see you?" she asked softly. I told her the walls would talk if she did.

"The walls will have little to say. Where do you live?" I gave her my address, which was the house at 18 West 11th Street.

154

"What time shall I come?" she asked.

"Come at 6," I said.

"I'll be there tomorrow at 6. I'll only be able to stay for 20 minutes."

"One minute would be a gala," I said, "you'll come for 20 galas."

At one minute to 6, I went to the door. Coming up the brown steps, wearing a cloth coat and a big floppy hat, was Greta Garbo. "You're a punctual visitor," I said.

"I'll be punctual in my departure," she said.

She wasted five of the 20 minutes looking over the house. She also looked at my paintings, which achieved some recognition in easily awed circles. We settled in the library. Then she whipped two letters out of her straw bag.

"I will appreciate it if you will tell me all you can about this person."

I sighed. "You don't believe that I have supernatural powers."

"Tell me what you see in the handwriting."

"But I was telling a joke last night, I was trying to amuse, I was guessing."

"Guess again," said the irresistible Swede. She took the letters out of their envelopes and I reluctantly took over. The salutations had been cut off, and there was nothing but solid blocks of English prose. They were from a man.

"He is an international type," I said, noting that the number 7 had a line across it. "He might be a Swiss or even a Belgian, judging by the symmetry of the spacing. English is not his native tongue, but he was educated in England. He is almost always in a hurry, the way his dashes are consistently left behind. The extra forward thrust of his 'h's' suggests that he is not shy about women. But he is a lover and can be relied on to be faithful to his word. His handwriting does not disintegrate. He doesn't make love in taxis. He is a careful dresser and doesn't like to mess himself up."

Miss Garbo looked at the clock and realized her self-al-

155

lotted time was up. She reached over and took the envelope. "I must go now," she said, getting up and complimenting me on the house. "I enjoyed the surroundings," she said, not mentioning the paintings she had seen nor commenting on the handwriting effort.

"Will you dine with me on Monday?" I solicited.

She replied from the front door, "How do I know I'll be hungry Monday?" She thanked me and made a determined departure. She can be a precise and punctual person at the same time she is very elusive. Her manner implied that my diagnosis of the handwriting she had shown me was correct, and I'm inclined to believe that despite my protestations she still thinks I'm a graphologist. Perhaps I am, for all I know. If things get bad, I may buy myself a turban.

The star director in the days of silent pictures was Marshall (Mickey) Neilan who had a reputation for being reckless. He was a great disciplinarian and made the actors toe the line, but would not discipline himself. He was a maverick, perfect material for publicity as he did ridiculous and reckless things.

Once when Neilan and I were both staying at the Ambassador Hotel, I was dressing for a dinner to be given by Norma Shearer when Neilan phoned my room. "Come right down, I have a present for you," he said. "I'll meet you in the parking lot." I put on my pants and hurried down. Neilan was there, occupying one of those graceful baby Austins that flourished in the 'twenties. "It's yours," said Neilan. "Get in and I'll show you its stamina. I'll drive it first because I have no license." Strange logic, but I couldn't refuse him.

He stepped on the gas and the Austin flew out of the lot, smashing a traffic stanchion in the Ambassador Hotel driveway. "See," said Mickey, "it's tough." I was sorry to see the beautiful machine get treated so badly. Mickey backed away from the stanchion and flew onto Wilshire Boulevard heading for downtown Los Angeles. He came upon another traffic signpost and bumped it. "I just want to show you that the body can take it," he said. I was convinced, but Neilan kept aiming at signposts and traffic posts until the Austin was a piece of flattened tin.

Neilan kept saying, "I know a place where you can get nickel whiskey." We got to the bargain-price saloon, Farmer Page's. You could get whiskey for a nickel but you had to buy the beer which was 95¢. It was a coincidence, but the night we were there was the night Farmer Page was shot. After the pistol shot, I pulled Neilan out of the melee in the bar and over the fence bordering the saloon and shoved him into a taxicab. If the police had found Mickey Neilan on the spot, he would likely have become involved and it would have been difficult to explain the car. It was hard enough explaining it to Norma Shearer who had waited dinner.

The most successful producer of money-making films for MGM was Irving Thalberg who had hardly brushed up against the real world. He thought in motion-picture captions. He wooed with motion-picture gallantry. He had risen to the top of the screen world where he talked in millions, crushed villains and made stars.

He was thoughtful when he thought of you, but he rarely thought of you unless you were useful to a picture project. He picked brains. He seemingly had shelves on him to hang telephones. He married Norma Shearer. She became the biggest star on the MGM lot—he didn't notice anyone else.

He had one admirable negative trait: he didn't care about publicity and didn't even want his name in the billing. He was the only producer in Hollywood who was self-shrinking. It was great strategy, and made his competitive producers not so competitive.

I never had a conversation with him about anything except movies. When I was at the studio, I waited 10 hours in his outer office to find out what he wanted to see me about. I got saddle sores from sitting on leather. When you were ushered into his presence, he forgot that he had called you.

He was sensitive and handsome. Many people thought he would make a movie star himself, but they didn't realize that his was the most valuable skill on the lot. His main talent was his editing and cutting. It was said that all MGM films were made and remade. It was Retake Valley. Thalberg worked every minute of the day and he expected every creative person on his studio staff to do the same.

He had a one-car locomotive built and furnished with a degree of taste. This was used for transport to and from previews which MGM scheduled in Riverside. On the trip to the preview, dinner would be served, and on the trip back, there would be an exchange of ideas about the film, so that Thalberg got the benefit of the entire producing, writing, and directing staff.

For some reason, he valued my opinion and often telephoned me from California. I suppose I should have felt flattered by his frequent calls but I knew it would get me nowhere. He was sorry if he had interrupted dinner but he didn't stop talking.

Later on, I was spending about half the year on Long Island at Sands Point and commuting to my office at 45th Street and Broadway. I went in and out in one or the other of my Chris-Craft speedboats, the "Stuff" and the "Nonsense." The "Stuff" had a top on it in case of rain.

The evening of the Louis-Schmelling fight I went back in the "Stuff" to Sands Point to pick up the tickets. I had invited six people to the fight and had left the tickets at $100 apiece in the house. I had to get them and then go to the Grand Concourse Hotel where I was to pick up my guests at 7 o'clock. It was a close call whether or not I would make it in daylight, and I was on my way back to the dock when the telephone rang—Thalberg!

"Listen, Irving," I said, "I've got to pick up a flock of

guests. I'm taking them to the Louis-Schmelling fight. I'll call you as soon as the fight is over."

"Do that," Irving said, "I'm glad to see you're having a little recreation, you've been working too hard. Call me up after the fight is over."

I said I was taking the speedboat and I didn't want to go on the Sound in the dark. "I'll call you at the first opportunity," I said.

"Just one consideration before you hang up, Howard, just answer me yes or no. Do you think we should make *Romeo and Juliet?*"

"Offhand, no," I replied, "but we can discuss it after the fight."

"What do you mean, 'no?' " said Thalberg. "It's the greatest love story ever told, it's a work of art."

"Who'll play Juliet?" I asked.

"Norma," he replied.

"I doubt if she would be right for it," I said. "She's not that young."

"Juliet can be any age."

"I don't think *Romeo and Juliet* is box office."

"With Norma, it will be a cinch."

Thalberg attacked a few more problems in doing the picture and I eyed the dark water.

"But you'd better go to your fight," said Thalberg solicitously.

The fight was over.

The horror-show master in those days was Tod Browning, who dreamed up silent pictures designed to shock you or disgust you and was marvelously successful at it. His most-noted work was *Freaks*. Irving Thalberg himself felt it was imaginative art and edited Browning, who was flattered that his work should attract the production genius.

Freaks brought together many paraplegics, an eight-foot giant, and a pinhead who was representative of the intellectual content of the screen play, as were Tom Thumb (riding a hamster) and all the famous misfits seen in vaudeville or more recently on the television screen. The freaks stuck together and had their own elections and national conventions. There was an army of midgets. The midgets could conceal themselves in the upholstery, and I got accommodations for them in the best hotels. They preferred small rooms.

Browning asked me if I could suggest a writer for the new film he had in mind. "Actually I don't need a writer," he said, "I can do the writing myself. I want someone who can answer one big question that I will put to him. I need someone who can clear up the plot. It might even be a woman. After all, Mary Wollstonecraft created Frankenstein."

It wasn't my business to suggest writers, but since my advice was solicited, I suggested Herman Mankiewicz but pointed out that he was expensive.

"This is going to be the greatest movie I've ever made," said the macabre director, "and merely getting screen credit will enhance any career. Here's the story outline.

"It opens with Lon Chaney wearing a white wig and an inverness cape, playing 'The Last Rose of Summer' on the violin. He is blind and has a tin cup hooked onto him, and the crowd divides before him as he slowly walks in a measured tempo while scratching away at his fiddle. He continues on his way and suddenly darts down five or six steps in front of a brownstone house. He taps a mysterious code on the door and rings a doorbell in between taps. The door is opened. We hear strange screams from inside. Lon Chaney removes his white wig and inverness cape and appears in a complete surgical outfit. He enters the room from which the screams emerge, the screams get louder and Chaney gets covered with blood. The prison-like cells are filled. We see him cutting off the heads of half a dozen nude ladies. He also cuts off the heads of half a dozen apes. Lon Chaney now is busy putting the heads of women on the bodies of apes and the heads of apes on the bodies of women.

"Now I'm coming to the question," said Browning. "What business is Chaney in that he should want to put women's heads on apes and the apes' heads on women?"

I told Browning that if anyone knew, it would be H. J. Mankiewicz.

I n the early thirties, Fanny Holzman, a shrewd lawyer with distinguished clients, came to my office and told me she was about to sue MGM for maligning her client, Princess Youssoupoff. In the film, *Rasputin and the Empress*, Rasputin had raped her and the princess did not appreciate this, even if only on celluloid.

The film story was based on the actual assassination of Rasputin by Prince Youssoupoff. Rasputin was supposed to have cast a spell over the Czarina and left a trail of sexual adventures. The prince decided that the monk must go. He lured him to the palace and served poisoned cakes as hors d'oeuvres and goblets of wine heavy with cyanide. When the poison failed, the prince took a pistol and shot Rasputin twice. Still the monk did not die but began attacking and chasing the prince who managed to grasp a cane and club Rasputin nearly to death. The prince's bodyguard threw Rasputin into the river where he swam for a while and then drowned.

The film was the first and only one starring the three Barrymores. John played the prince, Ethel was the czarina, and Lionel played Rasputin. It was directed by Richard Boleslavsky, produced by Bernard Hyman, and also featured Diana Wynyard and Ralph Morgan. It was a big box-office attraction.

"I have a big publicity stunt for you," Fanny said. "I'll sue you for libeling the princess. I'll demand a quarter of a million dollars and I'll settle in advance for $10,000 which you will give me right away because the princess is broke.

Your losses are limited; the trial will capture public attention. It will be a noisy case."

I told the story to J. Robert Ruben, MGM's legal executive. "That's champerty," he said. I looked it up. Champerty is the sharing in the proceeds of a litigation by the one who promotes it. I told Fanny it was champerty; I appreciated the publicity stunt but we couldn't use it.

"It's not champerty," she said. "I'll bring this suit in London; they don't like Hollywood there."

The following year, Princess Youssoupoff won a $125,000 suit against Metro-Goldwyn-Mayer in England, and another $50,000 in other countries.

hen we were making the film, *The Big House*, I went to San Quentin to see Warden Smith, thinking he might provide access to the atmosphere. I took the quick tour of San Francisco. Chinatown, Fisherman's Wharf, the cable cars, the Top of the Mark, before returning to my hotel, the St. Francis. I dropped into the bar to see if anybody was there —there is always someone at the St. Francis bar—and there was John Barrymore, large as life and drinking it away. He was having an argument with a man from Warner Brothers. It seems they were giving the great Barrymore a banquet in the St. Francis ballroom downstairs, only the great Barrymore preferred to stay at the bar and not go down to the dinner and make a speech.

Mr. Barrymore remembered me from a comment I once made at the Players Club about his much-touted delivery of the famous lines "To be or not to be" and "Alas, poor Yorick." I had contended, not knowing whether I was right or wrong but certain that I was provocative, that Shakespeare had meant the lines to be read "That *is* the question," not "*That* is the question," and "Alas, poor Yorick, I knew *him*, Horatio," not "I *knew* him." I was saying a lot about iambic and anapestic meter and why Shakespeare used meter to emphasize his meaning. "That *is* the question" emphasized that living life itself was in question and "I knew *him*" meant that Yorick was not a mere acquaintance but that he, Hamlet, had probed Yorick's conscience, his soul.

Barrymore asked me if I had ever got straightened out on the bard's significant accents. He ordered Courvoisier for me and a whiskey for himself, and magnanimously invited the man from Warner Brothers into the inner circle of Shakespearean investigators.

But the man from Warner Brothers was weeping. "Please come to the banquet table," he pleaded. "It's too embarrassing; they want you in the ballroom."

Barrymore, growing indignant, said, "I am talking to this gentleman here. He speaks intelligently about intelligent things. Surely, it's much more important to get to the bottom of Elizabethan cadences than to make speeches to people who can hardly talk. If they want to hear a speech, send them up here and I'll make a speech about Shakespeare."

The man from Warner Brothers looked at me helplessly and I felt sorry for the treatment he was getting. I told Barrymore that I had to leave as I had to get up at 5 o'clock the next morning to go to San Quentin and have breakfast with Warden Smith. Barrymore reached into the inside pocket of his jacket and took out a long vial containing what I believe was ether. He opened it into his whiskey and stirred it with the vial.

"If you're going to San Quentin," he said, "will you give this to Kid McCoy? I owe him some money, from an account I ran up in his saloon before he shot his wife." He took a roll of bills and handed it over to me. I demurred from taking it but he forced it on me. I gave the money to Warden Smith and told McCoy I had delivered $80 from Barrymore. McCoy thanked me for the thought but said he doubted that he would ever see it.

Why Am I Singing in the Morning

Running the risk of being styled repetitive, vulgar, unfunny, labored, and adequate, Arthur and I began work on our fifth revue, *Flying Colors*, in 1931.

When writing the script for a revue I tried to make it as complete as that of a play with descriptions of all the dance routines and ballets. But when one has in the cast outstanding special performers, one must be prepared for the new thing that bobs up at rehearsal, the inspirational notion that comes from seeing talent at work. Yet it is dangerous to rely on anything but advance preparation. I usually left the show slightly long to allow for future cuts. We would open in Boston or Philadelphia with about a half hour more show than we would have in New York.

There is no way of being sure that a show will be a hit, a failure, artistic, or crude. Too many factors enter into it. The timing of things, the routining of them, the mechanics. Many a scene that was funny in print and rehearsal laid the well-known Broadway egg when dressed up and presented. Many a dance that was exciting when the girls did it in practice clothes lost something when the wide skirts were put on. Many a novelty becomes a cliché overnight. If the music is good perhaps overorchestration will cloud the melody, perhaps the lyrics will not be heard, perhaps they will be. The big effect that was to startle and amaze might not work right.

So often audiences are a failure. Many an audience has been so bad that it should have been panned by the reviewers.

Before you get near rehearsal day you have to hold regular auditions in some dusty, dark theatre with a pilot-light effect, listen to and observe hundreds of entertainers you couldn't possibly use, but who were sent over either by some friends or by that curious coterie and speckled band known as the agents. The singers all think it ingenious to render one of your own songs and they get the lyrics wrong. The tap dancers do Fred Astaire and Clifton Webb routines. Then there are the magicians with conversational patter and no lights, the novelty boys, and the knockabout comedians.

One day I was sitting with Helen Broderick at an audition watching a man whose act was to do a violent and comic prizefight with himself. He actually made his nose bleed. Incredulous, I asked if he made his nose bleed at every performance. "Oh no," replied Helen, "only at auditions."

Flying Colors was produced by Max Gordon and starred Clifton Webb, Charles Butterworth, Tamara Geva, and Patsy Kelly. It was a well-paced show and had four successful songs: "Fatal Fascination," "Shine on Your Shoes," "Louisiana Hayride," and "Alone Together."

FATAL FASCINATION

(The man reminisces and his part is spoken throughout.)

Girl

It isn't the clothes you wear,
  Though I like your style.
It isn't your jaunty air
  Or your winning smile.
It isn't your clever phrases
Makes me give these adoring gazes
You've got that je-ne-sais-quoi
That appeals to moi.

Man

I was in France—

Girl

You've got a fatal fascination
  Don't know what it can be—
You've got a fatal fascination
  For me.

Man

I went over on the double S. Paris in 1926—

Girl

I've got a new infatuation
  For it's easy to see

167

You've got a fatal fascination
 For me.

Man
I sat at the captain's table.

Girl
You're not really my first affair

Man
I was only sick once.

Girl
With the wine that is love.

Man
It lasted five days.

Girl
I knew from that cursed affair
 If I got one more sock I'd
 Be cock-eyed.

Man
And five nights.

Girl
What gave me my intoxication
Something stronger than tea—
You and your fatal fascination
For me.

(*The orchestra starts the second verse. Man pays no attention to the music, but talks thru it.*)

Man
Gay Paree! Champagne a dollar and a half a quart—$3 a pint. I lived in a little hotel on the left bank—what they call a pension. Room and bath a dollar and a half, and what a bath! A nice, big bathtub—large washstand, and a little tiny washstand to bathe your feet in. One night in the Montmartre one of those French girls wanted me to

buy some of those postal cards. I said, "Do you think all of us Americans are Americans?"—Do you want to see the cards?

Girl

You've got a fatal fascination
Don't know what it can be—
You've got a fatal fascination
For me.

Man

When I returned the boys hardly recognized me—
I'd changed so.

Girl

I've got a new infatuation
For it's easy to see
You've got a fatal fascination
For me.

Man

As soon as I got home
I had to take a long rest.

Girl

You're not really my first affair
With the wine that is love
And I knew from that cursed affair
If I got one more sock I'd
Be cock-eyed.

What gave me my intoxication
Something stronger than tea
You and your fatal fascination.
For me.

SHINE ON YOUR SHOES

Go away you good-for-nothin'!
Never amount to nothin'
Hangin' round the corners—
Can't you see you never will be gettin' anywhere.

If you want to get employment
Tidy up your face
And amount to sumpin'.
Those big men that got up there
All declare:

When there's a shine on your shoes
There's a melody in your heart.
With a singable happy feeling
A wonderful way to start
To face the world every day—
With a deedle-um-dee-di-di-
Little melody that is making
The worrying world go by.
When you walk down the street
With a happy-go-lucky beat,
You'll find a lot in what I'm repeating—
When there's a shine on your shoes
There's a melody in your heart—
What a wonderful way to start the day!

There's the shine that you get in the barber shop,
While the barber's going "ziggy-ziggy-zig" with his strop.
There's the shine that you get in the pullman car
While the train is going chug-chuggy-chuggy-chuggy-chug
   going far away—
There's a shine that you get on the ferryboat
While the water's going wishy-washy-wishy-washy-wishy-
   washy-WOO.
But it doesn't matter where you get it
It'll do a lot of good if you let it
With a little bit of polish
You can certainly abolish
What's bothering you.

My old friend Norman Bel Geddes of the war-game days was the designer. Norman was a perfectionist and he determined to achieve every stage effect he had planned, even the impossible. In Philadelphia, he worked out a remarkable effect with the staging of "Alone Together," by constructing a receding stage. The dancers, Tamara Geva and Clifton Webb, disappeared as they gradually danced their way upstage.

The Imperial Theatre where we were playing in New York had a gas pipe which would not allow for this spectacular effect in the Geddes plan. Norman decided to remove the pipe which was 6 inches in its circumference. He was sawing away feverishly, while Tom Farrar, the artist, who was Geddes's assistant, viewed the scene with alarm. We had a hard job making Norman desist but managed to get the effect without blowing up the theatre, an event which would have pleased Mr. Geddes.

In the early Thirties, the movie companies had big offices in New York. Schenck spent most of his time there and most of the talent for film productions came from Broadway. Two or three times a year I would go to Culver City to see to problems or promote a picture but my life was centered around our house on 11th Street and the MGM office at 1540 Broadway. Those were the days! Broadway was alight with shows, and Harlem spots meant a good time drinking and dancing until morning. There was Small's, The Hideaway, The Cotton Club, and many good bands and dance halls. Everybody wanted to dance—or maybe I was just younger and didn't feel the Depression that was supposed to be on.

I was a bridge from the movies to the stage and I kept in touch with all phases of the theatre, saw all the shows, and went to all the parties. I didn't worry about finances because all my extravagances were paid for by MGM.

But it wasn't all music and flowers for Arthur Schwartz. Despite *The Band Wagon, Flying Colors,* and a show in England, *Nice Goings On,* the insecurity of living from show to touch with all phases of the theatre, saw all the shows, and none of the eccentricities that go with talent. He could not rely on me, as my movie job came first. There followed an unproductive period during which he debated a possible re-embrace of his law practice. I tried to help Arthur but the show angels had had their wings clipped in the Depression. Between February 1933 and June 1934, he could not get started on any project. He gave himself until September, deciding, if nothing developed by then, to return to the torts and the trials.

Something developed. It was a chance meeting with the orchestra leader Don Voorhees that saved the legal profession from the return of the prodigal. Voorhees had made a 99-and-44/100 percent pure contract with Proctor and Gamble to help create a radio program for Ivory Soap. A script had been written by Courtney Riley Cooper and it was to be a musical comedy serial entitled *The Gibson Family.*

A musical Diogenes, Voorhees had been training his lantern on every composer capable of writing an original score that would unwind for 39 weeks. It finally lighted on Schwartz, who was ready for anything. "The price is right," said Voorhees. "But you'll have to write at least three songs a week. Won't that take a lot out of you?"

Schwartz agreed. "Yes," he said, "it will take a lot out of me, but it will also take a lot out of Bach, Beethoven, and Brahms."

We wrote 94 songs in the next 39 weeks. In that period, it seems to me, I never came out of the shower without a new lyric. And Arthur always had a tune for it.

Arthur also had tunes for an operetta with Libby Holman called *Revenge with Music* based on a story by Alarcón, *The Three-Cornered Hat.* Libby, in the shadow of the Reynolds case, wanted to get back to work and I gave her the part but she was miscast. She had been taking singing lessons and it seemed to spoil her voice. She lost her ability to project the lyrics so that every word was understood.

Though the show did not survive long, one of the songs did, notably, "You and the Night and the Music."

YOU AND THE NIGHT AND THE MUSIC

Song is in the air
Telling us romance is ours to share
Now at last we've found one another alone.

Love like yours and mine
Has the thrilling glow of sparkling wine
Make the most of time ere it has flown.

CHORUS

You and the night and the music
Fill me with flaming desire
Setting my being completely
On fire!

You and the night and the music
Thrill me but will we be one
After the night and the music
Are done?

Until the pale light of dawning and daylight
Our hearts will be throbbing guitars
Morning may come without warning
And take away the stars

If we must live for the moment
Love till the moment is through!
After the night and the music die
Will I have you?

REPRISE

Tell me, Maria, how could you
Destroy what was more than divine?
I am no longer your lover
For you're no longer mine.

I'll give my heart to another
Tear out this feeling for you
And with the morning you'll find
What my revenge will do.

I asked C. B. Cochran, the British theatrical producer, what he thought of *Revenge with Music*, which had just opened.

He said, after a quiet reflection, "It's dire!"

Grist
for de Mille

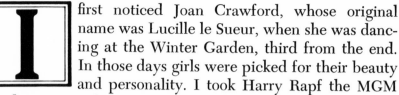**I** first noticed Joan Crawford, whose original name was Lucille le Sueur, when she was dancing at the Winter Garden, third from the end. In those days girls were picked for their beauty and personality. I took Harry Rapf the MGM producer to see her and he agreed she was a natural for pictures and we signed her for a contract. Joan was an exceptional looker and you didn't have to have 20/20 vision to notice it. Her personality knocked you over.

Le Sueur had to be changed and I ran a contest to select a screen name for her in *Motion Picture Magazine.* The name Jane Crawford was the winner, but consulting with Miss le Sueur we made the final name Joan Crawford.

I called her "eyes Benedict." She was the first star with a big mouth and broad shoulders and she started the square-shouldered style that lasted into the forties.

Hedy Lamarr came to this country in 1933, having been persuaded by Mr. Mayer to appear in American films.

When she arrived here, the press dwelt on her beauty, emphasizing her looks more than her talent as an actress. They wrote that she had appeared in the nude in a film called *Ecstasy* and she was the first star to do that. She was driven to tears.

Mr. Mayer called me up. "I have a hysterical star on my hands," he said. "Come up and save the situation."

I hotfooted it to the Plaza and went in to see Hedy. "You Americans are terrible," she said through her tears, "you have no artistic appreciation."

"Did you appear in the nude?" I asked.

"Yes," Miss Lamarr answered shyly.

"Did you look good?"

"Of course."

"Then it's all right," I assured her, "no damage has been done."

I convinced her that all Americans care about is success. If you're a successful nude, you're ahead of the game.

Tallulah Bankhead was pretty noisy, but she had an effective personality; she was loyal to friends beyond question. She lived at the Elysee Hotel and she kept everyone busy admiring her beauty. Tallulah could wear one out. I said, "A day away from Tallulah is like a month in the country."

The agent grew in stature in the thirties. They ceased being mere 10-percenters and were more or less in a position to offer their clients 10 percent. One rich agent was Leland Hayward—the dashing Tybalt. Hayward was never known to be without a woman, he had been wooing Katharine Hepburn heavily, and Margaret Sullavan lightly. He carried a suitcase filled with sleeping pills wherever he went.

Hepburn thought that she was going to marry Leland and I met her at one of George Cukor's Sunday afternoon gatherings in the dramatic instant when news came over the radio that he had run off with Margaret Sullavan. Cukor was the most sympathetic person you could have in time of trouble, and with Hepburn it was a time of trouble though she could not admit her grief; she was too embarrassed.

Though Margaret married Hayward, things did not go well. I ran into her on Fifth Avenue one day and she asked me if I were free to take her on a shopping tour. We went to a well-known couturier salon and the saleslady quoted the prices of the costumes. She presented Margaret with a gaudy creation priced at $1,200. Then she showed another that looked just like the first for $1,400. I asked her what the difference was between the two dresses; why one cost $200 more than the other. "This one," said the vendeuse holding up the second, "has a belt." Margaret didn't buy anything.

She went on her way, which was a difficult way, as she was not able to tame Leland and there was no place else she wanted to go. She got divorced and married Kenneth Wagg, who was so in love with her that Margaret couldn't refuse him. Finally she fell asleep once too often from Hayward's valise.

Almost successful Hollywood agent in the thirties was Phil Berg, who would have received an Academy Award if they had one for agents.

Although he took in $1 million a year, it wasn't enough for the way he lived, so he invented what is now known as "the package deal," that system in which all the key people in the making of a film have their contracts cleared through one channel. This channel usually was Phil Berg, who used me as part of the package deal, getting publicity for the star.

Phil would start by taking an option on a current bestselling novel. Then he'd get a good screen writer to make a synoptic treatment. Then he'd interest a director and a star who was looking for a vehicle big enough for her many talents. Then he got a few studios bidding for his "package" and had them fighting over it. He called his firm "Pooh Bah, Inc." and he called his yacht "Pooh Bah" and he deducted the operating expenses from his income tax.

Phil had a beautiful wife, Leila Hyams, who had been a star but was not sufficiently talented to warrant a campaign build-up, so Phil assigned her to keep house in their modern cliff dweller marble edifice.

There is no doubt about Phil's resourcefulness, and no doubt that he called the shots, as he used to say. Unfortunately, the more successful he got, the more he delegated matters to his staff and the more isolated he became. He got bored with his yacht and tried an experiment with a specially built Greyhound-type bus, which he equipped so that a guest could be housed there when it wasn't on tour. It was a compact and luxurious trailer. It lived in a hangar next to the house and parked flush up against the side of the house with a doorway connecting.

He got drivers from the Greyhound Bus Company and it took them three days to get him to New York. One would drive to Kansas City, the second to Chicago and the third on to New York. When he got there, he would park in the "21" lot, getting his meals and other essentials delivered in the bus.

But even so, he was not content. Money was what he dealt in, and he encroached on his wife's domain just to have something to do.

"Leila," said Phil one day, "what progress are you making toward getting rid of that maid Olga?"

"I'll have to get up my courage," Leila said.

"That's the trouble with women," said Phil, "they're too soft, and that's why they're no good in business."

"I'll do it tomorrow," said Leila.

"No," said Phil, "I'll do it. Have her serve my breakfast tomorrow at 9." Nine came, and Olga entered through the swinging door from the kitchen. She carried no orange juice, no cereal, nor other requested breakfast staples. Her emptiness relieved Phil, who was getting nervous himself. But before he could formulate words leading to the dismissal, Olga spoke up hurriedly. "Mr. Berg, may I have a word with you, some advice? I know you're busy, but there's a man at the back door. You see, I bought some property up in Coldwater Canyon with my earnings, two acres in fact. This man tells me they've struck gold on my property and he's offering me $50,000 for it. Would you be so kind as to tell me what I'm to do about it?"

Phil pulled out a chair. "Sit down, Olga," he said.

One night in the depressing thirties, Henri D'Agand, a theatrical agent, and I were standing at the bar at "21" discussing a radio series which might be sold to one of the networks. D'Agand felt that all I had to do was talk to a certain influential vice president in my quiet way and he would sign a contract on the spot. The trouble was me. I had made several appointments with that influential VP, and had broken them every time. This had brought D'Agand to tears. It wasn't the loss of the 10 percent commission that bothered him; it was the loss of prestige, and prestige was an essential commodity in his profession. Failure to deliver a promised client at the appointed hour damaged an agent's standing, and D'Agand was desperate. He made an appointment for the next day at 9 o'clock and made me solemnly swear that come the following morning, I would be where the elevator lets out on the twelfth floor of the Grand Central Terminal Building. For him it was Armageddon.

The proposed radio series was somewhat different from the usual format in tune with the pre-Rooseveltian Depression. It had two characters, somewhat like Bob and Ray. One leaps off the roof of the Empire State Building and the other jumps from a window on the 100th floor. They meet in mid-air and for 13 weeks (or more, if the option is taken up), they are falling down and discussing the journey in a casual way, not unlike the dialogue passengers on a transatlantic steamer might have: "They tell me you don't come in sight of land for quite a while," sort of thing. In the course of their fall, each reveals that he is committing suicide because of the stock market. One owes his broker an impossible amount. The other turns out to be the broker he owes.

D'Agand paid the check and I repeated my promise to show up the next morning. I stayed at the bar for a solitary nightcap.

The theatre was out, and among those who drifted into the bar was Jean Harlow. She was accompanied by a good-looking chap, whose name I didn't catch, as I was preoccupied with Jean who was a good friend. I called a waiter who got a corner table for the three of us. We talked about the good time we had together the night we rode all over Hollywood with Howard Strickling who wanted to take us to a gambling joint. He couldn't remember the name and got tied up with stuttering, which often happened when he had a few drinks after hours.

Jean was grateful to me for a successful publicity plan

which restored her popularity when she had shown signs of slipping. I had arranged a personal appearance tour for her to about 30 Loew's theatres and her platinum hair and seductive figure had captured the public. When she resumed picture making, she rose rapidly to the height of stardom in such pictures as *Red Dust, The Blonde Bombshell,* and many, many others. She was an unpretentious personality and wore her success casually. That night I was full of compliments.

But the young man who was her date felt ignored and insulted. He didn't react favorably to my infiltration and got up and left. I ran after him, but he had stepped into a cab before I could catch him. Feeling a bit of a heel, I returned to Jean.

"I'm sorry," I said, "I should have been more considerate. I don't blame him for being sore."

"Don't worry about it," said Jean. "I'll call him tomorrow and help him get over his soreness. You've got me on your hands exclusively for the rest of the evening. Where are you going to take me?"

We went to the Club 18 where Jack White was an M. C. and Pat Harrington ad-libbed and to Leon and Eddie's to hear the song about "Hudson the Trapper." We invaded Harlem: Small's, the Hideaway and other joints which are not easy to remember. Jean was her voluptuous self. She danced all night. Harlem was hers. I didn't get her back to her hotel until after 7 o'clock when I kissed her goodnight and took a cab home.

Then it came to me like a blow on the chin! The date with D'Agand. How was I to keep it? I thought of breaking my solemn promise but I couldn't do that—not even to an agent. I had little more than an hour and a half. I got under the shower, I rubbed ice cubes into my head.

It was 9 o'clock and bright sunlight when I crossed Park Avenue to the Grand Central Terminal Building. I felt like a case for a plastic surgeon, my mouth full of temporary fillings. I got out at the 12th floor and there was D'Agand, good old dependable D'Agand, always on time. He led me to the executive office where I was to outline my radio program to the prospective producer. The man waiting there was Jean Harlow's date of the night before!

I could understand how the playwright Molnar felt when he was sued for plagiarism and had to appear in court at the crack of dawn. Noticing the milling throng of white collar workers filling up the streets, he rubbed his eyes and asked his lawyer, "Are all of them witnesses?"

Joe Cohn and I go back to the custard pioneer days. We were there when Samuel Goldwyn bought the studio from Tom Ince. We were there when Marcus Loew merged with Mayer. We were there when Will Rogers and "Big Boy" Williams were lassoing goats every afternoon on the bare expanse of the Culver City studio acreage. Across the street, lots were being sold by a local realtor who sounded a gong every time he sold one. Rogers would then whirl his rope and shout to passersby, "Sam Goldwyn just sold another picture."

Joe became a big-time producer, but I'm afraid he'll go down in Hollywood history as the hatchet man of MGM. A hatchet man is an executive who weighs a script on a butcher's scales, puts a limit on the shooting time, and is always ready to substitute merely inexpensive sets for the right ones. Regardless of the profit or loss on a film, the H. M. measures its success by one yardstick: Did it come in under the budget?

Outside the studio Joe had a Falstaffian merriment. He was generous, hospitable, kind and his appearance embodied his spirit. He showed his teeth in a glowing smile. He was sunburned and strong, and whatever he had left of white hair was just enough to provide a sort of baldheaded crew-cut.

But inside the studio, he would count the dimes and act vindictively toward any producer, director or star who favored the great outdoors or any place on the continent of

Europe where he had to pay for standby grips. "A tree is a tree and a rock is a rock" was his most frequent reprise at production meetings.

He attempted to provide an all-purpose, harmonious background set on the lot by planting lush green hand-painted shrubbery and constructing an artificial lake which could represent any season you wanted anywhere. This topographical achievement was greeted with mixed emotions and many pros and cons as to whether or not the lake looked phony. The studio christened it "Cohn's Park" and used it for Tarzan pictures and predigested westerns.

But Joe was impervious to jibes as long as he was bringing in the pictures under budget. Whenever a small picture showed signs of promise at the preview, Irving Thalberg would have it made over again, correcting its faults and adding some authentic backgrounds.

There was a knotty problem when Joe and the other studio cost-calculators decided to buy lot #5. They bought up everything except a small piece of land owned by a man who played the cornet. He had a booth like a telephone booth on his property. He sat patiently, rain or shine, producing his screeching solo, and going full blast forte when a movie was being made. The situation became desperate. Sometimes the cornetist would be away for a few days, and Joe would hurriedly spring into action. The shooting would be about to start, when the raspy, foggy sound of the cornet would announce the return of the one-man brass band. This couldn't go on, and the studio had to pay through the nose. It was a long nose.

ietz is a man who writes shows on MGM stationery," the too-soon late Ernst Lubitsch liked to say. He was a warm and witty movie director who became noted for what was called "the Lubitsch touch." That sentence about me had "the Lubitsch touch."

Despite the Depression of the thirties, Ernst had produced

or directed a string of light comedies for Paramount that were respectable by critical standard and also made money. But it's dangerous to be a big success in Hollywood, because if you're a success in one field, they widen your panorama to include other skills. Lubitsch was put in charge of the entire studio. While bankers blinked, slapped both their cheeks, and made other gestures of despair, the great man moved in like a Vachel Lindsay poem, answerable to no one, excepting Paramount's president Barney Balaban.

Ernst's tenure as an executive didn't last long, however. Jerry, a man with muscles, would make his rounds before breakfast to put the executives in therapeutic shape for the rigors of the day. While rippling his fingers over the expensive stomachs, he would spread scuttlebutt like a town crier. He arrived about 6 A.M. at the Lubitsch gymnasium just off the swimming pool and, while pounding the hell out of his gifted client, said he felt terribly sorry.

"Sorry for what?" asked Lubitsch, whose pores were opening.

"About your dismissal," said Jerry.

"What about my dismissal? It's news to me," said Lubitsch.

"Well," said Jerry, "I just came from Mr. Balaban's and during the workout he was on the telephone with Y. Frank Freeman and. . . ."

Ernst leaped off the table, threw on his clothes and, one suspender dangling, whirled himself to Paramount, where he found that Jerry's rumor was fact.

There is an estate in New Jersey that was built and landscaped by the entertaining Joe Cook, the nonsense comedian who broke all records for the length of his vaudeville runs. Life there was different. Drive up to the entrance and the door would be opened by a pair of George Washingtons with covered knees and garters showing. When you signed the register, a stream of water was squirted in your eyes. In fact, squirting water was one of the main occupations on the estate.

The grand tour was an unbelievable adventure. You saw tennis courts with lines that could be pulled any way you wanted to score. Baseball fences that could be pulled by players to make home runs out of short flyballs. There was a fountain of beer, a mountain of suds.

Marc Connelly, the playwright, Harold Ross, then editor of *The New Yorker*, and I went to Joe Cook's for a weekend. I have never been the same since.

We were taken to a barroom. The walls and the ceiling were decorated with numberless objects, "each smaller than a man's hand," Joe explained. Mr. Sweeney, who was the stooge in Joe's act would wear different costumes. He had been George Washington at the door, he was Abe Lincoln at the bar, and Teddy Roosevelt at a weighing machine.

We went to bed after supper, which was the only conventional thing about the place. We were assigned bedrooms. I had just switched the light out when there was a knock on my door. The door opened, a bare arm came into the opening holding a mug of beer. As soon as I got there, the arm pulled back, and the beer disappeared.

We were due to play golf at 9 o'clock the following morning. At 8 o'clock, cathedral bells rang throughout the house. I put on the clothes I brought along for golf and was ushered on to the golf course by one of Cook's stooges. Each hole was a trick. The ball came out of the side of a hill where there was a desk and cards, making you a member of the hole-in-one club. The first hole was a 20-foot tall monument, 6 feet wide, with smooth grass for teeing off. The green was shaped like a cone. It was an easy pitch from the tee to the green. The second hole looked like a smooth grass lawn, but it was painted rock and the golf ball bounced back to you. The third hole was inside a house. I marveled that anyone would go to the trouble to construct such a bizarre series of structures. Joe loved his golf course and kept it in good condition.

The relationship between Mayer and Thalberg became delicate, and in the mid-thirties Thalberg took a trip to Europe. Mayer brought his son-in-law, David Selznick, to the MGM lot, and gave him *Dinner at Eight* to produce. I went out to the studio on one of my periodic visits and before I could get to my office, Mayer waylaid me and said, "David just finished *Dinner at Eight*. I want you to look at it. Come to my office as soon as it's over. I want your opinion."

I saw *Dinner at Eight* and went to Mayer's office. "Well," he said, "what do you think of it?" "With all those names in the cast, we'll put it over," I said. "We don't have anything to worry about." "What do you mean, we don't have anything to worry about. This is one of the biggest pictures ever made. No wonder we have so many flops with you handling them. Your opinions aren't worth a damn!" "In that event," I said, "my opinions can't possibly disturb you," and I started out of his office—it seemed the only thing to do. In the doorway, I ran into Selznick. It looked as though I were in for a repetition of the scene, with a slight change of cast.

"Well," said David, "how did you like *Dinner at Eight?*" I told him I had evidently offended Mr. Mayer because I didn't think the picture was a smash. David got mean: "You're just like all the rest of the New York smart alecks," he said, "George Kaufman, Dorothy Parker, Marc Connelly, the whole Algonquin clique. They think it's a crime to write for the box office!" "But, David," I said, "George Kaufman was the author of *Dinner at Eight*." He seemed to have forgotten that. I managed to escape and went to my office.

Mayer was giving a party that Saturday night, and everybody who was anybody at the studio was invited. It was now Thursday, and word had gotten around that Mayer and I had had words. A great number of people shunned me. They couldn't afford to differ with the big brass.

Ida Koverman, who was Mayer's secretary and, in fact, represented him in all political attitudes, confided to me that

Mayer didn't want to have a quarrel with me; he wanted me to come to his party. Mayer had been pressing me to take sides in his feud with Thalberg but I was above the battle. Thalberg would be on my side, and that made the opposition formidable.

Miss Koverman suggested that I apologize to Mr. Mayer to save the situation.

I said I had done nothing to apologize for.

Miss Koverman said I would not be obliged to make a profound apology, I could just say I was sorry.

I said I couldn't do that.

Miss Koverman then said I could apologize to her and she would give the apology to Mr. Mayer. That should be easy to do.

I said it didn't seem necessary that I apologize to Mr. Mayer and that I would have to quit anyway because there's no point in working with someone you disagree with.

She said, "You're pretty tough," and I replied, "It depends on what kind of a fight it is."

Later in the day, I received a card inviting me to the party. On Saturday night, I dressed in my best and went to Mayer's house in Santa Monica. Mayer came to the door himself and throwing his arms around me, escorted me to the bar. "This fellow is no softie," he announced. "He saw *Dinner at Eight* and thinks it's a great picture."

I didn't think it would serve any purpose if I refined his statement.

When Thalberg returned from Europe, his relationship with Mayer declined rapidly.

Thalberg's untiring effort, the delicacy of his health, and his unhappy situation with Mayer led to his untimely death in 1936. He was 37 years old. Thalberg had left a legacy to MGM which was to last for many years. It included such pictures as *San Francisco, Little Women, Grand Hotel, A Night at the Opera,* and *Mutiny on the Bounty.* In the early forties the company really felt Thalberg's absence. Mayer had been looking for another Thalberg, which was like looking for another Kohinoor. He hit upon Dore Schary, who had made some box-office winners at RKO: *The Bachelor and the Bobby Soxer, Battleground,* and some good pictures of minor stature. But Schary, unlike Thalberg, was interested in personal publicity and this upset the spirit of MGM, which had been a money-making spirit.

Shows and Hollywood

AN INTERNATIONAL BILLIARD MATCH

Bill O'Brien, classmate at Columbia and colleague at MGM. With his wife Mildred Lewis, who looked after my interests.

Pete Smith and I on a stage at MGM in 1925, posing for a short subject. When Pete's son, age six, took the train for New York, he was instructed to give his age as five. The conductor on the train asked young Smith how old he was and he answered, "Five, but for railroad purposes only."

The fabulous Barrymores, Lionel, Ethel and John, playing together for the first time in *Rasputin*.

Garbo and Gilbert in the silent days.

Judy Garland showed talent even then.

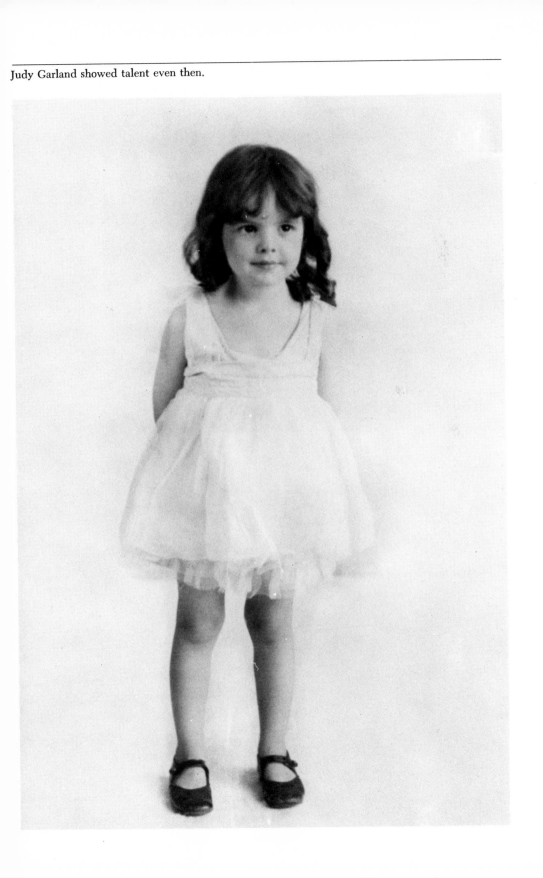

Our first song together, "Hammacher Schlemmer, I Love You."

"Won't you sit down?" says Clifton Webb to Tamara Geva in a sketch in *The Little Show*.

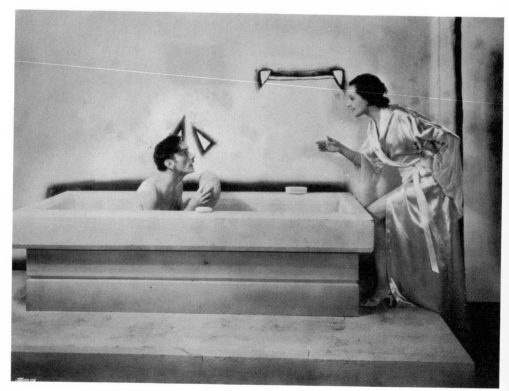

Clifton Webb strangling Libby Holman in "Moanin' Low" which was an outstanding success in *The Little Show*. Ralph Rainger was the composer.

The spectacular Tamara Geva in *Three's a Crowd*.

The merry-go-round designed by Albert Johnson for *The Band Wagon*. In the foreground center, Fred and Adele Astaire, Frank Morgan and Tilly Losch.

Max Gordon and Millie. Asked if he believed in reincarnation, the showman replied, "When you close here, you gotta open somewhere else."

George Abbott

We were in Philadelphia with *The Band Wagon* prior to coming to New York. Me, Fred Astaire, Jimmy Altemus, a friend of the company, Adele Astaire and Tilly Losch. We dropped into a local photographer's studio. You'd think we'd be tired of pictures.

Adele and Fred Astaire with hoops.

Tilly Losch. She floats through the air with the greatest of ease.

A quartet of show girls who appeared as decorations in *Flying Colors*. The blonde at the right is Bonnie Walters, the wife of Johnny Green the composer, arranger and conductor. Bonnie was a swimmer on the U.S. Olympic team.

Clifton Webb practicing surgery on Charlie Butterworth in *Flying Colors*.

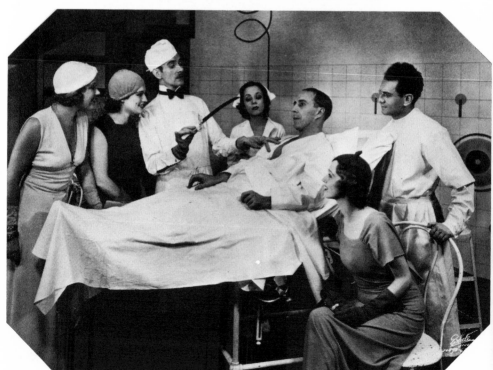

Jimmy Durante and Larry Hart with me in between. I wrote a number with Jimmy Durante and Jimmy McHugh entitled "I'm a Fugitive from Esquire" which Durante delivered in *Keep Off the Grass*.

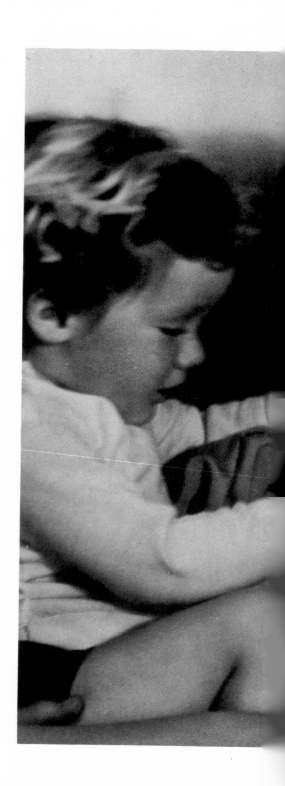

Marlene Dietrich. You'll notice nobody else.

oucho, Chico and Harpo Marx. If we use Zeppo we'll need more money.
n Harlow, a well-proportioned star.

Tanis Guinness studying America from a relative point of view. We were married in 1937.

lina Mehuys, who was maid to Tanis and also took care of me. She was bereft when we got orced. She is still with Tanis in the Domain de Migron, in Biarritz.

uis B. Mayer gave a wedding banquet at the Coconut Grove for Tanis and me. Among se present were Howard Strickling, Howard Dietz, Tanis, Mr. Mayer and a number of ests who have become strangers to me.

Herbert Bayard Swope. While there's life, there's Swope.

Tanis and Mrs. John Barry Ryan in the library at Eleventh Street.

Croquet at Margaret Emerson's, Sands Point. Herbert Bayard Swope, Jr., and me, with Margaret Emerson doing woman's work.

RICHARD CARVER WOO

raldine Fitzgerald and her husband Stuart Scheftel, weekend guests at Sands Point.
orge Kaufman. When Hi Bloomingdale backed the musical *The Garden of Allah*, Kaufman
vised him to close the show and keep the store open nights.

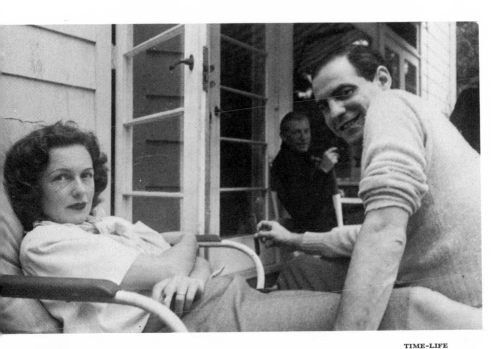

Dick Rodgers has Dorothy as well as his talent.
Randolph Churchill and his wife Pamela, who later married Averell Harriman.

Spencer Tracy played Father Flanagan, the patron of Boystown. Father Flanagan was on the set every day telling Tracy that he should be more saintly in his interpretation.

Margaret Sullavan. She left the scene too soon.

I took Rita Hayworth to the opening of *Allegro* and got mobbed by the crowd, who got me out of their way to get at Rita.

role Lombard and Clark Gable at the Atlanta opening of *GWTW*. In the background,
ht, Margaret Mitchell at the mike.

Lassie was on paw to greet me on one of my many trips to the studio.
She greeted Elizabeth Taylor too.

za imitating her mother in the studio on Eleventh Street.

oadcasting the "Transatlantic Quiz" in 1939. This was a program in which an English
m tried to stump an American team in identifying well-known localities and vice versa.
e English were Denis Brogan and Jack Buchanan and the Americans were Christopher
orley and me. Alistair Cooke was moderator.

A meeting of the MGM publicity staff. Seated left to right: William Ferguson, Frank Whitlock, Howard Strickling, me and Si Seadler. Standing: Ernest Emmerling and Ralph Wheelright.

Joe Cohn, who joined MGM at the same time I did.

Harry Ruby and Sammy Fain, popular songwriters and witty fellows. Ruby wrote "Three Little Words" and Fain "Love Is a Many Splendored Thing." Harry has a formula for the acquisition of wealth. Especially recommended to wives. Every night before going to bed, empty your husband's pockets and take out $50 or $100. If you do this for a reasonable length of time, you will be surprised how it will add up.

MANNY GREENHAUS

ith Howard Strickling, publicity director at MGM.

nsy Schenck, a great beauty, wife of Nicholas Schenck, MGM president. He said, "There
nothing wrong with the movie business that good pictures can't cure."

Mary Martin as Annie by Lucinda.

Lucinda was designing costumes for such shows as *Annie Get Your Gun, Streetcar Named Desire, The Sound of Music, The Gay Life*. She was a designing woman.

That's
Entertainment

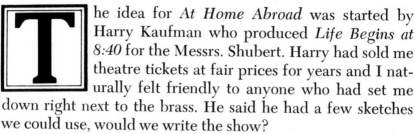he idea for *At Home Abroad* was started by Harry Kaufman who produced *Life Begins at 8:40* for the Messrs. Shubert. Harry had sold me theatre tickets at fair prices for years and I naturally felt friendly to anyone who had set me down right next to the brass. He said he had a few sketches we could use, would we write the show?

"I've got a good idea for a number," Harry said. "The chorus would come out looking like Fred Astaire and singing 'We're Fred Astaires from Buenos Aires.' "

He was full of ideas like that. I always told him it was a good idea, but I didn't like it. I got tired of coming to the telephone, and after a while my indifference to his ideas showed. I ran into him and courteously said, "You haven't called me up in the last two weeks."

"I know," said Harry. "I was going to call you up last night. I had a good idea, but I didn't like it."

We signed up Bea Lillie to be a geisha girl, a premiere danseuse, an alleged smuggler, the bride of an Alpine guide. Ethel Waters was a French lady and a Hottentot potentate. Eleanor Powell danced as an Eton boy, a Balkan spy, a Samoan girl. We also had Herb Williams and Reginald Gardiner.

One of the most effective numbers was "Get Yourself a Geisha."

GET YOURSELF A GEISHA

If you have merely looked at a Japanese print—
Hokusai, Hiroshige, Hokusai—
The chances are you have but a casual hint—
Hokusai, Hiroshige, Hokusai—
Of how—of how we live in Japan.

If you have only read Lafcadio Hearn—
His books—his books upon Japan
We don't see how on earth you could possibly learn
Anything about the isle of Nippon.
It's an island you should take a trip on

Do you mind if we give you a tip on
The way you should really see Nippon?

CHORUS

Get yourself a Geisha—a gay little Geisha—
A Geisha girl's the surest—
The surest guide for the tourist—
If the tourist is no purist
He can have a lot of fun
Doing what he ought to do in Tokyo.

Get yourself a Geisha—a gay little Geisha—
She's free and Japanesy.
She's debonairy and breezy
And she dances hot-strip-teasy
Even in Japan it's done.

She will take you on the town from dark till dawn.
You'll drink a lot of Japanese gin
When you've had enough of Japanese gin,
You can take her home and maybe carry on.
When you enter a house you take your shoes off.
It's better with your shoes off.

Get yourself a Geisha—but only in case ya
Would pass up what's in guidebooks.
The tourist knows if he's tried books
That the best things aren't in guidebooks.
Let yourself go—Go get yourself a Geisha girl.

She will shower you with Oriental charm
In the land of the radiant sun.
You'll wait up nights for the radiant sun
Then together you will wander arm in arm
And sleep in the forest of cherry blossoms.

(BEA LILLIE)

It's better with your shoes off.

CHORUS

Get yourself a Geisha. The flower of Asia.
She's one with whom to take up

At night your bed she'll make up
And she'll be there when you wake up.

Let yourself go. Go get yourself a Geisha.

Let yourself go. Go get yourself a Geisha girl.

Bea Lillie at first refused to perform in it. I planned the scene so that she was dressed up like the rest of the chorus. You didn't recognize her until she sang her one line, "It's better with your shoes off." But she said she wouldn't sing it unless she could sing the whole song. The song was written for that one line and I persuaded her. When she sang it, the reaction was electric.

Ethel's main numbers were "Thief in the Night" and "Hottentot Potentate."

THIEF IN THE NIGHT

Slinky Johnson, if I just had you here
I'd tell you what's on my mind.
I ain't seen you in the best of a year
But I understand your kind.
You'll come repentin' for the way you carried on
Hopin' I'll be relentin' and let bygones be gone.
Though I love you still
Our love affair's through
I'm takin' no chances on you.

You're just a thief in the night.
Nothin' but a thief in the night.
You came without a warnin'
And left before the mornin' broke through.
I never knew
I'd ever see you again
You're an education in men.
The one I had belief in
Turned out to be a thief in the night.
Oh, how I've worried and fretted
And got myself in a pet

Wishin' we'd never met.
Mopin' and hopin'
And swearin' I'd square accounts yet.
Folks declare my eyes are always wet
Because a thief in the night
Stole my heart and vanished from sight.
I knew I'd come to grief in
Believin' in a thief in the night.

Oh, how I've worried and fretted
And got myself in a pet
Wishin' we never met.
Mopin' and hopin'
And swearin' I'd square accounts yet.
Folks declare my eyes are always wet
Because a thief in the night
Stole my heart and vanished from sight.
I knew I'd come to grief in
Believin' in a thief in the night.

THE HOTTENTOT POTENTATE

Hailed from Harlem, settled here
Knocked the Congo on its ear.
I came, I saw, I conquered a nation
With my trickeration.

My witchcraft made 'em make a crown for me.
The natives do a lot of bowin' down for me.
And everyone of them would go to town for me
The Hottentot Potentate.

I brought my bottle of Chanel with me
I took along a script of Lulu Belle with me
I win them all; but, oh, it raises hell with me.
The Hottentot Potentate.
I fool 'em . . . playing a part
I rule 'em . . . I've got an art
I fool 'em . . . right at the start
I gave 'em that hotcha . . . je ne sais quoitcha.

227

The new name for the Congo stamping ground
Is Empress Jones's Africana vamping ground
I don't allow no camping on the camping ground.
I'm hot and potent. Potent and hot.
The Hottentot Potentate.

The jungle now has lots of chic to it.
A touch of cloisonné and Lalique to it.
And who put all this drawing room technique to it?
The Hottentot Potentate.

This wild and savage open-airy land,
With lions and with tigers was a scary land
Until I made of it a savoir-fairey land.
The Hottentot Potentate.

I slayed 'em . . . right from the start.
Okayed 'em . . . when they were smart.
I made 'em . . . copy my art
I gave all their movements modern improvements.

The Congo's not what one supposes now.
The heathens live upon a bed of roses now
And Cartier rings they're wearing in their noses now
For the hot and potent
The hot and potent
Potent and hot
Potent and hot
The Hottentot Potentate.

Vincente Minnelli was the director. He was doing an adept job, considering that it was his first show, but his staging was not entirely to my satisfaction. I went down the aisle and spoke to him in a low voice, then took a seat in the back of the orchestra. Minnelli didn't accept the correction I had made in the scene. I shouted, "Vincente, what are you doing?"

He said, "I'm doing the same thing for *At Home Abroad* that Hassard Short did for *Three's a Crowd* and your other shows."

I said, "You're not a Hassard Short, you're just a hazard!"

I found out that I had a contract with the Shuberts which stated that I was in charge of the show. Vincente Minnelli had the identical contract. A deal with Lee Shubert is a deal indeed.

It would be a faint statement to say that the Shuberts were difficult to deal with. Yet there was something likable about Mister Lee, as he was called. It was his consistency as an unreasonable trader. Mister Sam was spotty in his sense of justice. He was more apt to fit the coffin to the corpse. What they call procrustean.

The Shuberts owned a working percentage of *Between the Devil,* which was almost a good show. The plot was bigamy and the triangle featured Evelyn Laye, Jack Buchanan and Adele Dixon. I didn't make it hilarious enough. As a result, Jack Buchanan tried to provide what the script lacked, but Jack left to his own comical inventions was as funny as a blow with a cosh. *Between the Devil* had three entertaining numbers: "Triplets," "I See Your Face Before Me," and "By Myself." "Triplets" was an incidental cabaret song. Later Danny Kaye, Vivien Leigh and Laurence Olivier sang it for a benefit at the Palladium in London.

TRIPLETS

Three little unexpected children simultaneously
*   The doctor brought us and you can see*
That we'll be three forever and aye—e—i—o
You wouldn't know how agonizing being triple can be
*   Each one is individually*
The victim of that clinical day—e—i—o
Every summer we go away to Baden Baden Baden
Every winter we come back home to Walla Walla Walla.

We do everything alike
We look alike, we dress alike
We walk alike, we talk alike
And what is more

We hate each other very much
We hate our folks. We're sick of jokes
On what an art it is to tell us apart
If one of us gets the measles
    Another one gets the measles
Then all of us get the measles
And mumps and croup.
How I wish I had a gun—a little gun
It would be fun to shoot the other two
And be only one.

Mrs. Whiffenpoofer loves to talk to Mrs. Hildendorfer
Of the day she went to Sloan's and had her silly Willie
Mrs. Hassencooper loves to talk to Mrs. Goldenwasser
Of her major operation when she had the twins.
But when mother comes along she silences the others
She accomplished something that is very rare in mothers
For example just to prove that she was more than ample
She admits Lane Bryant thought that they were measuring
  a giant.
Doctor Hemerdinger almost broke his middle finger
On the day that he first looked upon us three.

We do everything alike
We look alike, we dress alike
We walk alike, we talk alike
And what is more
We hate each other very much.
We hate our folks. We're sick of jokes
On what an art it is to tell us apart.
We eat the same kind of vittles
We drink the same kind of bottles
We sit in the same kind of highchair (highchair, highchair)
How I wish I had a gun—a little gun
It would be fun to shoot the other two
And be only one.

We do everything alike
We look alike, we dress alike
We walk alike, we talk alike

And what is more
We hate each other very much
We hate our folks. We're sick of jokes
On what an art it is to tell us apart.
We play the same kind of soldiers
We fight the same kind of battles
We shake the same kind of rattles
How I wish I had a gun—a little gun
It would be fun to shoot the other two
And be only one.

I SEE YOUR FACE BEFORE ME

I see your face before me
Crowding my every dream
There is your face before me—
You are my only theme.
It doesn't matter where you are
I can see how fair you are,
I close my eyes and there you are
Always.

If you could share the magic
If you could see me too,
There would be nothing tragic
In all my dreams of you.
Would that my love could haunt me so
Knowing I want you so—
I can't erase
Your beautiful face before me.

BY MYSELF

The party's over, the game is ended
The dreams I dreamed went up in smoke
They didn't pan out as intended
I should know how to take a joke.

I'll go my way by myself
This is the end of romance
I'll go my way by myself

Love is only a dance.
I'll try to apply myself
And teach my heart how to sing.
I'll go my way by myself
Like a bird on the wing
I'll face the unknown,
I'll build a world of my own;
No one knows better than I myself
I'm by myself alone.

I'll go my way by myself
Like walking under a cloud
I'll go my way by myself
All alone in a crowd
I try to apply myself
And teach my heart how to sing
I'll go my way by myself
Like a bird on the wing
I'll face the unknown,
I'll build a world of my own;
No one knows better than I myself
I'm by myself alone.

 movie company wanted to buy *Between the Devil*, but Mister Lee stuck to his price, which was not practical. I sat across the table from him in his tiny office and I was determined to be as tough as he was. He slapped a sheet of paper in front of me. On the sheet were the names of several producers, Dillingham, Frohman, Ziegfeld, and others.

"What's this for?" I asked.

"What does it tell you?" countered Lee.

"They're all dead," I guessed.

"Right," said Lee. "What else?"

"I'm sure I don't know," I said.

"They all died broke," said the producer.

I had several dealings with the Shuberts. When Arthur and I had our big success with *The Band Wagon*, Harry Kaufman told me that the Shuberts wanted to make a deal with me that involved my services as an editor. They would produce any musical show that I recommended, and they would give me 1 percent of the gross receipts.

I believed there should be more experimental work done on musical shows, as music heightened the dramatic effect. I told Mister Lee that I would take the job provided he turned over one large theatre like the Majestic for a ballet, a dramatic musical, a revue. The theatre would become a school and stars would be teachers. The Shuberts turned me down, and I turned them down.

The Shuberts were sharp about royalties. I had bought 38 tickets for the opening night of *At Home Abroad*. They were $10 apiece, and when I received my first royalty check, they had deducted 100 seats for their expenses. The Shuberts refused to pay me, and I said I refused to work for the Shuberts any more until they paid me the royalties they owed. I asked them to give me the list of their 100 critics.

Years passed and time came they they were producing *Keep Off the Grass;* in the midst of rehearsals, McHugh's partner fell ill and the Shuberts chased Harry Kaufman after me. There were three numbers needed and I told Harry that I would write them if they paid me the overdue royalties from *At Home Abroad*. They said, "Oh, don't worry about that." I said, "I *do* worry about that."

They were slow to capitulate.

Beautiful as it was, time took away the quiet demeanor of 11th Street and the most attractive block in town no longer completely charmed the Village. Double parking was at the doorstep.

I had developed an infatuation for golf, and was lost to the art, although it was not an art as I practiced it. The Sands Point polo club had been converted to a golf course and my friend Herbert Swope proposed me for membership.

Betty and I rented a house called Sands House and the

Long Island weekend became a way of life. I made a good many friends: George Backer, Jack Baragwanath, Ogden Phipps, Neysa McMein, John Wheeler, William S. Paley, Leonard Lyons, Edward Lasker, John O'Hara, Irving Berlin, Abe Burrows, Turner Catledge, Marc Connelly, Russel Crouse, Morris Ernst, Edna Ferber, and others, who regarded the Swopes as a port of call.

Mrs. Herbert Bayard Swope was an amazing and lavish housekeeper. When her husband, who was the renowned executive editor of *The New York World* sold out his interest in the paper for $6 million, Maggie set up housekeeping on a grand scale. She engaged two shifts of servants. If you happened to be hungry at 4 in the morning, you could get a steak. Everybody drifted Swopeward.

Croquet would take up the afternoons Friday to Monday. Croquet was played on several Long Island courses, notably Margaret Emerson's, Ellen Doubleday's and the Swopes's.

Croquet is a difficult and highly strategic game, involving, as it does, accuracy in shots and maneuvering for position. The team with good tactics can usually beat a team superior in shotmaking but lacking in strategy.

Most players survive the "epithets" branding croquet a "sissy" game. It looks sissier than it is. If one decides to make it a gambling game he does it by allowing the contestant to double as in backgammon. But gambling is not necessary to its enjoyment. Horace Elisha Scudder, an expert on croquet, whose book was brought out by Abercrombie & Fitch, claims that Lewis Carroll established the game in 1863. We all remember our *Alice in Wonderland* and the Queen's croquet ground. Scudder says croquet is a French word meaning "crooked stick."

Alexander Woollcott, who was not athletic by any stretch, wrote several articles about this game of outdoor chess, which he was good at, and called them "With Mallets Toward None."

234   Croquet brings out the competitive spirit. Herbert Bayard

Swope was a ruthless opponent. On the lookout for breaches in the rules, he was merciless in making everyone stick to them. He treated his partners as if they had never played before. Alexander Woollcott carefully described Swope in a letter to a friend, quoted by Scudder:

> *I suppose you want to hear the latest Swope story. Burdened with Gerald Brooks as a croquet partner, he [Swope] became so violent that Brooks agreed to do only what he was told and thereafter became a mute automaton, a condition which Swope enjoyed hugely. Brooks never moved his mallet or approached a ball without being told by Swope: "Now Brooksy, you go through this wicket. That's fine, now you shoot down to the position, perfect!!" And so on. Finally, before an enthralled audience, Swope said, "Now you hit that ball up there on the road. That's right. Now you put your little foot on your ball and drive the other buckety-buckety off into the orchard. Perfect!!" It was only then, from the shrieks of the on-lookers, that Swope discovered it was his own ball which had been driven off.*

Herbert Swope, Jr., was also a difficult but brilliant player. The only one who could match up to him was Averell Harriman: Harriman was steady and brilliant, while young Swope was always brilliant. I played a fair game myself, but the nearest I got to a title was in the semi-finals of a tournament at Mrs. Emerson's. I was playing Harriman and had him all but beat, but he was too patient for me.

Almost every evening ended with games. Sometimes canasta or backgammon or whatever game was in vogue at the time, and sometimes parlor games. Whenever the party was at the Baragwanaths, Neysa would already have organized something. She was the queen of party games.

One of the games she liked was called "Curtain Lines." One might win with such lines as "Good God, people don't do such things" said by Judge Brock after Hedda Gabler shoots herself, or "I'm sorry for everybody in the whole world" immortalized by Jeanne Eagels as "Sadie Thompson." I prefer the line from Hecht and MacArthur's *The Front Page*, "The son-of-a-bitch stole my watch."

Neysa, the illustrator and magazine-cover artist, was married to John Baragwanath, the architect, but they led libertarian lives. One day when Neysa was painting a portrait, her model was impatient to knock off. "Have you got a heavy date?" asked Neysa. The model said, "Yes, with a great guy, Jack Baragwanath."

The three dashing blades of Long Island were Jack, William Rhinelander Stewart and George Abbott. They took an annual week's vacation from their wives and they called it "freedom week," meaning they were free to do whatever they wanted to. Their wives were liberal wives and very desirable, if not as liberal as their husbands.

One night at the Abbott's, Jack, who had just returned from abroad, introduced a new parlor gimmick. He picked up the game which had been a success on shipboard. One side wrote down a word and their opponents had to draw likenesses from which their team could guess what you had in mind, either a slogan, a song or book title. I proposed a variation on the game, a form of charades. The group was divided into two teams and the captains of each were given several phrases by an anchor man. The captains acted out the words and the first team to guess won. Thus was born "The Game." It was popular in the forties and fifties and is still played at some gatherings.

Alice Duer Miller had asked me to take her to dinner in Oyster Bay at Sagamore Hill, inherited by Theodore Roosevelt, Jr. They were interested in playing The Game. I was chosen as the anchor man to explain the rules and pick the phrases that were to be guessed. All my phrases were popular during the regime of the man who discovered "The River of Doubt"; "Delighted," "a big stick," "Byzantium logothete," "velvet glove." Alice was the captain of one team and Teddy, Jr., was pitted against her on the opposing team. Despite the fact that all the answers were literally hanging from the walls, Teddy's team lost.

Later when I was married to Lucinda we went to Dottie Parker's re-wedding to Alan Campbell, which was celebrated with a reception at the Charlie Bracketts. The Game erupted and raged for hours. All the guests who could still walk played, until Dottie got mad at Alan for guessing she was the wolf suckling Romulus and Remus when she was acting out the Brooklyn Bridge.

Another time after dinner at Alfred and Jeanne Vanderbilts we chose teams and played The Game. Joe Alsop was on my team. We all decided that even though it would cost us the game, we wouldn't guess what he was acting out. He had gotten "Tramp, Tramp, Tramp, the Boys Are Marching" and confidently started tramping and making flag-waving motions. We guessed "Tipperary," "Rumpelstiltskin," "Spanish Dancing," "Stamping Out the Grapes." Joe tramped and stamped and finally jumped up and down. Everyone was laughing so hard that he finally caught on—just in time to save the floor.

I Guess
I'll Have to
Change
My Plan

For a brief period, I had a boat craze. I bought myself a craft that looked like an ocean liner. It was black and gold and called "L'Apache" and had been used by Carl Fisher to cast his lines in southern waters. It was 72 feet long, and felt at home in Long Island Sound where its thirst for gasoline drank up 75 gallons a day. It had a crew of four. Its mooring was off the Bath and Tennis Club at Sands Point, near the house we rented called the Sands House. I bought two additional sea craft: speed boats, one with a top to ward off the rain, and one without. They were called "Stuff" and "Nonsense." "Nonsense" had been owned by Fred Astaire and it was as graceful.

It was a mad collection, as I knew little about boats. I felt like Jack Hazzard in the musical *Night Boat,* playing a role in which he deceives his wife by telling her that he spends his nights guiding a ship on the briny and it happens to be the Albany night boat. The wife is worried over what her friends tell her is her husband's dangerous career, and she begs him to lead a more normal life. "What! Give up the sea?" says Jack.

If I wasn't seagoing myself, I had a barfly friend, Nat Curtis, who was at home on deck and below. He was shameless and he fancied his looks, and I must say he was impressive in the brass he had me buy for him. He wore it all the time.

Just as I was getting very much attached to "L'Apache" and Sands House, I had to spend more time in Hollywood. When I went to the studio, I thought I would be there for only a week but I was to remain a month. I left Betty in charge of the eccentric Captain Curtis, who relished the assignment, and I subsequently found my hold on her weakening.

In Hollywood I met Tanis Guinness, who had dropped in from overseas with a group of English friends. Tanis had just been divorced from Drogo Montagu, the son of the Earl of

Sandwich. I met her at a party she gave with Ethel Borden who was the daughter of Daisy Harriman, the ambassador to Norway. I had gone to the party taking Lupe Velez with me. Lupe, though married to Johnny Weissmuller, often traveled alone.

I said to Tanis, "I must get you out of all this."

She said, "Wait till I change my dress." She went off stage and came back in no time at all.

"Wherever we're going, I'll have to take the two of you," I said.

"Who is the other one?" she asked. I said it was Lupe Velez, "the tempermental, reckless Mexican wildcat."

"We three will make a good couple," Tanis said, and even though she was the hostess of the party, she left it to go along by itself, and we went to the Colony Club. I gave Lupe $500 and Tanis $500 and told them to gamble, but not to expect any more, and I would take back my $500 and half the profits, if any. It was an exciting night with the glamour of Hollywood at its most exotic. Lupe didn't win any money, but Tanis won $2,000 and insisted on my taking back the $500 I had invested in her and the $500 invested in Lupe. I took the girls home, Lupe first. Tanis wanted to go on to another gambling place, so we went to the Clover Club, where Tanis, playing roulette, was lucky again. She was excited about her month in Hollywood and said she felt she could win enough to support us both, and if I was staying for an overlapping time, perhaps we would work out happily together. I improved on her proposition. I suggested we make a date for every night and call only to break it. This switch was popular with her. I told her that I couldn't make it for the following weekend—Harpo Marx had invited me to go to Palm Springs. I hired a limousine and a chauffeur to take me there. The limousine drew up in front of the Beverly Hills Hotel and Tanis arrived in her light yellow Cadillac convertible at the same time. She dismissed my car and chauffeur and took me to Palm Springs herself.

I put Tanis at the top of my top echelon and canceled my

dreams with Aileen Pringle, Sheila Graham, Tallulah Bankhead, Ethel Borden, Jean Harlow and Lupe Velez.

It wasn't smooth sailing. Many men were trying to date Tanis, but I had the best track. We stuck to our breaking-the-date plan, and though I stayed in Hollywood three weeks longer, we broke only one date. That was when an Englishman she fancied, named Teddy Phillips, made the trip to Hollywood to save Tanis from sinking into the arms of an American. I found myself on the farewell night in a *diner à trois*, and we stayed up all night, winding things up at dawn on the tennis court.

Back home on Long Island, I didn't trust the cordiality of Betty and Curtis. Even though I had fallen for this charming visitor, I didn't want to lose Betty. It was my own fault that an aloofness between us had set in and our relationship had become forced. I wasn't sure I wanted to marry Tanis and I didn't want Betty to know about her. I was very fond of Betty. She was a lovable person and life with her was comfortable and convenient. I hesitated to disturb it even for such an entertaining beauty as Tanis. On the other hand, though we had been married nineteen years and were fond of each other, we had no children, nor any compulsion to stay tied together.

Lord (Porchy) Carnarvon had whipped up a flame about Tanis, and when she thought that I was a hopelessly married man, she gave in to Porchy's proposal. She agreed to meet him in Washington where they would be spliced by the British ambassador. They rendezvoused at the Mayflower and intended to be married the next day. They said goodnight at midnight and went to their separate rooms. Tanis's maid of a lifetime, Celina, listened to Tanis arguing with herself, and decided that all was not right.

"What is the trouble, Madame?" she asked, as if she didn't know.

"I don't want to marry Porchy," said Tanis.

"Then don't marry him," said Celina. "Marry that nice Monsieur Dietz."

Tanis said, "Let's get out of here."

Celina repacked and they took the first train out of Washington. It was a news story. Carnarvon, the son of the great Carnarvon, had been jilted. "You may say I have been jilted," he confirmed to newsmen when the people involved in the wedding plans found that these plans had gone awry. Tanis telephoned me and said, "What shall I do?"

I said, "Go back to England and I'll go to California to prevent more column gossip."

Celina called me up and said, "Please don't let anything happen to Madame."

Betty and Curtis were getting along fine and they only then realized that the breakup between Porchy and Tanis was significant. I sold my boats to the Coast Guard as gasoline was getting hard to get, and Curtis, an admiral without a fleet, was about to go on to a job in Hollywood. Betty told me that she was going to marry Curtis, and I said, "If that's the case, I'm going to marry Tanis."

Tanis wrote that she had been told that I had become free, and indeed I had, but I was reluctant about rushing into matrimony. Celina was doing sentry duty and she called me from the St. Regis at 7 o'clock one morning and said that Madame was on the window ledge, what should she do?

"I'm too sleepy to cope with problems of life and death," I said, "call me back at 9."

Betty and Curtis went to Chihuahua where you buy instant bliss on short notice and Betty freed herself from the bonds of matrimony. Tanis and I also married across the border, in Juarez. I went to the old market and bought her a wedding ring for a dollar.

The British press somehow found out about my work at

the creamery 20 years before and they ran the headline "LA-BORER WEDS HEIRESS."

We spent our honeymoon with the family of the Earl of Sandwich, Tanis's previous in-laws. We had a second honeymoon in Hawaii where we traveled on the ship the "Lurline." Samuel Goldwyn was aboard and he was anxious to play bridge. Frances, Sam's attractive wife who was dedicated to pleasing Sam, spent most of her time beachcombing for bridge players. Sam found us pleasant partners, but wasn't pleasant himself and managed to lose $1,500. Tanis adored bridge and found winning attractive. When the Goldwyn avalanche came in, we put our winnings in a little house on the sand Tanis found, with servants and a Chevrolet. Our marriage seemed sound.

Tanis was a daughter of Benjamin Guinness, the chief financier, cousin of the beer baron who pressed out the stout that was good for you. Benjy's main corporation was the EBIT Corporation which meant Evasion of British Income Tax. He summoned me to the LaRue restaurant in Paris and over the rare luncheon he wanted to know all there was to know about my cash and credit situation.

I was accepted by this gold mine of a family because I got a big salary and they were humble in the face of cash. They reasoned that their children would feel safer if they married money. The money part didn't affect me. I remembered what Harry Ruby, the songwriter, had said: "If you marry a drunk you become a drunk, if you marry an artist, you become an artist, but if you marry money, you never get rich."

Guinness learned that the one thing I needed most was a pocket full of dollar bills so I would always have money for taxis. When Christmas came he sent me 150 dollar bills and I have received 150 dollar bills from his estate every Christmas since. It makes me feel rich.

ur dinner parties at 18 West 11th Street were special events. One such was inspired by a letter from Alec Woollcott.

Bomoseen, Vt.
January 4, 1942

My dear Howard:

On January 19th, Ethel Barrymore, by beginning her Chicago engagement in The Corn Is Green, *and Kit Cornell by launching the new Bernstein play in San Francisco, will fittingly observe my birthday. But so far I have not heard what you are going to do about it. Your plan to give a dinner party, to which, of course, I would wear my fur cap and red mittens, will be frustrated by the circumstance that I have to be in Washington that night. Instead, will you give the dinner on the night of January 13th, when I shall be in New York?*

I leave the whole matter of place and menu to you, but in dread lest you fill the table up with Morrie Ryskind and the like, I must stipulate that you ask only Tanis (Dietz) unless you could manage to have Bob and Madeline Sherwood, Raymond Gram Swing and Vilhjalmur Stefansson, a foursome who admittedly have nothing in common beyond the fact that I would like to see them while I am in New York.

A. Woollcott

It never occurred to me that Woollcott was joking. I started by telephoning the Sherwoods who were old friends. Then I worried over invitations to the other two who were very celebrated just then and whom neither Tanis nor I had ever met. Although Woollcott never showed up, it turned out to be one of the best parties we had. Woollcott never explained his absence. He didn't believe in explaining.

Tanis was an excellent hostess and she invited the perfect complement of guests. For one gathering I wrote poems for placecards. I quote a few of them.

245

COLE PORTER

Cole Porter on a summer's day
Was idly ambling in the city
When as would be his mind gave way
To fashioning a little ditty.

He sang his love on Bowling Green
And all the way to Dyckman Street
Named every highway in between
No Baedeker was more complete.

He set it in chromatic style
And put it in a Broadway show
They hummed it up and down the aisle
They kissed to it when lights were low.

But not content with this, the dog
Went on to cover other ground
A Sears and Roebuck catalogue
Was rhymed and harmonized for sound.

His perfumed jazz massaged the soul,
His graceful couplings told a story
Long live the King whose name is Cole
The artist of the inventory.

GEORGE BACKER

There once was a digger from Perth
Whom the ladies thought heaven on earth
With them he was regnant
They often got pregnant
But few of them ever gave birth

LINDA PORTER

She used to come visiting Washington Square
And light up the rooms that were shadowy there
And with her return to the Village, why then
The shadowy rooms can be brilliant again.

TILLY LOSCH

The smile that borders on her lips
The enigmatic eyes that dance
The Central European hips
Are invitations to romance.

The walk that's balanced on the toes,
The hats that look like summer squash
The Renoir cheeks, the puppet nose
These piquant things are Tilly Losch.

What does she do with all her days?
Does she take lonely little strolls
Or sit at window panes and gaze
At people and debate their souls?

What goes within that sheltered mind
Wearing its pastel mackintosh
Behind a pink venetian blind?
I'm silly over Tilly Losch.

MAGGIE

It's hard to cope with Maggie Swope
But I'm a glutton for the work
More ponti-fickle than the Pope
It's hard to cope with Maggie Swope
I've never yet relinquished hope
Though she declares that I'm a jerk.
It's hard to cope with Maggie Swope
But I'm a glutton for the work.

Tanis had a sister, Meraud, who lived in the French village of Aix-en-Provence. Painting was the principal product of the place. Cézanne was born in Aix, and the motif of most of the village artists was Cézanniste.

Tanis had left me in Aix; she couldn't take the table d' hôte and no baths. Meraud, surprisingly, for a Guinness heiress, found hardship a way of life. She lived just off the road on a narrow promontory. A car couldn't make it to the front door as the incline was too steep. Meraud was married to Chile Guvera. They were both painters. Chile was slightly superior to his wife in reputation in canvas circles.

After I had lived with the Guveras a few days, I was infected with the spirit of modern art and I took up painting as a side line. I bought some canvases and proceeded to paint things from memory. I was constantly warned not to paint literature, but I didn't know what that meant. Then I realized that meant you shouldn't indulge in clichés. Suppose you isolate yourself from everything and paint something you've never seen before. You are a modern artist.

Liza, my first and only child, was born in 1938 and grew up with many of the attitudes of her delightful mother. Almost at once she was placed in charge of Miss Drinkwater, an English nanny whom Tanis imported. Miss Drinkwater practically ordered me around. She thought she was my nanny as well as Liza's. When Liza was old enough, I put her in a school in the Sixties run by Miss Hewitt.

Liza was creative. She could paint watercolors which were colorful and humorous. At the age of eight she wrote a short story with a remarkable first sentence: "Once upon a time there was a bad witch and she lived in a dark bathroom." She also wrote a piece about a magician who could take things out of a hat.

"He was a poor magician and his name happened to be Eliri Santaho," she said. "When I say he was a poor magician, I don't mean his magic was poor. I mean he had no money. He was broke. He could do marvelous tricks but they could only last for 15 minutes. Then they would disappear.

"He would pull eggs and bacon out of a hat, and that was all right because he could finish eggs and bacon in 15 minutes. But most things aren't any good if they could only last 15 minutes. He prayed that he could pull something out of his hat that would last.

"He dreamed of going to China on a magic carpet, but he could not risk it. His carpet would not stay up long enough. However, he said, nothing ventured, nothing gained and he pulled a carpet out of his hat and bravely flew off for China. Ten minutes passed, 15 minutes, 16 minutes, 17 minutes. Suppose the magic carpet should disappear? But it didn't. 'Eureka,' he shouted, 'I have made things last,' and he landed in China and had a wonderful time."

Randolph Churchill, Winston Churchill's son, was a close friend of Tanis's, and he came to our house in Sands Point for weekends whenever he was in New York. He had been divorced by Pamela Digby, a great beauty who married Leland Hayward and is now the wife of Averell Harriman.

Randolph was a creature who required drastic disciplinary measures. He drank a great deal, and was stubbornly determined to have his way. He liked to play bridge, but he wasn't a good player, which didn't keep him from playing for high stakes. In fact, the higher the better. When you reluctantly consented to play for the stakes he drove you to, he would then blame you for his losses. He was insulting.

Randolph liked the Swopes. One time, when our house was full up, Tanis arranged for the Swopes to take him in. But Randolph didn't return to his host's at a reasonable hour. Instead, he went to the George Backers and played in a costly poker game. Randolph would not let anyone quit. He pointed out that he was a visiting Englishman, our spiritual ally if not our material one. The game must go on. It was 4 in the morning when they broke it up, and Randolph, knowing his way around that part of Long Island, didn't bother to arrange transport. He said he would walk.

He arrived at the Swope house at an ungodly hour and roused the household. He went to sleep on the veranda on a glass table which wouldn't bear his 200 pounds, and Maggie wasted no time in calling the police. When the police asked Randolph if he had anything with which to identify himself, he said he was the son of Winston Churchill, and the cop said sure, *he* was the uncle of General Eisenhower.

Swope took charge, magnificent in his Charnet dressing gown and pince-nez; he swept Randolph in and the police out.

Harry Kurnitz, the playwright, screen-right, and everything-right, spent a weekend in Sands Point, where life went on around the swimming pool. The pool was cleaned by a stream of water flowing over the sides. "The Hollywood version of the 23rd Psalm," Kurnitz said. "My pool runneth over."

My close friend and regular weekend guest at Sands Point was Stuart Scheftel, who attracted all the girls but he didn't try to marry them. I felt his celibacy was a waste, and I determined to get him attractively harnessed.

As a marriage broker, I have had quite a few successes and some that were not so hot. Once when I had a date with Madeline Hurlock to take her to see *The Little Show* I asked Marc Connelly to join us at "21" afterwards. He no sooner saw Madeline than he lapsed into a series of his best stories, and Madeline fell for him, but this marriage didn't last long. She saw too much of Robert Sherwood, although he's one man you can't see too much of. I introduced George Kaufman to Leueen McGrath but this wasn't a successful mating. Moss Hart and Kitty Carlisle were a great success and Sally Scheftel met Buzz Scheftel at our house.

Stuart told me the only girl in the movies (which was my territory) he would go for was Geraldine Fitzgerald. I admired his taste, and since Geraldine was a close friend I promised that on her next visit to New York he would have the opportunity to give her close scrutiny. About a month later, Geraldine came to New York, and I told her I would deliver a charming gentleman for dinner. Tanis called up Scheftel and said, "How about your coming to dinner, Geraldine Fitzgerald will be with us." Stuart said no, he was too busy and had to eat dinner on a tray and go to bed. That was all he had to say, and he hung up with thanks. A minute later he called back. "Did you say Geraldine Fitzgerald?" "Yes," said Tanis. "I accept your invitation, I'll be there at 7:30," said Stuart. All four of us went to dine at the Lafayette. He and Geraldine were married a month later and are still.

I saw a good deal of Mrs. Patrick Campbell, the celebrated British actress, but not enough. She came into my life by way of Tanis, whose mother, Bridget Guinness, was her benefactor to the tune of about $1,000 a year—not enough to suggest this unique personality in her moods and indifference to money. Stella, as Mrs. Campbell was called when she was called by her first name, was a frequent visitor to 11th Street.

Tanis gave her a Pekinese named "Moonbeam," which caused complications in her life. Mrs. Campbell was in a taxi on her way to see us. She had Moonbeam with her. Usually Moonbeam behaved in public places, but she misbehaved this time. When Stella stepped out of the cab and was sorting out the fare, the taxi driver pointed to the mess Moonbeam had left behind on the seat and said, "Who did that?"

"I did," said Mrs. Campbell.

When she returned to England she was stopped at the port where they would not let the dog enter without serving time in quarantine. Stella said, "Love me, love my dog," and settled down in Paris where she wrote letters to and received letters from Bernard Shaw in a famous correspondence.

She was a gifted actress, but indifferent to the parts she played. Her figure bulged as she got along in life. Her stubbornness about London didn't help. She came to New York and stayed with us. I invited some well-known theatrical figures to dine, hoping they would be captivated by her wit and reminded of her ability, which had yet to be introduced to the New York stage.

Present were Bob Sherwood, Noel Coward, Gilbert and Kitty Miller, Ina Claire, Dwight Wiman, Steve Wiman, Clifton Webb, and others. They had all been briefed and were anxious to do her a good turn. But she succeeded in insulting most of them. She said of Constance Collier, "She comes toward you like a chest of drawers and she has a mouth like a galosh." Of Ina Claire, who was the reigning stage favorite of the time, she said, "She's quite pretty; it's too bad she can only play minor roles." To Joseph Schildkraut; "Young man, you ought to be on the stage."

He said, "My name is Joseph Schildkraut."

Stella said, "You can change that."

She told Noel Coward that his play, *Point Valaine*, in which he was appearing, was, "Quite good, a little dull for the first two acts, but when you jump out of the window, the interest picks up considerably."

She was no less lenient when she went to Hollywood. She told Irving Thalberg that his wife, Norma Shearer, was "a great beauty with those tiny little eyes."

Tanis was an international flame. She had would-be lovers in every port. I held her in check for 14 years. There was always an element of doubt and I wrote a song to that effect.

THAT ELEMENT OF DOUBT

I got a gal, keeps me out on the limb
Whether she loves me depends on her whim
I never know where the wind's gonna blow
If I'm in or I'm out of the swim.

There's always that element of doubt
Am I the one that she's crazy about

Am I the one that she can't do without
Does she love me
There's always that element of guess
She never gives me a positive yes
I'm never certain I'll be a success
Or what I'll be
I even went to see a gypsy
To find out whether or not she loves me
The gypsy studying the tea leaves
Came up with possibly so, possibly no
There's always that element of doubt
Am I the one that she's crazy about
I never know if she's in or she's out
Of love with me.

Sic Transit, Gloria Monday

n April 9, 1865, at Appomattox Court House in Virginia, the War Between the States, commonly called in the North the Civil War, came to an end. There was no funeral: the corpse remained in the house. The Confederate point of view was presented in 1915 with D. W. Griffith's *The Birth of a Nation,* and again in 1939 with *Gone with the Wind.*

As MGM had invested Clark Gable and $2.5 million in this latter picture, and as I represented MGM in promoting it, the marketing with all its complications was in my care. David O. Selznick, brilliant producer though he was, was also in my care, in a sense. His fixation was telegrams. Not a day went by that he didn't send me a yard or two from California. They usually arrived in the dead of night and, living in a town house with several stories, as I did, I found it especially annoying to be summoned to the door at an ungodly hour. One Selznick telegram totaled a record 4 feet high in my stocking feet. I was ashamed to let the servants see the size of this extravagant memo that woke them up.

It read in part: I WANT YOU TO BE VERY CAREFUL OF THE PAPER YOU SELECT FOR THE PROGRAM—STOP—SOMETIMES THEIR CRACKLING MAKES IT DIFFICULT TO HEAR THE DIALOGUE—STOP—PROMISE YOU WILL ATTEND TO THIS. I telegraphed back: RECEIVED YOUR EPIGRAM—STOP—YOU CAN REST ASSURED ABOUT PROGRAM NOISE—STOP—HOWEVER HAVE MADE TIEUP WITH *GONE WITH THE WIND* PEANUT BRITTLE COMPANY ASSURING EACH PATRON OF THE PICTURE A BOX OF PEANUT BRITTLE AS HE ENTERS THE THEATRE. Another Selznick wire read: I DON'T RECEIVE ENOUGH ANSWERS TO THE POINTS I RAISE HAVE YOU FOUND A BRIDGE CLUB DOWN THERE?

I had sent Norman Kaphan, an advance photographer, to Atlanta about a month before. His function was to photograph still backgrounds against which portraits could be taken. Experience proved that if we tried to photograph a star in the usual way the result was a mob scene. Taking the foregrounds and backgrounds separately, the stars could be photographed anywhere, indoors or out, whenever the coast was clear; and Norman was an expert. I asked him how he liked the South, and he said, "I've been 'honeyed' and 'sugared' so much I got diabetes."

In Atlanta as the opening approached the first problem was tickets—opening-night tickets, second-night tickets, anynight tickets. Politicians were deluged with requests from their constituents, salesmen were solicited by their bag accounts. One elderly lady almost lived in my headquarters at the Georgian Terrace.

"But you don't understand," she kept repeating, "I am president of the local chapter of the D.A.R."

At the end of my patience, I said, "But *you* don't understand, madam, this picture is about another war."

The solution of the ticket problem came inspirationally. Using my temporary high office, I decided to press the governor of Georgia and the mayor of Atlanta into service. Each one wanted to be reelected to his high post in city or state. Both were Democrats, if of different sorts: Rivers, the governor, was a New Dealer, while Mayor Hartzfield was an Old Dealer, if there was such a thing.

I met with the mayor first. We decided that the Community Chest would receive the combined total of the theatre admissions and the Junior League Ball, to take place the night before the premiere. It was understood that preference tickets would be subtracted from the list, which totaled about 1,400. The press was to have a special, exclusive screening. Mayor Hartzfield was beside himself with joy, feeling that he had triumphed over the governor.

When Rivers heard about the deal, he went into a rage and got me on the phone. "What will become of the Southern governors?" he demanded furiously. "I've promised them they could bring their wives; now they can't even bring themselves."

"You'll go through with your commitment," I told him.

"And you'll give them a banquet before the opening. MGM will pick up the tab."

"You mean you'll get by Hartzfield?" the governor asked.

"Exactly that," I said.

When I delivered the houseful of tickets minus the governor's quota, it was the mayor's turn to vent his fury, but I was ahead of him. "How would you like Clark Gable to take your daughter to the Junior League Ball?" I asked.

Silence. Finally: "You could do that?"

"Consider it done." I made a note to consult Carole Lombard.

The day of the premiere, a million people crowded into a city built to hold 300,000. They came from New York and Hollywood and all the towns, villages and hamlets along the way. They didn't come to Atlanta expecting to see the picture, they came to see the stars. One constituency lined the street. Leaning from the rooftops was another solid mass of rubber-necked humanity, waiting for the open cars as they came the 14 miles from the airport to the carré of Peachtree Street. The congestion was so great that Bill Goetz of 20th-Century-Fox, the one who bought the fake Vlaminck, complained of having his toes stepped on. "We don't make pictures as good as MGM," he said, "but at least we don't annoy people."

Howard Strickling had arranged for the parade. As the planes arrived, the stars got into open cars and made their way along the avenue of cheering humanity. The first to come down the ramp was Gable. A wild cheer went up as an officer led him to his car.

A 40-piece band had been provided. It was beautifully uniformed, brass shining blindingly in the sun, but it could play only one tune—the only one it knew—"Dixie"! Another wild cheer went up as the band began the opening bars. "Oh," said Vivien Leigh, "they're playing the song from the picture." A reporter from the *Atlanta Journal* heard that and asked me who said it. I thought fast and said, "Olivia de

Havilland." Had I admitted it was Vivien, we would have been sunk. It was bad enough that "Scarlett O'Hara" was an alien in real life.

To the tune of "Dixie," the Star Spangled Banner was raised above the Confederate flag—the first time this had been done since the Civil War. They played "Dixie" when the parade was about to break up, "Dixie" when Clark Gable escorted Vivien Leigh to her room in the hotel. It was a useful tune.

When the parade came to a halt, the fans rushed in for the autographs. One woman with an erotic tendency went to the hotel desk clerk and asked what room Gable would occupy. "We can't give out such information," the clerk said. "Well," said the woman, "will you promise to reserve it for me after he's gone? And don't make up the bed!"

The premiere lasted a weekend. Several notables from New York and Washington came down for the ball: Herbert Bayard Swope, John Hay (Jock) Whitney, who had an investment in the film, Carole Lombard, Myron Selznick, William S. Paley and many others. Gable took the fluttery daughter to the ball. It didn't require too much explaining to Carole Lombard Gable, who was the perfect sport. Though dressed to the nines, the daughter was, I'm afraid, under the eclipse of the movie stars. All the cast members were in costume, and the dancing went on till North and South feuds were forgotten.

The next day, to finish up, Margaret Mitchell gave a party at the Riding Club. *Gone with the Wind* had opened.

Not long afterward, David Selznick, dissatisfied with his business arrangement with MGM covering the distribution of the picture, told his partner Jock Whitney that MGM was raping them. When the early returns from the road show, amounting to $6 million, came in, Whitney said, "It may be rape, but it feels awfully good!"

Clark Gable's attraction to women seemed universal. When Gable was making his first postwar film, *Adventure*, there was widespread speculation as to who would play his leading lady. Greer Garson was picked and to publicize the vital union I wrote the line, "Gable's back and Garson's got him."

One day in the early fifties, Clark Gable sent me a wire asking me to reserve quarters for him in the St. Regis Hotel. Howard Strickling was in town, and together we formed a reception committee.

On hearing the news of the invasion, every staff member of the St. Regis was alerted. The chambermaids never polished the woodwork so lethargically. Indeed, they polished it four or five times. They jolly well weren't going to be finished in Clark Gable's suite until he arrived.

Finally, the door swung open and the most desirable male in the country entered. The three chambermaids in their cotton uniforms were swept up in the arms of none other than himself and kissed by him. It was the most romantic moment in their lives.

I n 1942, I was elected a vice president of Metro-Goldwyn-Mayer. Even though my domain was publicity and advertising, I hadn't sent out a press release about the appointment.

This bothered my then secretary, Mildred Lewis, who wanted me to think big. "Surely it's news," she said, "when a goof with aesthetic tastes like yours enters the arena of dog-eat-dog and comes out more than holding his end up."

I explained why I hadn't sent out an announcement. "It would be too embarrassing," I said, "to say I'd been elected a vice president when everybody thinks I'm president."

Soon after this appointment a call came from Sam Goldwyn. He asked me how well I stood with Nick Schenck. I told Sam that I stood in pretty well with him, as I had been

in his employ for more than 20 years.

"Then you can do me a favor," said Sam. "I have a picture, *The Westerner.* Gary Cooper is the star. It's a great picture, even better than *Gone with the Wind,* but not as long."

"I congratulate you," I said. "*Gone with the Wind* is hard to beat."

"Right," said Sam, "but *The Westerner* does it. Unfortunately, we didn't know how good it was until after the salesmen sold it to the Loew's circuit for less than half of what they paid for *Gone with the Wind.* Now somebody has to talk Schenck into tearing that contract up. Until that's done, we can't get the price *The Westerner* deserves from the other circuits. That's where you come in; you stand in so good with Nick that he'll do it for you. I'm asking you to go to bat for me for old times' sake."

"But, Sam," I said, "that's an impossible request."

"They paid 70 percent of the gross for *Gone with the Wind,*" said Sam. "All I want for my *Westerner* is 50 percent of the gross."

"Let me get this straight," I said. "You sold your picture to the Loew's circuit for 25 percent of the gross?"

"It's another *Gone with the Wind,*" said Sam.

"And you want me to persuade Nick to tear up the contract so you can sell it back to him at twice what he paid for it?"

"That's it, now you understand my position."

"I'm afraid Schenck might ask me who I'm working for."

"I guess you don't stand in so good with him!" said Goldwyn.

 few months before Pearl Harbor the Senate appointed a committee to investigate neutrality. Whatever was not neutral was subversive and should be stopped. The committee consisted of Senator Clark of Idaho, Senator Tobey of New Hampshire, Senator Brooks of Illinois and Senator MacFarland of Arizona. They tried to censor movies, books and plays like *Confessions of a Nazi Spy, The Mortal Storm, Escape,* and other works which showed the Germans in an unfavorable light. Leading figures in the motion picture industry were summoned for a hearing in Washington.

As its defense attorney the movie industry engaged Wendell Willkie, the liberal Republican who had just been defeated in the presidential campaign of 1940. The votes had gone heavily against him, but anybody who had to run against Franklin D. Roosevelt at the height of his popularity would have felt the crushing blow of a landslide.

I was appointed as aide to Willkie and charged with supplying him with any information about the movie industry that he might need. We both went to Washington a few days before the hearing, taking the train from Hoboken, where we were less likely to encounter inquiring reporters. We shared a suite at the Mayflower Hotel. Willkie asked me a lot of questions. He knew I was against Hitler but he wanted to know who I was pro. He was satisfied that any propaganda that was against the Third Reich would find favor with me.

We went to bed early. At 7 o'clock the next morning Willkie came into my room in his BVDs. He was shaving in an ambulatory fashion, the lather heavy on his face, and he brandished the safety razor while he talked. He had one unique extravagance when he was away from home: He didn't bother to send his clothes to the laundry. He wore his underwear and shirts just once and threw them away. Every day he sent a bellboy out to buy a new set of BVDs and a Brooks Brothers shirt. I found this lavishness attractive.

"Dietz," Willkie said, waving his razor, "I like your attitude. I even forgive you for voting for FDR." He felt that in the hearing our side was going to come through the cross-questioning with flying colors.

The senators put Nick Schenck on the stand. They took turns throwing questions at him, and whatever he couldn't answer he referred to me. My name was used so frequently that they decided to put me on the stand. Willkie was a little apprehensive about this because, even though he approved of my views, he was afraid I might take an overly partisan stance.

Since the hearing dealt with constitutional fundamentals, I was confronted with questions designed to get at my idea of Americanism. Senator Toby asked me my definition of freedom of speech. I said that it was the right to say what you wanted to say within the limitations of license, and that I hoped we would have it after this investigation—an answer which appealed to the gallery and to Willkie, who nodded his approval from his vantage point behind the senators. I was shameless, but I was satisfying the ham in me. At the same time, I couldn't understand United States senators revealing even a hint of pro-Nazism.

The day's hearing was adjourned and never reopened as the next day Pearl Harbor was attacked.

When the war came, the Coast Guard enlisted Vernon Duke, widely known as a composer of songs, among them, "April in Paris," "I Can't Get Started with You," and the score of *Cabin in the Sky*. In the theatrical market his stock was a nervous blue chip, but listed on the curb. Duke was born in a railway station in Minsk. His life was a conflict between popular music by Vernon Duke and serious music by Vladimir Dukelsky. Jazz won from the day he played "Swanee" by George Gershwin.

The Coast Guard gave Vernon $84 a month and a dazzling uniform and he was allowed to provide entertainment. I was already a part of the Coast Guard which served under Secretary of the Treasury Henry Morgenthau. The Coast Guard had bought my power boat "L'Apache" which had made two trips to Florida and used 75 gallons of gasoline per day.

Duke and I thought up *Tars and Spars* as a good recruiting agent. The remarkable thing about this show was the talent it revealed—Sid Caesar, an exceedingly funny man, Victor Mature, a handsome leading man, and Gower Champion who made his way in Broadway and in Hollywood as a director. *Tars and Spars* had a commendable score and was performed several times to the financial benefit of the Coast Guard.

In the next few years we wrote three shows together, *Sadie Thompson, Dancing in the Streets,* and *Jackpot.* They were flops.

Shortly after World War II began, Mussolini's fascist government in Italy declared a monopoly on all films from foreign sources. Count Ciano was administrator and the U.S.A. was the victim most victimized.

J. Robert Rubin, the legal light of MGM, was appointed chairman of an American committee to negotiate with the Italians and insist that they make fair payment for their imports. Rubin appointed me a member of his committee. A meeting was scheduled for a few days later after lunch in Rubin's office.

On the day of the meeting, I had lunch with a pretty girl at the Stork Club. When the lunch was over she said she wanted to go to the Cyclax beauty parlor, right next door. I went in with her. I had never been in such a place before, and I facetiously asked if they did men. They said it wasn't customary but they'd make an exception in my case. A beautiful brunette with an intoxicating smell took off my shirt and put me to sleep with a chest and facial massage.

I woke up with an alarmed jerk, and rubbed the cold cream off at the startling realization that I was late for the meeting with the Italians. "Oh, my God," I said, putting my shirt on over my slippery chest and dashing out without paying my bill. I grabbed a cab, combed my hair and arrived my tardy self at Rubin's office. Five Italians were listening to Rubin's apologies for me. Rubin was indignant at my keeping the committee waiting. He demanded to know where I'd been.

"At a beauty parlor," I said. "They were massaging my chest and I fell asleep."

The Italians roared with laughter and Rubin was puzzled by their cavalier attitude. But we made a better deal with them because despite their fascism, they were sympathetic to someone falling asleep in the afternoon under the hands of desirable women.

One day Joe Bryan, the journalist and handsome patriot, knocked at my MGM door on urgent business. He was organizing a committee to fight fascism and wanted me to sign up; he wanted my services to help with posters and slogans. We were supposed to get American corporations to contribute space in Italian media so that no Mussolini would rise again. I was enthusiastic and my reaction pleased Bryan, who loved dark intrigue and devious plans.

The first thing he had us do was choose a name. All the members of a sub-group had identical terminals to their names. The members of our particular team had nom de plumes which terminated in "igi." My name was "Saligi"; other names were "Louigi," "Maligi," "Cappigi," and so on. If your name ended in "igi" you belonged. There was a practical reason for this: When you gave your name to a member of the group at large, he immediately knew your call-group connection.

A few days later, Joe called me from Washington. My secretary, who hadn't been informed of the alias, insisted there was no one in the office by the name of Saligi. Joe was furious and sent me a telegram: "Why don't you tell your secretary your name?"

Secretary of the Treasury Morgenthau had issued bonds for defense at an early indication that we would be caught in the act of war. He spoke to Nicholas Schenck about drafting me to promote the sales. Of course I was willing.

Fred Allen called his radio program *The Treasury Hour* and he agreed to turn it over to me for promoting the sale of Defense Bonds. I, in my turn, pressed many prominent performers to appear on my air. Irving Berlin wrote a theme song "Any Bonds Today." Alexander Woollcott, who had established himself as a radio personality, appeared and well-known authors were interviewed. Herman Wouk, who hadn't written his novel as yet, was an assistant editor of the program. When war broke out, the Defense Bond Program became what might be called the Attack Bond program.

We also sent movie stars on tour to sell bonds. I had instructed all the stars to travel by train as planes were considered too risky for the outstanding personalities of the industry. Carole Lombard made a personal appearance in Indianapolis. Otto Winkler was the publicity man in charge. She wanted to get back to her husband, Clark Gable, so she didn't wait for the train. Otto and Carole took a private plane together and they never reached California.

When Clare Boothe Luce got elected to Congress in 1942 I remembered a few remarks she'd made some time earlier about the war. She intended to give the impression she was anti-Hitler, but I thought she was being anti-Roosevelt and even anti-American. All this inspired the following lines, which were published in *P.M.* in December, 1942.

AU CLARE DE LA LUCE

O Lovely Luce!—O Comely Clare
Do you remember—way back there—
Holding your lacquered nails aloft,
"The war we fight," you said, "is soft."

And while the vote hung in the balance
You turned the trick with all your talents.
You were the keystone brave and buoyant.
By Lucifer, you were clarevoyant!

Time marches on, events apace—
Are you a hoarder, saving face?
What say you now that Eisenhower
Has Africa within his power?

What say you of the bold attack
Where sea is blue and sky is black
"Vive la Liberté" for all!
"Soft" was the word, do you recall?

"Soft" where the dauntless Callaghan
Gave life itself, where every man
Rode through the fire with flag aloft?
Say it again—did you say "soft"?

O Lovely Luce, O Comely Clare!
The brave deserve the less unfair.
You are elected now, that's that—
The ring, we'd say, is in your hat.

But ere you pack your Vuitton grip
To take the Washingtonian trip,
While still responding to the toasts,
Remember this: That words are ghosts.

And when it's mealtime, never stoop
To see the letters in the soup
The ghosts may form like homing birds—
"My God," you'll cry, "I ate my words!"

Years later I got a note from Elliott Roosevelt, who was editing some of FDR's correspondence. He had found a memorandum from the president to Representative McCormack mentioning the poem and asking him to find a freshman congressman who would read it in the House the first time Mrs. Luce made a speech there. He also asked my permission to reprint the poem. This I was glad to grant and in my reply to Elliott Roosevelt I added that though Clare is a friend of mine she never even gave me a dirty look after the poem appeared in *P.M.*

Chacun
a Son Gout

A star is a star is a star. If you're a producer or director or librettist or composer or lyric writer, Ethel Merman or Mary Martin will get you if you don't watch out.

I wanted to hire Miss Merman for *The Second Little Show* when she was first brought to Broadway by Al Seigel. I gave her a tryout in vaudeville at Loew's 81st Street and she was dynamite with "Sing You Sinners." I turned gleefully to Dwight Wiman sitting next to me. I felt I was presenting him with the Kohinoor. But his reaction was negative and she was immediately hired by Vinton Freedley for *Girl Crazy*. She sang Gershwin's "Embraceable You" and "I Got Rhythm."

Some years later, it seemed to me that *Rain*, the Somerset Maugham story which Jeanne Eagels had played so brilliantly, would fare well as a musical for Ethel Merman. I put the idea up to Ethel and she reacted enthusiastically. I told her I was getting Rouben Mamoulian to direct it and Vernon Duke to compose it. I had an exchange of correspondence with Mamoulian as elaborate as Chopin and George Sand's. Duke had the score half written by the time we finished a few letters. The book I had written was good and I hadn't looked for any problems with the lyrics, but an unexpected force moved in—Ethel Merman's husband, a fellow named Robert Levitt. Unfortunately for our project, he had ambitions to be a lyric writer and thought he could get his work played by making changes in *Sadie Thompson*.

Subtle changes began to appear in Merman's lyrics. For instance, in "The Love I Long For,"

> *But I'll make much of*
> *I have no right to demand*
> *But I'll make much of*
> *The touch of*
> *A tender hand.*

He changed the word "tender" to "gentle." It was a seemingly harmless change, but I was very particular.

My verse read:

> Everytime I get to the edge of a dream
> I have to turn back
> I'm a fish who tries to swim upstream
> From the water murky and black
> Too late—too late—says a voice inside me.
> Would there were no conscience to guide me.

And Mr. Levitt replaced the fish in the murky water with "I just thought I'd caught a bright sunbeam/ But my hands are empty, slack." The "voice inside me" became "Dismal words deride me."

"Poor as a Churchmouse" got a special going over by Levitt, and I give both lyrics.

POOR AS A CHURCHMOUSE (MY VERSION)

> I'm an easy-going breezy-going cookie
> And I don't care whether school is keeping or not
> When I have a dime I hand it to a bookie
> And the nag I bet on has a passion to squat
> I despise anyone who's pennywise
> Money to me is only the second prize.
>
> Poor as a churchmouse—but rich in friends
> Sharing the joy-ride until it ends.
> Friendship is real and warm
> And a safe port in a storm
> That's my manner
> That's my banner—I won't reform
> Never unhappy when I'm with friends
> I always go for the one whose elbow bends
> Someone who will share a toddy
> There is where I park the body
> Poor as a churchmouse but rich in friends.

271

Ethel's version left only the title line and a sentiment about friendship intact. My lines are in italics.

> Just because I'm busted, do you think my shag
> is draggin'
> *That's not the way I'm gaited,*
> When the trouble's thickest, that is when my
> flag is waggin'
> *That can't be over-rated,*
> Happiness depends
> On what your fortune sends
> In the way of pals, chums, mates and friends.

> *Poor as a churchmouse—but rich in friends*
> Never too straightlaced, my elbow bends
> *Friendship is real and warm*
> *And a safe port in a storm,*
> But the fact is
> You must practice
> To keep in form
> Never too busy to say hello
> First at a party, and then the last to go
> Some folks say I'm most bewitchin'
> Playin' house without a kitchen
> *Poor as a churchmouse*
> *but rich in friends.*

Ethel preferred her husband's lyrics and said she couldn't get any message from mine. She recited a couplet of mine as an example:

> *You must put some black pencil*
> *on your peepers*
> *And some mal maison on your lips*

I told her it was a provocative kind of lipstick. We were deadlocked.

Ethel said she would get Sammy Worblin, her agent from the William Morris office, to settle the dispute. Sammy came to my office where I had arranged two folios, one of Ethel Merman's husband's lyrics, and the other, mine. Only I had shuffled them around so that his lyrics were in my envelope and my lyrics in the one marked for him. I said, "Are there any lyrics of his that you could point to that you think are better than mine?" He looked through the sheets and said, "All of them; I'm surprised that he is so good. I'm sorry, Howard. There's no doubt about it. Levitt's are the lyrics you should use." Sammy said he didn't like to hurt my feelings, but he had to act faithfully in a case like this. The more I pressed the question the more positive he became of his choice. I then told him that he had chosen my lyrics.

But Merman wasn't satisfied. She came to rehearsals and sang her husband's lyrics. I told her that she would have to sing my lyrics or leave the show. She resigned and we hired June Havoc, who was talented, but lacked the voice. The show would have been a perfect vehicle for Merman and there is little doubt that had she played Sadie it would have been a hit, but my pride which went before the fall couldn't take it.

Mary Martin who made her initial fame by singing "My Heart Belongs to Daddy," Da da dya, da da dya, grew more proper as her role in musical comedy became more certain.

We did a show for her called *Jennie* soon after *The Sound of Music*. There was always a nun or two or a priest watching rehearsals and Mary fell under the spell of one of the nuns. The nun couldn't act, sing, or dance but she could influence Mary.

One of the best songs that Arthur and I ever wrote was "Before I Kiss the World Goodbye," but Mary said she didn't like it; it was filthy, she said, and she wouldn't sing it. The couplet that roused her ire went this way:

> *Before I go to meet my maker*
> *I want to use the salt left in the shaker.*

Mary's nun had triumphed.

Mary Martin was a great performer and fun. She was victimized by her lack of trust in anyone but herself.

he best lyric writers are the ones who write the most singable words. They need not be fancy words (I fain would choosa sweet lollapalooza), but words you can lean on, which is to say solid substantial words you can put your teeth into. (Oh! tell me what street compares with Mott Street). They are a lot of a's and o's and I's and ah's. Even e words are not openly singable.

A good lyric writer can put words to music and have it come out as though he'd put music to words. Every song that has a popular quality is not necessarily a popular success, but every song that is a popular success must have popular quality. It is surprising how few popular songwriters of my era write both the words and music.

Jerome Kern who has written more than 1,000 songs has written only a few that made their way without a show or a film to plug them into popularity. The one of Kern's that I like is "The Last Time I Saw Paris." Oscar Hammerstein, the champion lyric writer, wrote the lyric.

Richard Rodgers has had a mountain of hits with help from Lorenz Hart and the perennial Hammerstein. I don't know any song that Richard Rodgers wrote that wasn't tied up with a show or a picture.

The composers of show songs, with a few exceptions, such as Stephen Sondheim, write either the words or music, but not both. The death of Cole Porter and Frank Loesser left Irving Berlin chief possessor of the title to complete songs. He finds himself the owner of most of our holidays, particularly Easter and Christmas, as well as author of a possible replacement of our national anthem.

By providing lovers with their songs for the last 60 years, he has increased the population of the world by millions. All this he has done by picking out melodies on a specially made piano which shifts the key for him. He is as good a lyric writer as he is a composer and he counts the open vowels better than most of his contemporaries.

The lyric writers that I single out to admire have collaborated with the composers I admire. They are Ira Gershwin (*Of Thee I Sing*), Alan Jay Lerner (*My Fair Lady*), Oscar Hammerstein (*Show Boat*), Lorenz Hart (*Pal Joey*), P. G. Wodehouse, Harold Arlen, Dorothy Fields, Yip Harburg (*Wizard of Oz*), Johnny Mercer, Sammy Cahn, Walter Donaldson and Hal David.

My favorite song has music by Kurt Weill and lyric by Maxwell Anderson, "September Song."

The most remarkable organization for song writing and composers is ASCAP. Though millions have heard of ASCAP, there are those, even among the musically inclined, who look blank when you mention this performing society. Some think you are referring to a space project, a patent medicine, or perhaps a Washington bureau.

ASCAP is an agent, a go-between. It collects money for the wares of its members. Its members are lyricists, composers and publishers. It gives licenses to its customers. Its customers are restaurants, radio and television stations, hotels and similar public places that benefit by music.

If there were no ASCAP the business side of music would be in Chaos, or Frenzy or some sort of Thesaurus land. The discomfiture on the part of the creators of music and the users of music would be mutual. A new contract would have to be exchanged with the performance of every song.

That's the way it was B.A.—Before ASCAP. Today the professional user of music can relax, knowing he has the right to play the full catalogue written by some eight thousand ASCAPians which contains the great standard numbers of the twentieth century. There are some restrictions, such as theatrical duplication which constitutes what is called a "grand" right. Even then special permission to perform is often granted.

I give ASCAP a simon-pure bill-of-health. It has a harder working board than that of any corporation I've seen in action. The board members get no pay, except a small pourboire for monthly attendance. The president, Stanley Adams, is conscientious enough and smart enough to be president of anything. Anything can use a man like Adams.

Ten years ago when Variety said Cheerio to ASCAP on its fortieth anniversary, I imagined a wave but didn't make a ripple when I suggested that the ASCAP technique might be applied to other arts—that there might be a Novelist's ASCAP, a Poet's ASCAP, a Playwright's ASCAP. After all, I am told that horse breeders keep a claim of a sort on horses they once bred. If there can be a Horse's ASCAP, why not an artist's.

rthur Schwartz had gone to Hollywood in 1938 and he lingered there for 10 years. He wrote a score with Frank Loesser, also a score with Leo Robin. Having also tried his wings there as a production executive with *Cover Girl* and *Night and Day,* Arthur decided to come back to Broadway and produce shows as well as write them. John Gunther's *Inside U.S.A.* suggested a revue. He made a deal with Gunther and one with me and we resumed our old habits of collaboration.

During the writing of *Inside U.S.A.* Bea Lillie, the star, was in London and Arthur and I would telephone to tell her that all was going well. On one occasion she asked me to sing a couple of numbers and I sang "Come O Come to Pittsburgh" and "We Won't Take It Back," a song about selling Manhattan to the Indians. Bea said she loved the songs and would I please sing them again. I thought about the $15 a minute and said, "I'll be glad to when you call *me.*"

"First Prize at the Fair," our best song in the show, was admired by the lyric writer I most admire, P. G. Wodehouse. It was sung in the finale of the first act.

1st Boy
I never did place in the piggy-back chase
Fell on my face in the sack-race
Still I won the first prize at the Fair.
I couldn't eat fast
When the apple-pie passed
Finished up last in the track-race
Still I won the first prize at the Fair.

1st Girl
When we were dancing the square-dance
You said: "I love you, I do!"
The man called "Sashay left!"
But I sashayed right to you.

1st Boy
I never came up
With a ribbon or cup
Still I came up in the clover.

1st Girl
When the Fair was over I knew—

Both
That I had won the first prize in you.

2nd Girl
I want to wilt
When my eiderdown quilt
Lost in the tilt for the trophy
Still I won the first prize at the Fair.
Joanna came through
Marianna came through
Hannah did too, even Sophie.
Still I won the first prize at the Fair.

2nd Boy
While we were dancing the square-dance
Your true affection came through
The man called "Do see do!"

2nd Girl
How I "do see dote" on you.

2nd Boy
So what did I care
Was there anyone there
Who could compare with my winning?

2nd Girl
Life was just beginning, I knew

Both
For I had won the first prize in you.

Man
Your sugar-cured ham
Didn't pass the exam
They thought your jam was Tabasco
Still you won the first prize at the Fair.

Woman
My pickled pig's feet
Wasn't fitten' to eat
Seemed to complete my fiasco
Still I won the first prize at the Fair.

Man
I gave my all in the hog-call
But the hogs rejected my song
I called and I called and I called them
Then you came along.

It started to rain
But I didn't complain

Woman
Not when you had my umbrella.

Man
Bought a sasparella for two—

Both
For I had won the first prize in you.

"Haunted Heart" became the best-known. It was later recorded by Perry Como.

HAUNTED HEART

In the night, though we're apart,
There's a ghost of you within my haunted heart.
Ghost of you, my lost romance,
Lips that laugh, eyes that dance.
Haunted heart won't let me be.
Dreams repeat a sweet but lonely song to me.
Dreams are dust—it's you who must belong to me
And thrill my haunted heart,
Be still, my haunted heart.

Time rolls on
Trying in vain to cure me.
You are gone
But you remain to lure me.
You're there in the dark and I call—
You're there but you're not there at all.
Oh what can I do
Without you,
Without you.

In the night, though we're apart,
There's a ghost of you within my haunted heart.
Ghost of you, my lost romance,
Lips that laugh, eyes that dance.
Haunted heart won't let me be,
Dreams repeat a sweet but lonely song to me.
Dreams are dust—it's you who must belong to me
And thrill my haunted heart
Be still, my haunted heart.

Inside U.S.A. ran for two years and then Arthur invented a television program based on the idea. It used our songs, starred Peter Lind Hayes and Mary Healy, and was a "first" variety show of its type on the visual air.

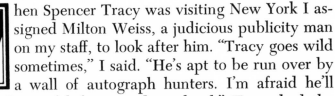hen Spencer Tracy was visiting New York I as-
signed Milton Weiss, a judicious publicity man
on my staff, to look after him. "Tracy goes wild
sometimes," I said. "He's apt to be run over by
a wall of autograph hunters. I'm afraid he'll
resort to violence if he's pressed too hard." Tracy had the
mistaken idea that a movie star can have the freedom of the
city and the right to put it into practice. He had no idea how
to handle people, and he drank in an unpredictable rhythm.
On previous trips to the big city he had inundated himself
in a friendly bar.

Weiss had his hands full. "I'm at the Sherry-Netherland,"
he said on the phone one afternoon, "and the big man is
drinking vodka martinis and smashing the glasses against
the mirror back of the bar. He says you should be looking
after him, not me, and he won't stop drinking until you show
him that you care. You'd better come up here."

I found Tracy with his feet on a chair, which he rocked
back and forth in time to his swallows. The bartender would
occasionally suggest that Tracy go slow as it might cost him
his job, but he might have been drunk too as Spencer had
been flattering him. "You're a great bartender," Tracy said,
"one of the old school. You made vodka martinis before they
even thought about them. You started when martinis were
one-third gin, one-third French vermouth, and one-third
Italian Cinzano."

"So you're here," he said, when I put in an appearance.
"You were too stuck up to come and meet me yourself. Well,
we'll see if you can do better than Milton. Milton has it all
over you as a diplomat. You think you're too high class to give
aid and comfort to an actor. You've had shows on Broadway and you go for actors like Fred Astaire, Clifton Webb,
and dancers. It makes you a high-class press agent. Furthermore, you look like me. Well, I won't go back to California
unless you come with me." He threw a glass at the mirror.
"Have a drink. Let's see how you handle yourself."

I managed to whisper a message to Milton whose subsequent departure Tracy didn't notice.

I got Tracy up to his suite on the seventh floor, and worked on him. I finally got him to agree to go back to California. "But only if you come too," he said. We took a limousine to La Guardia, and the three of us, Tracy, Weiss and I, boarded the plane. Tracy's consciousness was sketchy, so I left him in the hands of Milton, who gave instructions to the pilot to go west after I had climbed out. The plane took gracefully to the air and I sank into a gratefully relieved sigh and headed for home and bed.

The phone rang at midnight. It's your guess who was on the wire.

"You thought you were rid of me," the voice said. "Well, I'll meet you in the bar of the Sherry-Netherland at 9 o'clock. You'd better relieve Milton, he needs some sleep." Tracy was calling from Chicago.

s a promotion stunt for a picture called *The Romance of Rosy Ridge*, I gave $1,000 in Confederate money to all the leading motion picture critics in the country. The Confederate bills were worthless, but it was a colorful promotion and lots of items appeared in the papers.

Some months later, I was cleaning out my desk drawers when Paul Hochuli, a critic from Texas, came by. I was taking him to lunch. I was transferring a stack of Confederate bills from one drawer to another.

"That was a pretty good stunt," he said.

"Yes, it was," I agreed, "and I never dreamed it would turn out so profitably. I'm glad I kept some of the bills, I hope you've still got yours."

"No, I gave it all to my kids and they played Monopoly with it."

"That's too bad. You might find out if they still have it. I blame myself for not notifying the people on the list I sent it to."

"What do you mean?" he said.

"Congress has passed a bill making all moneys used in the Civil War legitimate and worth 100¢ on the dollar."

"You're kidding," said Hochuli, turning pale.

"Not at all," I assured him, "we'll see what we can do after lunch. We'll eat at '21,' which will charge you as though you printed the money."

We went to "21" and ordered drinks at the bar. When my guest went to the men's room, I had a chance to talk to the headwaiter and tell him I would pay my check with a Confederate bill; he was to honor it, and we'd straighten it out later. I ordered steaks and when the lunch was over, I got a check for $21. I gave the waiter a Confederate $100 bill which he took and brought back $79 on a plate. I gave him a $5 tip and pocketed the rest.

I thought Hochuli would go crazy. He was like a man who had just found $1,000. He said he'd better call Houston to see if any of the Monopoly money was still in existence. But I stopped him and told him it was only a joke. He recovered slowly.

Someone to Watch Over Me

I've had three wives
Which isn't bad
Though not as many
As Bluebeard had

I married Elizabeth
Bigelow Hall
After nineteen years
She said
"that's all"

And then I tied up
Tanis Guinness
After fourteen years
We called it finis

And now I'm yoked
To the fair Lucinda
Divorce and such
Are out the winda.

ucinda Ballard, the theatrical designer whom I had known for many years, came romantically into my life as Tanis, who had been gently and lovingly leaving me for several years, finally left.

Tanis was in Europe almost all the time and it was fortunate that as I developed an attachment for Lucinda, Liza did too. Liza had become almost dependent on her English nanny, Miss Drinkwater, as I was too busy to do any looking-after. Finally I got rid of Miss Drinkwater and from sheer cowardice retired her on full salary and sent her back to England as payment for years of devoted snobbishness. Liza struck gold with Lucinda, who firmly believes that it is wrong for a child to be unhappy or even cross. To Cindy, no child is unattractive or in the wrong.

When Lucinda and I decided to marry, her children,

Bobby and Jenny, and Liza were delighted. Liza chose Lucinda's dress and Bobby chose the wedding ceremony. We were on our way to the registry in Connecticut when we passed a Christmas-card church—small, white, New Englandish. A sign said "nondenominational." Bobby was overcome by the charm of this miniature cathedral and wanted us to go there instead of to a registry. We found it easy to see the pastor, minister, priest, whatever he was. The only thing he was surely not was a rabbi.

The reverend on being asked what the nondenominational service consisted of said "anything you like." Cindy and I were both silent so he undertook to ask me about my religion. "I haven't any." I saw no point in explaining that, though Jewish, I had never been near a synagogue. Lucinda's family, Early American and Protestants all, came through.

"Episcopalian" she answered and the reverend was overjoyed. "That's my favorite," he said. Now Cindy was alarmed, remembering how long a High Episcopal service is. "We want something simple," she said.

The reverend reassured her. "I'll cut it, add here, take off there, don't worry."

But he put us through all the pomp and circumstance he could get his hands on. I was so dazed and stunned by the long complicated ceremony that instead of handing the reverend $50, I gave him $200. Delighted, he wrung my hand and urged me to come see him again soon.

Gradually, almost without noticing it, we became a family, something I had never had before. We have remained one ever since.

Almost the first thing my new wife Cindy did was to get $2,000 from the telephone company. Getting 2¢ out of the telephone company is remarkable.

She was awed by our telephone bill. She saw a charge for a direct telephone wire to Wall Street. Recourse to the files showed I had paid this from 1930 to 1951.

It was logical that there had been such a line, since Charles Merrill, the head of the brokerage firm that sounded like a trunk falling downstairs, was the previous owner of 18 West 11th Street, but it was not logical that I should pay for it.

Cindy went to war with the telephone company. They searched the house, a vestigial remain was found, but no line. The telephone company would not admit defeat. The walls of neighboring houses, as well as our own, were covered with telephone linemen.

A day came when a minor official named something like Kelleher admitted the company was wrong. Next day he had disappeared. Cindy decided he had been fired as he was not supposed to let things happen that could cost the company $2,000. They did all they could to deny or lessen the refund but Cindy did not like Kelleher losing his job and they finally reinstated him and paid me the $2,000.

It was a famous victory.

All three of my wives lived on 11th Street but not at the same time. They all enjoyed the scenery. There didn't seem to be any reason for having a magnificent establishment unless you gave big parties and Lucinda knew how to give them. When we gave a large party, one that occupied every room, so that the tables and chairs and beds had to be moved, we would make arrangements with Robert Day Deane. They would come with a moving van and take out all the furniture, leaving only the bare walls. Another van would deliver the required number of conventional tables, chairs, knives and forks, glasses, sometimes for more than 250. The van, loaded with our belongings, would park on 11th Street, usually just outside our house. About 7 A.M., when most of the guests had left, the moving crew would clean and vacuum and return our furniture as they had found it. If you walked into 18 West 11th at 8 A.M., you would find it hard to believe a party had been going on all night.

Counting all the guests on 11th Street, a representation of the most desirable partygoers in New York could be mustered for any deserving occasion. A list of those who visited my house at various times sounded like *Who's Who*. The names were so heavy you couldn't fail to drop them.

Both Jenny and Liza made their debuts at 11th Street and the parties were courageous affairs. Jenny's was first and I had misgivings about the conduct of the young guests. Tommy Tailer's daughter had just come out and he alarmed me with stories of how the premises had fared.

But our party, seen to by some of Robert Day Deane's bouncers disguised as guests, went off perfectly. The girls were dressed in long full skirts and it looked like *Gone With the Wind*. The only one who showed signs of staggering was my friend, Bill Chadbourne, the well known attorney, who, carried away by the spirit of the event, had a drop too much. He was weaving in his walk and in his talk. The girls found him too affectionate and did not want to dance with him. He had to be moved and Lucinda and I hit on an ideal method of doing the moving painlessly.

Sir John Foster, the distinguished Englishman, was one who never took a drop. The party had arrived at his time limit and he was about to go home. I pointed out to him the obvious condition of Chadbourne and asked him if he would mind taking Chadbourne home. I told him the plan.

I would tell Chadbourne that he, Foster, was obviously under the weather and ask Chadbourne if he would take him home. In this way Foster would get to bed on time and Chadbourne would leave the party a trifle less out of control. The scheme worked. Chadbourne lurched up to Foster "Come along, Foster," he said, "let's get you home." Foster acted difficult at first and then succumbed, and they both waved alcoholic goodbyes.

The rest of the party stayed until 6 when the furniture

started coming back and Lucinda left for Philadelphia, where *Silk Stockings* was in rehearsal, with a portfolio under her arm. I never understood when Lucinda did her drawings.

There is a melancholy postscript to the story of the house. In 1970, years after we had sold it to live full time in Sands Point, Lucinda and I were sitting serenely before the television when a broadcast flashed the startling news that our dream house at 18 West 11th Street had been dynamited. The smoldering ruins of the blast which tore the Georgian facade to sand in a cruel and sudden way flashed on the screen. The newscaster announced that two women, both nude, were found in the first floor of the house by the first rescue workers to enter the building. The body of a man was found under rubble in the cellar of the house. He was not identified. The owner, James Wilkerson, was cruising on the Caribbean. Cathleen Wilkerson, 25 years old and a graduate of Swarthmore College, was reportedly a Weatherwoman. It was rumored that when her father went away, his radical daughter called a meeting in the house for the purpose of manufacturing sticks of dynamite. The dynamite exploded prematurely.

One Sunday in Sand Point Lucinda and I were walking across the lawn to our garage. The lawn was as smooth as a golf green and was marred only by the presence of an alien element. There were three alien elements, in fact. I at once recognized the man in the center of the trio, the other two were as if bodyguards. It was Frank Costello, who had only recently made news by moving to Sands Point—from rackets to riches. He was our first gangster. They were heading toward a huge oak tree, and Costello had a measuring tape around his shoulder. "Hello, Dietz," he said from 10 feet away, "you got a nice place here. I'm Costello and I just rented a house on Barkers Point Road. Bloomer is a good real estate agent."

"I don't care who you are," I said, "this is private property, and no trespassing is allowed."

"Come on, Dietz," said the gangster, "I never knew I could be sent up for *trespassing*. I've got a good score in the other events."

"Get going," I said, marveling at my courage. The bodyguard became alert.

"Oh, gee," said Costello, "we don't mean any harm, we're just trying to spend a Sunday in the country. We made bets on how thick the tree trunks are. For instance, we would like to make book on that one over there. The guess is 6 feet in diameter."

As he started to leave, he noticed a small sign at the side of the road. "Watch Out for Children." "They even put up birth control signs out here," Costello remarked. "So long, Dietz," he added, "when you get to know me you won't believe all those things they print about me."

In 1949, Garson Kanin, who wrote *Born Yesterday,* asked me if I wanted to do the English lyrics for a Johann Strauss opera, *Die Fledermaus.* He had agreed to write the "book" and direct it for Rudolf Bing, who ran the Metropolitan Opera House. Bing told me that I would not have to make a literal translation, but that I shouldn't change the intent of the play, which was to amuse. I enjoyed the job. I was pleased with two of my lyrics, a high percentage. They were "Look Me Over Once," widely known as the "Laughing Song," in the first act, and the couplets in the third act. Both were originally sung by Patrice Munsel.

THE LAUGHING SONG

Look me over once, look me over twice,
You will not remain in the dark.
Look me over once, look me over twice,
And laugh at your own remark.
You'll quickly discover, I think
My blood is as blue as your ink,
You'll find I'm well-appointed, aesthetically jointed
So look me over once and take a look again
In me you'll surely see an unplebeian strain
A lady's maid, upon my soul,
Excuse me if I lose control.

COUPLETS

I am portraying a farm girl
A typical pail-on-the-arm girl,
Endowed with bucolic allure
And incontrovertibly pure.
As I go calling upon my cows
The gesture that seems to arouse
The ubiquitous male is the swing of my pail
But I must mind my p's and q's
And what he wants I must refuse
I must refuse, I must refuse.
To give him what I mustn't lose
But when a handsome man pursues,
It's hard to guard the p's and q's.

Fledermaus was a hit and the Met performed it 21 times in one season. On its road tour, people came for hundreds of miles to hear a great company sing in English.

The success of *Fledermaus* led to an offer by Franco Columbo of the Ricordi company, owner of the Puccini copyrights. *La Bohème*, star of the Italian repertory, was nearing the end of its copyright. Columbo figured he might establish a vehicle of value if he had the Puccini masterpiece done in respectable English. I had actually started to write *La Bohème* before I was appointed by Columbo, and it became a three-cornered coincidence involving Bing, Columbo, and me.

Bing wanted to produce Mozart's *Così fan tutti*, but I told him I was already working on *La Bohème*. He warned me that he had no need for an English version of a work everybody seemed to like in the original Italian and which always played to full houses at the Metropolitan. However, I pinned him down to consent to listen to it when the English version was finished. I told Columbo that Bing was less than half-hearted, and had said that he would not produce *La Bohème* in English under any conditions. Columbo nevertheless signed a contract to publish and market my libretto. As with *Fledermaus* I went to work with Tibor Kozma at the piano. I was paid a respectable advance and at the same time would have the fun of doing the job.

It was not a popular move by Columbo, especially in opera circles where there is outspoken jealousy. The critic and composer, Virgil Thomson, warned Columbo that he had better not sign a contract with me and when a letter came accidentally signed "Fiendly yours, Columbo," it seemed to reflect the second thoughts he was having.

The day came when I finished my English version, and Tony Bliss, Sonny Whitney, Rudolf Bing and their wives, gathered at the piano in Sands Point. I sang the entire opera to them at greater length than it takes in the opera house, as I sang all the parts which often overlap each other. I offered to quit at various spots, but my audience was loyal. Bing changed his mind. He said he would produce *La Bohème* in two versions, English and Italian. The motion picture producer Joseph Mankiewicz, brother of my old friend Mank, was engaged to direct the opera in both languages.

The juxtaposition of two versions of a favorite opera quickened interest in a long-existing controversy. Before the curtain had risen, a few negative articles had already appeared—

one of them in the *Saturday Review* by Dale Warren, who neither liked nor saw the need for opera in English unless it was written in English in the first place. Germans may like their Italian operas in German and the Italians their German operas in Italian, but when he heard these foreign works performed in his own language "the magic was dispelled, the romance shattered, the illusion destroyed." He quoted passages, such as Rodolfo's "*Chi son? Son una poeta,*" as defiant of paraphrase.

What appeared to be the hard core of musical opinion inclined to Warren's view. They seemed to like their operas served up in the recipe provided by the original chef. The music has a better taste to them when the words are imported. It was clear they were not going to like *La Bohème* in English no matter what it was like.

For myself, representing the soft core who go to the opera occasionally, I am more apt to like what I understand than what I don't. I agree with John Mason Brown that "every opera is too long except *Carmen!*"

The solution would be an authentic English opera, but with the exception of the late George Gershwin or such others as Virgil Thomson and Gian-Carlo Menotti, we haven't developed any musical geniuses who are in love with our poetic language. As a result our singers are trained in the European tradition and the entire musical atmosphere is conditioned by continental winds. Singers don't like to sing in English because they aren't trained in English.

The hard core did concede that one might adapt into English operas in the comic spirit as they are more amenable to translation being more "conversational." Cliché phrases, the equivalent of "how's tricks?," "what's cooking," and "long time no see," are apt to be used. But this conversational exchange is not exclusive to humorous operas. The true reason for the adaptation of these frothier items is that audiences do not laugh at jokes delivered in a foreign tongue. And they may not be sighing when they are supposed to sigh in the heavier ones.

Certain operas do not lend themselves to adaptation or translation. When a work is perfect in its original form, when the language has the handwriting of an individual poet, it had better be left alone. I would shudder at the idea of foreign adaptations of the Gilbert and Sullivan operas even though they are light works. There is often more poetry in these so-called light works than in those operas with large tonnage. But truly great librettos, from the poetic point of view, are exceptional, and even the excellent Verdi and Puccini texts, written by able craftsmen, lend themselves to English adaptation without generating the guilt of an artistic crime.

The song in *Bohème* that I felt best succeeded in imparting the spirit of the original was "Musetta's Waltz."

> *I go my way*
> *And gentlemen react to me*
> *At least nobody turns his back to me*
> *Time and again I try to*
> *Control my eye*
> *Not roll my eye*
> *But what I get*
> *I give in reply*
> *I do not hang a sign out*
> *But it's plain to see*
> *I'm one who will agree*
> *To dine out.*
> *A more than written invitation*
> *To the dance is conveyed*
> *In my glance*
> *Each day I say "hello, goodbye love"*
> *A butterfly love*
> *No heartbreak*
> *No sorrow*
> *No plans for tomorrow*

I go my way
And the one who's playing
False with me
Can watch the others
Waltz with me
You say "call it a day"
And I obey, as long as we're free,
Gay and carefree, darling
Why shouldn't I
Go my way?

An atmosphere of doom surrounded the rehearsals of *Bohème*. I had been surprised at how little on-stage rehearsal opera singers got. Perhaps one reason *Fledermaus* turned out well was that nothing much was changed except the English words and Kanin and I had things our way. With *La Bohème* Joe Mankiewicz contrived new directorial touches and there was little time for rehearsing new moves as well as new words.

I noticed that when singers have to give a performance at night and rehearse a new opera in the daytime, they are inclined to be careless with the new vehicle. One afternoon, Richard Tucker, who throws himself into the part when he sings, was not giving his all to the English which I had set. He mouthed the words instead of delivering them. I went up on stage and spoke to him. "You got that line wrong," I said.

"How would you know?" said Richard, "I wasn't giving out. I don't give out until I know the part."

"I was lipreading," I said.

The first performance of *La Bohème* in English was in December of 1952 and played to a charity Sunday matinee full of people critical of English and of me. The production had a shiny new look. The reception was apathetic, except for a few partisans of English in the audience who appreciated it in a filibustering way. By and large the critics, including two important ones, Thomson of the *Herald Tribune* and

Olin Downes of *The Times*, having said in advance that they would not like it, didn't like it. Bing didn't like it, Bing's assistants didn't like it, Virgil Thompson didn't like it, Elsa Maxwell didn't like it.

A few brave champions appeared. I had fan letters from such greatly gifted librettists as Alan Lerner, whose abundant talent allows him to be generous. Tony Bliss liked it and Samuel Chotzinoff liked it and gave it a great production on *Omnibus*. It was enthusiastically received by the audience. Many wrote letters saying that they had never understood *Bohème* or even liked it before.

The English version was performed seven times that season and has not been staged at the Met since, unless Columbo is slipping it in and not paying me royalties.

I n 1951 MGM bought *The Band Wagon,* and Arthur and I were called to California to consult. There is a vast amount of consulting when they make a musical. We had to consult about numbers, how they would fit into the story—the players, how they would fit into the plot. This plot was an ingenious one, because it converted a handicap into an asset. Betty Comden and Adolph Green, authors of "the book" based the plot on the discrepancy in height between the stars, Fred Astaire and Cyd Charisse. Cyd was an inch taller and had longer legs; and her long legs made her look streamlined like the Chrysler Building. Fred was General Motors.

Celeste Holm had her Brentwood house for rent at $2,500 a month. We were in an extravagant mood and took it sight unseen. Celeste had given us the impression that we were moving into Valhalla. When we arrived at the Brentwood house, I couldn't believe Celeste's eyes, no less my own. It was as bare as a bikini. Celeste's husband, from whom she was getting a divorce, had been making poaching raids on the house, as he believed in community property. We had enough beds, but not enough chairs and tables. There surprisingly was a color TV set, but on one of the raids he took it so our sources for divertissement decreased. Celeste said a car went with the lease, but the only car that lived in the garage was a four-year-old Plymouth mounted on cement blocks. A handyman went with the house, it was rumored, but I never found out what he was handy at; in fact, I never found him. I meant to call Celeste, but it seemed too much to add to her already complicated situation.

I hit on another idea. The MGM property department would fill in the empty spaces. Soon the driveway was cluttered with moving vans carrying lamps, tables, chairs, radio sets and wall decorations, everything we needed including a Steinway.

Arthur and I set to work in earnest to write more songs. The picture score was not exactly the same one as performed on the stage. It was more hitty. We used songs from our other shows and actually we only used one new song of the many we wrote. It was "That's Entertainment."

> *The clown*
> *With his pants falling down*
> *Or the dance*
> *That's a dream of romance*
> *Or the scene*
> *Where the villain is mean*
> *That's entertainment.*
>
> *The lights*
> *on the lady in tights*
> *or the bride*
> *With the guy on the side*

Or the ball
When she gives you her all
That's entertainment.

The plot can be hot—simply teeming with sex
A gay divorcee who is after her "ex"
It could be Oedipus Rex
Where a chap kills his father
And causes a lot of bother
The clerk
Who is thrown out of work
By the boss
Who is thrown for a loss
By the skirt
Who is doing him dirt
The world is a stage
The stage is a world of entertainment.

The doubt
While the jury is out
Or the thrill
When they're reading the will
Or the chase
For the man with the face
That's entertainment.

The dame who is known as the flame
Or the king
Of an underworld ring
He's an ape
Who won't let her escape
That's entertainment.

It might be a fight like you see on the screen
A swain getting slain for the love of a queen
Some great Shakespearean scene
Where a ghost and a prince meet
And everyone ends in mincemeat
The gag
May be waving the flag
That began

With a Mister Cohan
Hip hurray
The American way
The world is a stage
The stage is a world of entertainment.

Schwartz wrote a rhythmic ballet entitled *The Girl Hunt,* directed with ingenuity by Michael Kidd. It was a take-off on Mickey Spillane and James Bond, only we took off less than we do today. Arthur Freed produced the picture and Vincente Minnelli, who was in top form, directed.

Being in Hollywood reminded me of the time we wanted to play tennis. We had a court, tennis rackets and tennis balls. But there were only three of us: Charlie MacArthur, his wife Helen Hayes, and me. I felt an obligation to deliver the necessary fourth, as we were too old to play singles.

Leaning on the stone wall surrounding the MacArthurs' house in Beverly Hills was a good-looking blond young man wearing a cardigan sweater. He was trying to thumb a ride and watching the Cadillacs go by. I went up to him and said, "Tennis anyone?" The young man nodded an interest. "Hey, Charlie," I yelled back, "I've got a fourth." Charlie equipped this fourth with a racket and introduced him to Helen. He did a double take, as who wouldn't, on meeting the great star in so casual a way; but he conducted himself unexpectedly gracefully. He said his name was William Crawford and he was English. Charlie decided to rename him, and he was I. C. Nelson from London from then on. After we'd played two sets of doubles, he explained himself. He had a job as an accountant in London, but he decided to go to Hollywood. He had hitchhiked his way and had to get a job, as he was out of money. The studio he would most like to see was MGM but he couldn't get past the front gate.

We liked him, and I was about to say I'd be glad to send him on a trip around the studio, but I saw a gleam in Charlie's eye which told me to desist from that line.

"I'll put you up, I. C.," said Charlie, "but you must do everything I command you to." Charlie gave him a room and some clothes and discussed the English theatre with him. He was surprisingly well informed.

The next morning on the MGM lot he crossed the path of Sam Marx, the story editor. "Guess who's in town?" said Charlie.

"Who?" said Sam.

"I. C. Nelson," said Charlie.

"Who's that?" asked the editor.

"You mean to tell me you haven't heard of the man who is to the Continental theatre what Clive Bell is to London abstraction? And he's right here in the promised village and you never heard of him?"

"Of course I've *heard* of him," said Sam, "but I can't meet every celebrity who comes into town, I'm too busy. Where's he staying?"

"He's with Helen and me for a few days, but he won't be here long."

Charlie next encountered Eddie Mannix, the general manager of the studio.

"Guess who's in town?" he asked him. "I. C. Nelson."

"Who's I. C. Nelson?" Mannix inquired.

"You never heard of I. C. Nelson? That's like never having heard of J. M. Barrie."

"Who's J. M. Barrie?" asked Mannix.

MacArthur continued on to his office, where he was working on *The Sin of Madelon Claudet* for Helen. His phone rang: It was Ida Koverman from Mayer's office. "Hello, Charlie, this is Ida. I understand that I. C. Nelson is in town and he's staying with you."

"That's right," said Charlie.

"Mr. Mayer would like to give him a luncheon tomorrow. I understand he's here for only a few days."

Charlie thought that could be arranged. "Does Mr. Mayer understand what I. C. Nelson stands for in the theatrical world?" he said.

"I'm sure he does," Ida replied, "but you might jot down a few things so that Mr. Mayer will be well informed."

MacArthur talked to the English hitchhiker that night. "I want you to say practically nothing. If you're asked what you are doing in the theatrical world say I just came out to escape the fog and the rain. I never saw Hollywood and I've heard so much about it. Now rehearse that. What are you doing in Hollywood if you are not making a picture, Mr. Nelson?"

"I came over to escape the fog and rain," he said with an impeccable accent.

At the special luncheon in Mr. Mayer's bungalow, Mayer announced: "It's an honor for us to have as our guest the distinguished gentleman of the theatre who stands for what Gordon Craig stands for, what Clive Bell stands for, what George Balanchine stands for in the ballet and what we at MGM stand for. We'd like to hear a few words from I. C. Nelson."

I. C. Nelson responded: "This luncheon comes as a surprise to me. I just came over to escape the fog and the rain and I am honored. Thank you."

Mr. Mayer conducted his guest on a tour of the studios and offered him $1,000 a week to produce pictures for MGM. I. C. Nelson took it big and said he'd think it over. He couldn't wait to talk to MacArthur, who had been present at the luncheon.

"I'm proud of you," said Charlie. "You don't even need an agent. All you have to do is be yourself and not get entangled in picture projects. The story department will send you scripts to see if they can't elicit your interest, but you send the scripts back saying 'It's not up my street,' or you can vary that with 'It's not up my alley.'"

I. C. Nelson went to the studio at 9 every weekday and turned the radio on in his charming office. For six months he continued to say, "It's not up my street," or "It's not up my alley." Though later he made a daring innovation in his routine by rejecting a manuscript with "It's not my cup of tea." At that he could have kept his job indefinitely, even if he elicited interest, had he stayed away from any definite commitment.

Peter Freuchen, the writer and explorer, wrote a script dealing with the Eskimos and I. C. Nelson couldn't resist the adventuresome project. "That's definitely my cup of tea," he said. Cheers went up in the story department when they realized that at last I. C. Nelson had agreed to work on Freuchen's project. Freuchen was pleased thinking the great I. C. Nelson's imagination would help the direction of his film. But I. C. Nelson felt that the jig was up, and with the voyage far beyond the studio, he confessed that he was an accountant and not a producer and storyteller.

"You shouldn't have varied the script and rung in that cup of tea," said MacArthur. "You can get a job at another studio. Remember all you should say is 'It's not up my street' or 'It's not up my alley.'"

Moanin' Low

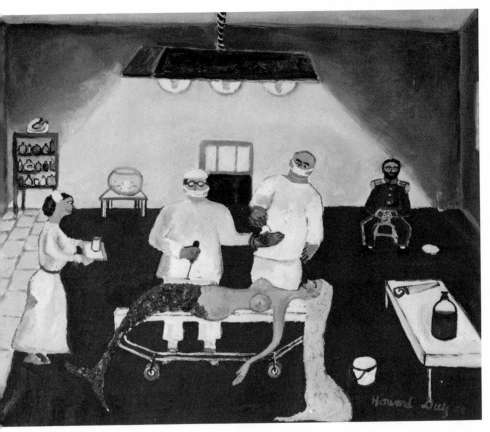

THE OPERATION

Cow Neck House, Sands Point, Long Island. Bought in 1936, sold in 1973.
Moss Hart and Kitty Carlisle. Moss Hart had a gold cigarette box, gold pencils and pens, everything gold. George Kaufman said, "When Moss dies, they'll bury him at Fort Knox."

...inda and me at Sands Point in 1952.

...n Jay Lerner, author of *My Fair Lady, Brigadoon, Gigi* and other brilliant librettos and
...cs.

Schwartz at the piano accompanied by Jack Haley and Beatrice Lillie. We were going over the score of *Inside U.S.A.*

Bea Lillie as the Massachusetts Mermaid in *Inside U.S.A.*

...trice Lillie and Jack Haley singing "We Won't Take It Back" in *Inside U.S.A.*

Vernon Duke (popular composer) and Vladimir Dukelski (classical composer).
Rudolf Bing of the Met and me at a rehearsal of *Die Fledermaus*, done in English.
Vivien Leigh on stage, graceful and beautiful and a Tovarich with Jean Pierre Aumont.

ty Carlisle dressed for her role as Count Orlofsky in *Die Fledermaus* at the Metropolitan.
k Gilford and Patrice Munsel in a scene from *Die Fledermaus*.

LEFT TO RIGHT: Clarence Brown, the movie director, and Madeline and Bob Sherwood in Hollywood.

Cyd Charisse and Fred Astaire. An intimate couple starring in the movie version of *The Band Wagon*.

"riplets" at home and abroad. In London at the Palladium left to right: Danny Kaye, Vivien Leigh and Laurence Olivier.

Hollywood at the MGM studio: Fred Astaire, Nanette Fabray and Jack Buchanan.

Jack Buchanan and Fred Astaire. Two nonpareils.
The Minnellis, father and daughter.

y Comden (of Comden and Green) making a trio with Schwartz and Dietz (of Dietz and
wartz). She and Adolph Green wrote the book for *The Bandwagon* Movie.

ulah, frightened by a critic.

Mary Martin drinking coffee and being a back-stage hostess.
Visiting the set of *South Pacific,* being welcomed by Oscar Hammerstein and Richard Rodgers.

nference with Marlon Brando on *Guys and Dolls*.

1 the movie set of *Guys and Dolls*. Me, Joe Mankiewicz the director, Samuel Goldwyn the oducer, and Michael Kidd the choreographer.

Sir John Foster. A man of all countries. He didn't drink himself, but took drinkers home.

Evie Backer, wife of George. Loved and missed in Sands Point, New York, London, Paris and you name it.

The house with the Georgian facade at 18 West Eleventh Street. This house was dynamited in March, 1970.

CECIL BEATON

LEFT: Jenny and Bobby Ballard in the library at Eleventh Street, December, 1953 for Jenny's 18th birthday party.

RIGHT: Liza at her party at Eleventh Street.

Helen Hayes and Alfred Vanderbilt at Liza's party.

TOP: Just before L-dopa I could not move. My face was frozen and my left side was a continuous tremor. I was in constant pain. Dr. Yahr annexed me as a Parkinson's guinea pig.

SECOND ROW: Two weeks after L-dopa, I could stand with Dr. Yahr's help.

Three weeks later I could stand alone.

THIRD ROW: After six weeks of L-dopa I had vigor in my stride.

No pain, no tremor. A free agent.

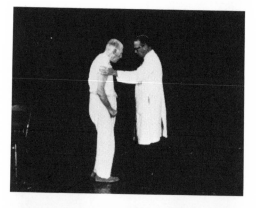

TOP ROW: Dr. Melvin D. Yahr formerly of Columbia Presbyterian now at Mt. Sinai. Always with The Parkinson Institute and his patients.

Dr. William Wagner of Port Washington, Long Island. He makes house calls and you never get into trouble unless he is on vacation.

Marian and Edmund Goodman. A beauty who paints and a handsome surgeon.

ARNOLD WEISSBERGER

TOP ROW: Tanis and Benjie Shaw, my grandchildren.

Jenny Ballard, wife of the architect Walter Ramberg, and her youngest, Julia.

Tanis holding Moonbeam's descendant with her own. Left to right: Dru Montagu and Claire, Sophy and Doone Montagu, Liza Dietz, wife of the publisher Christopher Shaw, Sarita Montagu and Tanis and Benjie Shaw.

ARNOLD WEISSBERGER

The ballet master handling his pupils. Lucy and Jenny-Sayre Ramberg, two of Lucinda's grandchildren.

Lucinda's grandson, Alexander Ballard, on the lawn at Sands Point.

Vivien Leigh reading *Winnie the Pooh* to Elizabeth Ballard, Lucinda's grandchild. Elizabeth loves to be read to by stars.

Charlie Lederer preparing to destroy.

Vivien Leigh at Cow Neck House.

LEFT: Katherine and John O'Hara, who deserved all the prizes, including Katherine.
TOP: Si Seadler, Lep Friedman and me at Sands Point in 1972.
RIGHT: Liza Dietz Shaw.

Pamela and Averell Harriman at The Dietz exhibit at the Museum of the City of New York, October 1972.

Mary Lee Leatherbee and Tom Prideaux. The staff of *Life*.

RIGHT: Cathleen Nesbitt and Maurice Chevalier at their birthday party. They were born in 1888.

Elizabeth Ballard (no mean painter herself) points possessively at her favorite Dietz in the museum show.

MANNY GREENHAUSE

Cornelia Otis Skinner, me, Josh Logan, Nedda Harrigan and Caroline Ballard, with part of "Adam and Eve" in background.

Leave My Pulse Alone

On September 15, 1954, lightning struck. The name of the lightning was "paralysis agitans." I was sitting in Nick Schenck's office while he read his mail. That was something I usually did: it enabled me to learn the problems of the company. Most press representatives don't realize that the mail the company gets is the key to the company's public relations. A manila folder I was holding dropped from my left hand. I reached to pick it up, but my aim was wide of the mark. Nick noticed the irregularity. I guessed my poor aim was connected to sudden tremors which had been coming over my right hand.

Having been a chemist before he became an amusement tycoon, Nick was familiar with the world of pills and knowledgeable about doctors. He himself took me to the eminent Dr. George Baer, who said I had paralysis agitans. Dr. Baer did not tell me so at the time, but paralysis agitans is the early stage of Parkinson's disease. No one knew how you get it or how you cure it. Dr. Baer said that the tremors might subside with medication, though new symptoms could appear and worsen unpredictably. Other problems besides the tremors soon presented themselves, such as rigid spasms in my hands. I felt tired a great deal of the time, though there were days when I was perfectly well.

Dr. Baer told me to relax, rest, travel—whatever doctors say when they are at a loss. Anita Loos suggested the Grand Hotel in Montecatini, Italy. Anita's complexion being a great advertisement for a spa, we went. While we were there my symptoms abated, possibly due more to Nunnally Johnson and other entertaining people also taking the cure than to the waters with names like Torrero and Inferno. Sylvia Lyons, the wife of Leonard, the columnist, noting that the chef put lemon juice on everything she said, "If there's one thing I like it's a sour lamb chop."

At the end of our three weeks in Montecatini, I felt so well that we decided to accept Tanis's invitation to visit her in Biarritz. We stayed for a couple of weeks, playing bridge in

French and invited Tanis to visit us in America, which she did.

But back in New York my symptoms returned. For the next few years, my condition remained about the same: unbearable, but not totally incapacitating. Having to fight for MGM's survival was no help. MGM had become a battleground. We battled the bankers, who were more than less in control. Arthur Loew had the right idea. The bankers wanted to sell the TV rights to all MGM movies, including *Gone With the Wind*, to pay the company's funded debt of $38 million, whereas Arthur and I believed the films could be leased for the same amount and MGM would still own them. Common sense prevailed and we won our point.

But then came the proxy fight. Mayer, whose contract had come to an end in 1951 and was not renewed, was bitterly opposed to Nick Schenck, chairman of the board of directors. He had support from Joe Tomlinson who was the largest stockholder in the company and wanted to restore Mayer as head of the studio. He was determined to present a slate that would be irresistable to the stockholders and started a proxy fight vowing that he could bring MGM back to its pristine glory.

Tomlinson didn't know anything about motion pictures or the motion picture business. I had a long talk with him. Whenever an MGM picture didn't click, Tomlinson thought it was because I was busy doing shows like *Inside USA*.

The doctor's warning that worry and overwork made Parkinson's worse was verified. My tremors and other problems had become so acute that I felt compelled to resign from MGM. I planned to devote my time to writing shows with Arthur Schwartz.

In the fall of 1959, Bennett Cerf and Donald Klopfer of Random House gave a surprise party for Moss Hart at Leone's restaurant. It was to be a big ballyhoo for *Act One*,

Moss's autobiography. Mossie had been directing the party's entertainment, assigning material and even rehearsing for one of the numbers, in total disregard for the surprise element.

Moss suggested that Arthur and I write a musical comedy based on *Act One* and perform it at the party and we did. We wrote a miniature musical which even included a parody of the kind of interminable ballet resolving the plot, which has clogged up most musicals since *Oklahoma!*

At the party, we performed sans scenery, costumes, or music except as provided by Arthur at the piano with me beside him, holding the typewritten lyrics I was to sing. By this time my hands were shaking so violently that when I rehearsed the crackling of my script drowned out the piano. We glued the pages to cardboard, which stopped the noise. Arthur and I sang all the parts, except that we had Kitty Carlisle appear at the end and sing a ballad called "It Only Happens Once in a Lifetime."

One of the high points of our show was "De Oily Boid." We took turns singing to the tune of "The Rain in Spain."

> *Comes the day when Moss gives up his job. He tells his friends, Dore Schary and Edward Chodorov, that he is headed for Broadway.*
>
> *Eddie Chodorov is played by Melvyn Douglas. Dore Schary is played by Ralph Bellamy.*
>
> *They tell Moss he had better drop that English accent because it wouldn't go on Broadway.*
>
> *"You mean I shouldn't chance it?" says Moss.*
>
> *"We'll test you," says Dore. "Repeat after me: 'De oily boid desoives de oily woim."*
>
> *The early bird deserves the early worm.*
>
> *No! No! Once again.*
> *De oily boid desoives de oily woim*
> *De oily boid desoives de oily woim*

I tink he's got it
I tink he's got it

De oily boid desoives de oily woim

De punk has got it
De punk has got it
Now once again what does de oily boid desoive?

De oily woim, de oily woim

And who gets de stinkin' woim?

De boid, de boid
De oily boid desoives de oily woim

Aha!

De oily boid desoives de oily woim
Good boy!

In Huntspernt, Kingspernt and Greenpernt
I got a goil named Goity
I woik on Toity-Toid Street

Now once again, who gets de oily woim?

De oily boid, de oily boid

And when does that friggin' boid get up?

Oily, oily
                    (Tambourines)
De oily boid desoives de oily woim

Bravo!

De oily boid desoives de oily woim.
                    (Tambourines)

I sang Mossie's part recounting his collaborative sessions
with George Kaufman.

> *He kept looking out of the window*
> *Never looking at me*
> *He studied a cat in the backyard*

Who was studying a bird in a tree
He picked some lint off the carpet
Then elaborately scratched his ear
And turned to me as if to say
What are you doing here?

He called me
Er-
Although he knew my name
He called me
Er-
Oh, how it galled me
When he called me
Er-
I could have murdered the guy
But he was king
Who was I?
Er-
I dreamed a dream in which I spoke up
Said before I woke up
Sir
To work with you is thrilling
But please don't make the billing
George S. Kaufman and
Er.

We would work from the early morning
  often into the night
I only had a meager breakfast
Me with my big appetite
There was no lunch but at teatime
Two cookies came in on a tray
This was the usual diet
But he varied it one day
Yes, he varied it one day.

He fed me
Fudge
Though I was feeling faint
He fed me
Fudge

He claimed to be a judge of home-made
Fudge
He said it had what it takes
But there was I
Craving steaks
Not fudge
I watched him wallow in a plateful
I couldn't hide a hateful
Grudge
I almost gave the show up
Rather than have to throw up
One more piece of that fudge.

hen Brooks Atkinson left *The Times* there was a dinner at Sardi's and Arthur and I sang a song I wrote called "The Critic."

THE CRITIC

The critic has a mother
Just like anybody else
Encountering an orphan
His heart melts
He's generous to beggars
Applauds what blind men play
He's a very human being
During the day.

But in the nighttime
He shows his other side
Jekyll becomes a Hyde
At night
He gives himself a potion
Like a witch's brew
So any play he sees
He'll be allergic to
Oh! in the night time
A critic really lives
Sharpening adjectives
That bite

333

God save authors from his lethal binges
God save plays that creak around the hinges
All but Tennessees and William Inges
Feel his might
Upon an opening night

Perhaps the critic's childhood
Will provide us with a clue
They say he got the way he got
Before the age of two
In fact upon his natal day
The moment he arrived
He looked up at the doctor
And he burbled, "It's contrived"
At feeding time
Though the bottle was required
He said,
"This formula leaves much to be desired"
When he grew up he sowed the first
Wild oat of his career
Holding her very near
He whispered in her ear,
"It's adequate, my dear."

But in the nighttime
There's one we all respect
One we never connect
With crimes
As candid as a camera
In his every line
Though he's very frank
He's not a Frankenstein
And it is high time
The theatre played the host
Offering up a toast
In rhymes
With integrity he has imbued us
Here's to one who has for years reviewed us
Now it's turnabout—he can't elude us
Ring out the chimes
For the critic of The New York Times.

By this time, I knew that I had Parkinson's disease. Besides the shaking of my hands, I was beginning to have spells of weakness when it was hard for me to find the strength to do anything, even to play golf and bridge. I had expected bridge to be the comfort of my old age, but now my hands shook so that it was hard to hold the cards. I could no longer type with my one-finger system but had to write in illegible longhand which made everyone nervous.

Nevertheless, when Fay and Mike Kanin came to Arthur and me with the idea of doing *The Affairs of Anatol* as a musical we got to work and emerged with *The Gay Life,* which Alec Wilder in his book, *American Popular Song,* generously called our best score since the thirties. "Why Go Anywhere at All" is one of the songs he liked. Cindy designed the costumes for *The Gay Life* and she got a Perry Award for them. Oliver Smith, most amusing of designers, got good notices for the scenery. Barbara Cook and all the singers liked their parts, but our leading man couldn't act, dance, sing or speak English, which was a handicap.

After the show opened, we left for Barbados and the sun and sea. We went down to the beach every day where we played bridge with Marietta and Ronald Tree who had a card table set up on the sand. At the hotel we watched T. S. Eliot and his protective young second wife play cribbage while we played bridge with Walter Hirshon, the Wall Street magnate, and the Gilbert Harrisons of *The New Republic.* We dined with Rebecca West and her husband. She was as natural as yogurt but more fun.

As we were set to do a show called *Jennie* for Mary Martin, Arthur Schwartz came down and we started work at Claudette Colbert's, who was looking as she did in *It Happened One Night.* She invited us to use her beautiful house and her piano and we went there every day as some people go to the office. But conferences regarding *Jennie* and problems with *The Gay Life* made it necessary to return to New York.

Back in the city my condition became worse. On Easter

Sunday, 1962, we had lunch at Sally and Buzzy Scheftels'. I was eating the good food always to be found at the Scheftels when I had to stop. My right hand had started to shake as badly as my left hand. On the way home I said I was determined to have the brain operation Margaret Bourke-White had had. I spoke to Dr. Peters, our family doctor, and he reluctantly agreed to make an appointment with Dr. Irving Cooper, an eminent specialist in this kind of surgery.

Dr. Cooper's office was in Manhattan, but he did his operations at St. Barnabas Hospital in the Bronx. He was expensive and so was the hospital, and it was all payable in advance. It was made clear that nothing was returnable if I died. But Dr. Cooper himself bore such a resemblance to the Angel Gabriel, that I felt hopeful. He seemed very skillful and his confidence gave me courage. I didn't know, that except for the day following the operation when he appeared in my room trailed by press agents and reporters, I would never see him again. He departed for Chicago where he was to deliver a speech and I have never laid eyes on him since.

I was fully conscious during the operation, which was intended to stop my right hand from shaking. The only anesthetic was Novocaine. The operation was almost painless, and worked a big improvement in my right side, although the right arm developed an involuntary motion, darting out when you least expected it to and acting like a sort of private poltergeist. It knocked things over and frequently caused me to burn myself with hot tea or coffee. As I was writing the show for Mary Martin, I visited her quite often, and broke her Venetian glass, which didn't make me popular with her.

Jennie presented more problems than just broken glass. *The Gay Life* had been difficult, but at least there had been a basic story and mood—something to work on. *Jennie* was originally based on some very funny stories by Dwight

Taylor. Mary Martin was to be a small-town gymnastic instructress who is wooed by a glamorous pursuer. Her first song was to be instructions and advice given by a modestly bloomer-clad Mary to an equally demure class of young ladies. Arnold Schulman was to write the script. Arthur and I foresaw a shower of gold that made Danaë's look tacky. We therefore bravely borrowed a lot of money and invested it in *Jennie*. After Arthur and I had written some entertaining songs for the version of *Jennie* we thought we were working on, it transpired that Mary and Vinnie Donahue, a TV director who was totally under the Halliday thumb, had decided that there were to be no funny songs. We had a different Schulman, Max this time, on the book. Suddenly the plot was switched: the gymnastic instructress vanished and was replaced with a tragedy queen.

We had not foreseen that with Mary and her husband Dick Halliday as producers, we would have little to say. We were not protected contractually and I was ill and couldn't take a firm position. Lucinda was uninvited from doing the costumes and replaced by Irene Sharaff, and our choice of Oliver Smith was passed over for George Jenkins. *Jennie* had more operations than I did, but despite the surgery it had trouble talking, walking, and being entertaining. To flatter it, one would call it a flop.

When I was in Boston with *Jennie*, I went to the Massachusetts General Hospital for analysis and treatment. Dr. David C. Postkanzer said they could get rid of the involuntary motion in my right arm and they did. My room in the Phillips House of Mass. General had a fireplace, and they cooked my breakfast when I woke up. Also, Vivien Leigh came to see me from New York on her day off from *Tovarich*.

In spite of the operation my general condition didn't improve. I grew worse in spite of the comforting attention of such beauties who came to Sands Point as Vivien Leigh,

Marie Harriman, Madeline Sherwood, Evie Backer, Vivien Wanamaker, Geraldine Fitzgerald, Sally Scheftel, and Marian Goodman. Dr. Edmund Goodman, Marion's husband, was to save me when prospects for the future seemed painful, even hopeless, and I was willing to try anything except more brain surgery. By 1968 I could barely walk. I was in constant pain and had developed Parkinson side-effects of a very disagreeable sort. It was then that Dr. Goodman persuaded Dr. Melvin Yahr, who was experimenting with the drug L-dopa on Parkinson's patients, to take me on as a sort of Parkinson guinea pig. I was the 94th person to be treated with the drug. I had confidence in Dr. Yahr and we were rewarded with progress. Dr. Yahr is a great man and I am a great guinea pig.

But there still had to be more surgery. Dr. Goodman made graceful incisions on me and reduced my colon to a semicolon. This was related to Parkinson's in some way I'm not clear about; I just lifted my skirts and let them cut and came out of the sixth operating room in a year with a stomach looking like a Picasso.

I have been on L-dopa for approximately four years, and while it doesn't permit me to behave as if I were well, it doesn't make life unliveable. Parkinson's still works to handicap me on small targets. It's difficult to type, and the world is deprived of much of my deathless prose. I deal awkwardly in playing cards, and that makes my participation in a bridge game uncomfortable. I come up empty quite often when I am playing golf. I am not safe when I attempt to swim in deep water, so I don't attempt to. I have some trouble with my voice.

Of course age is a factor, and never having been old before I cannot tell what my symptoms would be were I less than 77. Dr. Yahr comes on like "Onward Christian Soldiers" and interferes with my falling down and passing out. I don't know what keeps a staggering person alive. You've got to be lucky if you're in that shape. In my case, Dr. Yahr saves my life.

I'm yoked to L-dopa and I visit him once a month. There is great hope for Parkinson's victims if they stick to L-dopa and find people like Ed Goodman and Melvin Yahr when they're dancing in the dark.

Shows

1924
Dear Sir

Produced by Philip Goodman
Book by Edgar Selwyn
Lyrics by Howard Dietz
Music by Jerome Kern

Cast included
Walter Catlett, Genevieve Tobin
and Oscar Shaw

Principal songs:
Oh, What's the Use;
All Lanes Must Reach a Turning;
A Houseboat on the Harlem;
If We Could Lead a Merry Mormon Life.

Times Square Theatre
15 performances

1927
Merry-Go-Round

Produced by Richard Herndon
Lyrics and sketches by
Morris Ryskind and Howard Dietz
Music by Henry Souvaine and Jay Gorney
Staged by Alan Dinehart

Cast included
Libby Holman, Philip Loeb,
Frances Gershwin,
Leonard Sillman,
Margaret Byers

Principal songs:
Hogan's Alley, Happy Days,
Sentimental Silly,
If Love Should Come to Me.

Klaw Theatre
136 performances

1929
The Little Show

Produced by Tom Weatherly and Dwight Deere Wiman
Sketches mostly by Howard Dietz,
Fred Allen, Newman Levy,
Marya Mannes, and George S. Kaufman.
Lyrics by Howard Dietz
Music by Arthur Schwartz

Cast included
Clifton Webb, Libby Holman, Fred Allen,
Romney Brent, Portland Hoffa,
Bettina Hall, Helen Lynd,
John McCauley, Peggy Conklin,
Constance Cummings,
Adam Carroll and Ralph Rainger (duo-pianists)

Principal songs:
Can't We Be Friends, music by Kay Swift,
words by Jimmy Warburg;
Body and Soul, music by Johnny Green;
I Guess I'll Have to Change My Plan;
I've Made a Habit of You; Hammacher Schlemmer,
I Love You; Moanin' Low.
Music Box Theatre
321 performances

1930
The Second Little Show

Produced by Tom Weatherly and Dwight Deere Wiman
Sketches by Norman Clark,
Marc Connelly, William Miles,
Donald Blackwell,
James Coghlan, Bert Hanlon
Lyrics by Howard Dietz
Music by Arthur Schwartz
Directed by Mr. Wiman and Monte Woolley
Dances by Dave Gould
Settings by Jo Mielziner
Costumes by Raymond Sovey, Helen Pons
Music director, Gus Salzer

Cast included
Al Trahan, Jay C. Flippen,
Gloria Grafton, and Arline Judge

Principal songs:
You're the Sunrise; Lucky Seven;
What a Case I've Got on You;
I Like Your Face.

Opened September 2
Royale Theatre
63 performances

1930
Three's A Crowd

Produced by Max Gordon
A revue conceived and compiled by Howard Dietz
Sketches by Howard Dietz,
Fred Allen, Laurence Schwab,
Corey Ford, Groucho Marx, Arthur Sheekman,
William Miles, and Donald Blackwell
Lyrics by Howard Dietz
Music by Arthur Schwartz
Staged and lighted by Hassard Short
Dances by Albertina Rasch
Settings by Albert R. Johnson
Costumes by Kiviette
Music director, Nicholas Kempner

Cast included
Clifton Webb, Libby Holman,
Fred Allen, Tamara Geva, Portland Hoffa,
Earl Oxford, Fred MacMurray

Principal songs:
Something to Remember You By;
The Moment I Saw You;
Right at the Start of It.

Opened October 15
Selwyn Theatre
271 performances

1931
The Band Wagon

Produced by Max Gordon
under the supervision of Howard Dietz
Sketches by George S. Kaufman and Howard Dietz
Lyrics by Howard Dietz
Music by Arthur Schwartz
Directed by Hassard Short
Dances by Albertina Rasch
Settings by Albert R. Johnson
Costumes by Kiviette, Constance Ripley
Music director, Al Goodman

Cast included
Fred and Adele Astaire,
Frank Morgan, Tilly Losch, Helen Broderick,
Philip Loeb, John Barker

Principal songs:
Dancing in the Dark;
New Sun in the Sky; Hoops; I Love Louisa;
High and Low; Miserable with You;
Where Can He Be?; White Heat;
The Beggar Waltz.

Opened June 3
New Amsterdam Theatre
260 performances

1932
Flying Colors

Produced by Max Gordon
Sketches by Howard Dietz
Lyrics by Howard Dietz
Music by Arthur Schwartz
Production designed and lighted by Norman Bel Geddes
Dances staged by Albertina Rasch
Costumes by Constance Ripley
Music director, Al Goodman

Cast included
Clifton Webb, Charles Butterworth,
Tamara Geva, Buddy and Vilma Ebsen,
Patsy Kelly, Larry Adler,
Philip Loeb, Imogene Coca

Principal songs:
A Rainy Day; Mother Told Me So;
A Shine on Your Shoes; Alone Together;
Louisiana Hayride; Smokin' Reefers.

Opened September 15
Imperial Theatre
188 performances

1934
Revenge With Music

Produced by Arch Selwyn and Harold B. Franklin
Book and lyrics by Howard Dietz
Music by Arthur Schwartz
Directed by Komisarjevsky,
Worthington Miner, and Howard Dietz
Dances by Michael Mordkin
Settings by Albert R. Johnson
Costumes by Constance Ripley
Music director, Victor Baravalle

Cast included
Charles Winninger, Libby Holman,
Georges Metaxa, Ilka Chase, Rex O'Malley,
Joseph Macaulay, Ivy Scott, Detmar
Poppen, Margaret Lee, George Kirk

Principal songs:
When You Love Only One; Never Marry a Dancer;
If There Is Someone Lovelier Than You;
That Fellow Manuelo; Maria;
You and the Night and the Music; Wand'rin' Heart.

Opened November 28
New Amsterdam Theatre
158 performances

1935
At Home Abroad

Produced by the Messrs. Shubert
Sketches by Howard Dietz,
Marc Connelly, Dion Titheradge,
Raymond Knight, Reginald Gardiner
Lyrics by Howard Dietz
Music by Arthur Schwartz
Production staged and settings and costumes
by Vincente Minnelli
Dances by Gene Snyder, Harry Losee
Music director, Al Goodman

Cast included
Beatrice Lillie, Ethel Waters,
Herb Williams, Eleanor Powell,
Reginald Gardiner, Paul Haakon, Vera Allen,
Nina Whitney, John McCauley, and Woods Miller

Principal songs:
Hottentot Potentate; Paree;
Farewell, My Lovely; Love Is a Dancing Thing;
Get Yourself a Geisha; Got a Bran' New Suit.

Opened December 9
Winter Garden Theatre
198 performances

1937
Between The Devil

Produced by the Messrs. Shubert
Book and lyrics by Howard Dietz
Music by Arthur Schwartz
Directed by Hassard Short, Edward Duryea Dowling,
Fred DeCordoba, and John Hayden
Dances by Robert Alton
Settings by Albert Johnson
Costumes by Kiviette
Music director, Don Voorhees

Cast included
Jack Buchanan, Evelyn Laye,
Adele Dixon, Vilma Ebsen, Charles Walters,
The Tune Twisters

Principal songs:
I See Your Face Before Me;
Triplets; By Myself; I'm Against Rhythm;
You Have Everything.

Opened December 22
Imperial Theatre
93 performances

1944
Tars and Spars

A Coast Guard Show

Lyrics by Howard Dietz
Music by Vernon Duke

Discovering and starring Victor Mature,
Gower Champion,
Sid Caesar

Principal song:
The Silver Shield

1944
Sadie Thompson

Produced by A. P. Waxman
Lyrics by Howard Dietz
Music by Vernon Duke
Directed by Rouben Mamoulian
Settings by Boris Aronson
Costumes by Elizabeth Montgomery

Cast included
June Havoc,
Ralph Dumke,
Lansing Hatfield

Opened November 16
Alvin Theatre
60 performances

1948
Inside U.S.A.

Produced by Arthur Schwartz
Suggested by John Gunther's famous book
Sketches by Arnold Auerbach, Arnold Horwitt, Moss Hart
Lyrics by Howard Dietz
Music by Arthur Schwartz
Dances staged by Helen Tamiris
Settings by Lemuel Ayers
Costumes by Eleanor Goldsmith, Castillo
Musical director, Jay Blackton

Cast included
Beatrice Lillie, Jack Haley,
Herb Shriner, Valerie Bettis, John Tyers,
Eric Victor, Louis Nye, Carl Reiner,
Thelma Carpenter, Estelle Loring,
J. C. McCord, Rod Alexander, Boris Runanin,
Jack Cassidy, Talley Beatty

Principal songs:
Inside U.S.A.; Blue Grass;
Rhode Island Is Famous for You;
Haunted Heart; My Gal Is Mine Once More;
We Won't Take It Back; At the Mardi Gras.

Opened April 30
Majestic Theatre
399 performances

1950
Die Fledermaus

Metropolitan Opera Company,
produced by Rudolf Bing
English lyrics for Johann Strauss's opera
by Howard Dietz
Book by Garson Kanin
Directed by Garson Kanin
Scenery and costumes by Rolf Gerard

Cast included
Risë Stevens, Ljuba Welitsch,
Richard Tucker, Patrice Munsel

Principal songs:
When the Band Begins to Play;
When You're Away; Chacun a Son Goût;
Look Me Over Once; Some Days You're Lonely;
You and I; The Girl with Yellow Hair;
Oh, the Delight of a Night with You; P's and Q's.

27 performances first year.

1952
La Bohème

English version of Giacomo Puccini's opera
for the Metropolitan Opera Company
Produced by Rudolf Bing and Ricordi

Directed by Joseph Manckiewicz
English lyrics by Howard Dietz
Scenery and costumes by Rolf Gerard

Cast included
Richard Tucker

Principal songs:
Rudolfo's narrative; Mimi's aria;
Musetta's waltz; Song to a Coat.

1953
The Band Wagon (Movie)

Produced by Arthur Freed for MGM
Book by Betty Comden and Adolph Green
Lyrics by Howard Dietz
Music by Arthur Schwartz
Directed by Vincente Minnelli

Cast included
Fred Astaire, Cyd Charisse,
Nanette Fabray,
Jack Buchanan, and Oscar Levant

Principal songs:
That's Entertainment;
Dancing in the Dark; The Chase.

1961
The Gay Life

Produced by Kermit Bloomgarden
Book by Fay and Michael Kanin
Lyrics by Howard Dietz
Music by Arthur Schwartz
Directed by Gerald Freedman
Dances by Herbert Ross
Scenic Production by Oliver Smith
Lighting by Jean Rosenthal
Costumes by Lucinda Ballard

Cast included
Walter Chiari, Barbara Cook,
Jules Munshin,
Elizabeth Allen,
Jeanne Bal, Lu Leonard

Principal songs:
Why Go Anywhere at All; Bring Your Darling Daughter;
Now I'm Ready for a Frau; Magic Moment;
Who Can, You Can; The Label on the Bottle;
This Kind of a Girl;
I'm Glad I'm Single; Something You Never Had Before;
You Will Never Be Lonely;
You're Not the Type; Come A-Wandering with Me;
I Never Had a Chance;
I Wouldn't Marry You; For the First Time.

Opened October 17
Shubert Theatre
113 performances

1963
Jennie

Produced by Cheryl Crawford and Richard Halliday
Book by Arnold Schulman
Suggested by *Laurette* by Marguerite Courtney
Lyrics by Howard Dietz
Music by Arthur Schwartz
Directed by Vincent J. Donehue
Dances by Matt Mattox
Settings by George Jenkins
Lighting by Jean Rosenthal
Costumes by Irene Sharaff
Music director, John Lesko

Cast included
Mary Martin, George Wallace,
Ethel Shutta, Jack De Lon,
Imelda De Martin, Robin Bailey

Principal songs:
Waitin' for the Evening Train;
I Still Look at You That Way;
Before I Kiss the World Goodbye;
Where You Are; High Is Better Than Low.

Opened October 17
Shubert Theatre
82 performances

Index